To my daughter Barbara,
for all her love and patience during this translation.

Brother Thomas of Celano

The Life of St. Francis of Assisi

and

The Treatise of Miracles

Translated from the Italian by Catherine Bolton

Editrice Minerva
Assisi

Editing and publishing consultant: Pier Maurizio Della Porta

ISBN

© soc. coop. a r.l.
Editrice Minerva Assisi
Assisi – Vicolo degli Archi 1

Introduction

Much has been written about St. Francis since his death over 700 years ago and there is a wealth of information available about the man himself and about the Franciscan Order. Nevertheless, to understand exactly who he was and why his movement had such a profound and lasting effect on the Church, it is essential to see him through the eyes of those who knew him and thus to place the man within the context of his life and times.

Consequently, the works of Brother Thomas of Celano represent an invaluable source not only for scholars of Franciscanism but also for the lay person. But who exactly was Brother Thomas?

St. Francis' first biographer was born in the town of Celano in central Italy. Although the exact year of his birth has not been established, he is thought to have been born in around 1185. His surname is likewise unknown. He probably entered the Order between 1213 and 1216, but nothing is known about these early years. In fact, the first information we have about Brother Thomas comes to us from the *Chronicle of Brother Jordan of Giano*, which indicates that Thomas was chosen in 1221 to help found the Order in Germany under the leadership of Caesar of Speyer, who had been appointed as first minister provincial of Germany during the chapter held that year.

During the provincial chapter of Worms, Brother Caesar then chose Thomas to serve as vicar provincial in Germany while he attended the general chapter in Assisi. Thomas then returned to Italy shortly thereafter.

It is important to point out that Thomas had little contact with Francis during the Saint's last years. Consequently, in Thomas' *Lives*, his account is accurate, but it is based as much on what he was able to glean from others as on what he himself experienced. Nevertheless, his detailed description of the canonization ceremony (July 16, 1228) would seem to indicate that he was present. It also likely that it was around this time that Pope Gregory IX commissioned him to write the *First Life*.

It is unclear why exactly Pope Gregory chose Thomas for this assignment, other than the fact that he was a man of letters and was probably one of the "educated and noble men" admitted to the Order shortly after St. Francis returned from Spain. In any case, Thomas was an excellent choice, for he was a skilled writer and was painstaking in his research. In fact, as indicated above, he relied extensively on the testimony of Francis' early companions, such as Brother Leo, Brother Rufino, Brother Angelo and Brother Elias, who was vicar from 1221 until 1227. It also seems clear that Thomas had access to Francis' own writings, which he quotes frequently throughout this work. Thus, Thomas' *First Life* is an outstanding historical document on St. Francis since it was completed so soon after the Saint's death and was his official biography as commissioned by the pope himself.

There is no further information about Brother Thomas for the next fourteen years until Crescentius of Jesi, the newly-elected minister, asked him to write the *Second Life*. In fact, during the general chapter held in Genoa in 1244, Brother Crescentius asked the friars to send him all the information they had about the life and works of Blessed Francis. Between 1282 and 1288, chronicler Brother Salimbene wrote that Cresentius ordered Thomas "who had written the first legend of Blessed Francis, to write another book, inasmuch as many things had been uncovered about the blessed Francis that had not been written down".

Since the *Second Life* was written on the basis of the material contributed by a number of brothers, Thomas considered himself more of a spokesman in this case than an actual biographer and indeed, the prologue is written in the first person plural. Nevertheless, there can be no doubt that Thomas was the sole author of the *Second Life*.

Towards 1250, the new minister, Brother John of Parma, asked him to write the *Treatise of Miracles*, which he completed in around 1253. The reason for this request was that while the entire third section of the *First Life* was dedicated to Francis' miracles, the *Second Life* was considered somewhat incomplete, since no section of this sort had been included.

While many of the miracles described in the *Treatise* had already been set down in the *Lives*, it is nevertheless an important work as far as biographical information on the Saint is concerned, since 41 of the 198 numbered paragraphs deal with miracles that the Saint worked during his lifetime. Moreover, thirteen of these paragraphs offer new material that had not been discussed in the *Lives*.

It seems likely that Brother Thomas stayed in Assisi to write this work and that then he remained there to write the *Legend of St. Clare*, which was commissioned by Pope Alexander IV and was completed in around 1256.

He spent his final years in Tagliacozzo, in the region of the Marches, and probably had charge of the Poor Clares at the monastery of St. John of Varro. Brother Thomas died in 1260 and was buried in the monastery. In 1516, his body was laid to rest behind the high altar of the church there and then, at the turn of the eighteenth century, his remains were clothed in the habit of the Friars Minor Conventual and were placed under the high altar there.

At this point, it is essential to look at Thomas' works in the context in which they was written. First of all, the *Lives* were not written as a biography in the modern meaning of the word, but they were *legends* in the medieval sense. The word *legenda* itself means "(what is) to be read" and indeed, in his frequent asides to his audience, Thomas often refers to "those who hear this", as if the work were being read aloud. Secondly, in the Middle Ages, a *legend* was the life story of a saint, with particular emphasis on his or her miracles. This explains why Thomas did not follow a strictly chronological order in his account, since the very purpose of a *legend* was to offer the audience a religious lesson by examining a Saint's works rather than to look at the more ordinary and "human" events in his life. Consequently, any lack of chronology or even omission should not be taken to reflect inaccuracy or lack of reliability as far as the biographer is concerned: the whole intent behind Brother Thomas' *Lives* was to present a picture of Francis, the saint, to a very widespread audience that went far beyond Francis' Order itself. It is also worthwhile to note that the *Lives* were written as distinct works and not as a body, and therefore they should not be considered complements of each other, just as the *Treatise* itself, while written to fill in some of the gaps left by the *Second Life*, is not merely a footnote to the *Lives*.

As far as the translation of these works is concerned, as the saying goes, some things do indeed get lost in the translation. First of all, the English translation is based on Fausta Casolini's translation from Latin into lovely and flowing Italian. This means that Brother Thomas' painstaking attention to the artistic device known as *cursus*, or in other words the rhythmic pattern at the end of each sentence, which was used by both ancient and medieval Latin writers, is lost in both the Italian and English translations. Moreover, his frequent use of word play, which comes across in a Romance language such as Italian, is unfortunately lost in English. I have added several footnotes throughout the text in order to give the reader some idea of this stylistic device, which Thomas used quite frequently and to great effect.

Nevertheless, what comes across throughout Brother Thomas' works is the respect and love that he felt for St. Francis and it is Thomas' love for his subject that has given his *Lives* such force, grace and elegance. Thomas captured the joy and sheer delight that St. Francis experienced in all that he did and in everything that surrounded him, and this is what has given his writing its timeless quality.

The task that was given to Thomas of Celano was to make Francis' life and works known to a vast audience, not only during his own lifetime but, as he himself points out in his introductory remarks, for generations to come. Indeed, in his *Preface* to Part Two of the *Second Life*, Thomas states, "Handing down the excellent works of the fathers to the memory of their children is a sign of honor to the former and of love to the latter. Truly, those who have not had the fortune of knowing their forefathers in person will be led towards goodness at least through the account of their lives and will be induced to do their best...." In this, Thomas has more than succeeded in the task he set out to accomplish, for the Franciscan message, as he wrote it, is as fresh today as it was seven centuries ago when he first set pen to paper.

Catherine Bolton

FIRST LIFE

In the Name of the Lord, Amen.
Here begins the Prologue to the life of Blessed Francis

With the intention of recounting in order and with pious devotion the acts and life of our most blessed father Francis, always pursuing the truth as my guide and master since there is no one who can remember all his actions and teachings by heart, upon the request of the glorious lord pope Gregory[1] I have committed myself to set forth to the best of my ability but in a plain style, what I myself have at least heard from his own mouth or learned through what has been recounted by proven and faithful witnesses. I wish that I may at least be a worthy disciple of one who always avoided affected and obscure sentences and was unaware of the artifice of rhetoric!

2. I have divided all the material that I was able to gather about the Blessed One into three parts, arranging it in chapters so that there will not be any confusion about the episodes that occurred at different times, nor any doubt about their truth.

The first part follows the events in chronological order[2] and deals especially with the purity of his way of life, his holy works and his salutary teachings. It also includes just some of the many miracles that our Lord deigned to work through him during his lifetime. The second part narrates the events that took place from the next-to-last year of his life until his happy death. Lastly, the third part contains many miracles, overlooking even more, that were worked by the Saint starting from the time in which he reigned gloriously with Christ in heaven. It also describes the worship, honor, praise and glorification that, during his happy reign, Pope Gregory and all the cardinals of the holy Roman Church accorded to him by including him among the saints.

Thanks be to God Almighty who, through his saints, has always revealed Himself to be worthy of admiration and love.

---

[1] Gregory IX (1227-1241), born Hugolin of the Counts of Segni.
[2] Celano does not follow a strictly chronological order. However, the events that took place prior to September 1224 are grouped together in the first part.

PART ONE

To the praise and glory of God almighty,
Father, Son and Holy Spirit. Amen.
Here begins the life of our most blessed father
Francis

CHAPTER I
How he lived in the world

In the city of Assisi, in the area of the Spoleto valley, there was a man named Francis[1] who, from the very beginning of his life, was brought up badly by his parents according to the vanities of the world, and since he had long imitated their lifestyle and morals, he became even more frivolous and conceited.

This is because this vile custom was widespread among those who consider themselves Christians and this detrimental method of raising children this way right from the cradle had taken root everywhere, so that it seemed as if it had been decreed by law.

In fact, as soon as they learn to speak, or rather to babble, these poor little ones, who are barely even born yet, are taught ugly and abominable things through words and gestures. Then, once they have been weaned, they are urged not only to say but even to do decadent things. Out of childish fear, not one of them dares to behave honestly because he would be punished harshly. Therefore, as one of the secular poets says well, "Because we have grown up amidst the bad practices set by our parents, we thus pursue all evil things from the cradle."[2] And this is truthful testimony, for indeed the more harmful the parents' desires are to their children, the more often they come true.

---

[1] The Latin text begins *Vir erat (Jb I, 1)* and Celano would later use this same style at the beginning of the *Legend of St Clare*. Celano does not mention Francis' original baptismal name, John, until the *Second Life*, 3.

[2] Passage from Seneca in his *Moral Letters,* 1. VI, ep. 8.

But when these children are a little older, driven by their own instincts they move on to increasingly worse actions, for rotten roots will usually generate a tree full of faults, and once something has degenerated, it is hard to restore it to its proper state.

And how do you think they become once they reach adolescence? It is then that they truly let themselves float adrift towards debauchery of every kind, and since they are allowed to do everything they please, they carelessly fling themselves into a shameful life. Thus, by submitting voluntarily to the slavery of sin, they turn all their limbs into instruments of iniquity and no longer demonstrating the least sign of Christianity in themselves, their conduct or their morals, they take strength in being Christians in name only. These wretches quite often boast of having worse faults than they actually do, out of fear that the more innocent they are, the more despicable they will seem[3].

2. Such are the sad teachings with which this man, whom we worship today as a saint -- for he is truly a saint -- lived from his very childhood, miserably wasting and passing his time until he was almost twenty-five years old[4]. Indeed, since he had progressed even further in these vanities than all his other peers, he had become a great instigator of evil and a model of foolishness. He was an object of marvel to everyone and in his pompous conceit, he strived to surpass everyone in games, refinery, eloquent words, song and luxurious and flowing clothes, since he was very rich. Indeed, he was not stingy and was not avid in amassing wealth but a spendthrift, a cautious merchant yet very lavish out of vanity. On the other hand, he was very courteous, compliant and affable, unfortunately to a fault. In fact, precisely because of this he was courted by many – those evil instigators – and so, surrounded by hordes of sinners, he strode majestically through the

---

[3] See St. Augustine, *Confessions*, II, 3, 7.
[4] By comparing this relative date with other explicitly documented dates (Francis' initial conversion in 1205-6 and his death in 1226), it has been calculated that he was born in 1182 rather than 1181. See A. Fortini, *Nova Vita*, II.

squares of Babylon[5], haughty and lavish, until out of all His goodness God, who was watching over him from the heavenly heights, turned His rage aside and restrained him by putting the bit of His praise in the wretch's mouth to keep him from sinking completely to the bottom.

The hand of the Lord came over him and the right hand of the Almighty transformed him so that, through him, sinners might gain the hope of living a new life in grace and so that he would become for everyone an example of conversion to God.

CHAPTER II
How God touched his spirit with illness and a dream

3. Thus, while this man continued to live in sin with the zeal of youthful passion and was driven by the feverish impulse of his age to satisfy all his youthful desires as he pleased, since he did not know moderation he was easily driven to evil by the poison of the ancient snake. Suddenly, however, divine vengeance, or rather mercy, began initially to reproach his misled conscience, bringing anguish to his soul and illness to his body in accordance with the prophecy *Therefore, I will hedge in your way with thorns and erect a wall against it*[6].

Debilitated by a lengthy illness (so necessary against human stubbornness, which will only mend its ways through punishment), he began to think very different thoughts than usual. Then, since he was feeling much better, in order to regain his strength he began to wander here and there through the house, leaning on a cane. One day he went out and began to pay closer attention to the countryside that spread out before him, but the beauty of the fields, the pleasure of the vineyards and everything that is a delight to the eye no longer gave him any joy. He was amazed by this

---

[5] Here Celano's imitation of St. Augustine's *Confessions*, II, 3, 8 is evident.
[6] *Hos 2, 8.*

sudden change and considered foolish all those whose hearts are attached to possessions of this kind.

4. From that day on, he began to have little consideration for himself and to despise what he had previously loved and admired.

However, he had not fully and truly loosened the bonds of vanity yet, nor had he shaken the yoke of perverse slavery from his neck. In fact, it is difficult to abandon old habits, for once they have penetrated the soul, they are not easily uprooted. Even if it has been drawn away from them for a long time, the spirit will continue to return to its original habits and through duration, vice will usually become second nature. Thus, Francis still tried to flee from the hand of God and, forgetting about this paternal scolding for a short time now that fortune was smiling on him, he turned worldly cares over in his mind[7] and, unaware of God's designs, promised himself once again to accomplish great things for worldly vainglory.

A nobleman of Assisi was going around arming himself at great expense and, puffed up with vainglory, he had pledged to go to Apulia in order to gain more wealth or honor[8]. Upon hearing this, Francis, flighty and not just a little daring, agreed to leave with this man, to whom he was inferior in nobility of birth but

---

[7] *1 Cor 7, 34.*

[8] According to undocumented tradition, Francis put himself at the disposal of Walter of Brienne, head of the papal militia, to fight against Markwald d'Anweiler. The latter was allied with the Emperor to contend against Innocent III over the guardianship of young Frederick II.

However, since the expedition undertaken by Francis has been dated to 1205 and Markwald died in September of 1202, the enemy must have been Diepold of Vohburg. It is more likely that the conflict reported here was the one between Walter of Brienne, pretender to the principality of Taranto, and the three brothers, Walter, Gentile and Manerio of Pagliara, counts of Manoppello. In fact, both the *Legend of the Three Companions* and the *Legend of Perugia* mention a count named Gentile, whom Francis hoped would arm him as a knight. Walter of Brienne died in June of 1205.

superior in greatness of spirit, and was poorer than he in wealth[9] but more lavishly generous.

5. So one night, while he was completely absorbed with his preparations and was burning with the desire to leave, He who had struck him with the staff of justice visited him in a dream with the sweetness of grace, enticing and exalting Francis, who thirsted for glory, with the very heights of glory. It seemed to him that his house was filled with arms, or in other words, with saddles, shields, lances and other trappings of war, and while he reveled completely in this, he looked about in astonishment, wondering what it could be. In fact, he was not accustomed to seeing these instruments in his house, but rather piles of cloth to sell. And while he was more than a little amazed by this sudden occurrence, he was told that all those arms were for him and for his soldiers. When he awoke the next morning, his spirit still filled with joy, he got up and, interpreting the vision as an omen of great prosperity, he was certain that his trip to Apulia would be successful. But he did not know what he was saying[10] and was still unaware of the gift that was sent down to him from heaven.

He should have understood that his interpretation of the vision was not correct because, although it did have a certain relationship with war-like actions, the vision nevertheless did not give him the joy that he had been accustomed to feeling until then whenever he thought about his undertaking. Rather, he almost had to force himself to complete his plans and put his desired expedition into effect.

It is right to speak of arms at the beginning, for it is fitting that arms be given to a soldier who is about to battle against one who is strong and armed so that, like a second David, he can free Israel from the disgrace of its enemies in the name of the God of armies!

---

[9] Therefore, this cannot be the knight to whom he gave his clothing, as described in the *Second Life*, 5.

[10] *Lk 9, 33; Mk 9, 5.*

CHAPTER III

*How, changed in mind and lifestyle, he spoke
figuratively about the treasure he had found and about his bride*

6. Thus changed, but only in spirit and without giving any external signs of it, Francis refused to go to Apulia and attempted to bend his own will to the will of God. And so, withdrawing somewhat from the noise and business of the world, he made an effort to guard Jesus Christ deep in his heart. Like a prudent merchant, he hid the pearl he had found from the eyes of the scornful and later tried to buy it by selling everything else[11].

In fact, since there was a young man of Assisi, his peer, whom he preferred above all the rest and in whom he felt the urge to confide his secrets because of their long friendship, Francis would often bring him to secluded places that were suitable for meditation, declaring that he had found a great and precious treasure. That young man was jubilant about this and out of curiosity, he willingly went with him whenever he was invited.

There was a cave near the city and they often went there to talk about that treasure. The man of God, already a saint because of the holiness of his intentions, would go into the cave while his companion would stay outside to wait for him and, filled with unusual new fervor, Francis would secretly pray to his Father. He would rejoice that no one knew what he was doing there and, wisely hiding the good for the better, he would seek advice about his holy resolutions only from God. He would devoutly ask the true and eternal God to guide his steps and teach him to do His will. He was prey to a very intense feeling of excitement and would not resign himself until he had accomplished what he had planned. All kinds of thoughts continued to crowd his mind, greatly disturbing him with their insistence. A divine flame burned within him and he was incapable of disguising his ardent spirit from the outside. He regretted that he had sinned so grievously

---

[11] *Mt* 13, 45-46.

and had offended the eyes of the celestial majesty. Past and present vanities no longer delighted him, but he still did not fully trust that he would be able to stay away from the future ones. Therefore, when he would go back outside to his companion, he would feel so weak that he would seem very different coming out than what he had been when he entered.

7. But one day after he had invoked divine mercy with all his heart, God showed him how he was to act. From that point on, he was filled with such great joy that he could not contain himself and so, against his will, some of this joy overflowed to reach the ears of men. Although, due to the immensity of the love that was instilled in him, he was unable to remain silent, what little he did say he stated cautiously and in riddles, and just as he had talked to his best friend this way about a hidden treasure, he tried to speak allegorically to others as well.

He explained that he no longer wanted to go to Apulia, but promised that he would accomplish great and noble exploits in his homeland. The others thought he planned to get married and questioned him. "Could it be that you want to take a wife, Francis?" And he answered, "I will take the noblest and most beautiful bride you have ever seen, one who will surpass all others in beauty and wisdom."

And the true religion that he embraced was truly the bride of God, and the kingdom of heaven was the hidden treasure he had searched for so passionately, for the evangelical vocation had to be accomplished fully in him who would become the minister for the Gospel in faith and truth[12].

---

[12] *Eph* 3,7 and *I Tim* 2, 7.

CHAPTER IV
How, having sold everything, he spurned the money he had earned

8. Since the established time had come, the blessed servant of the Most High, prepared and confirmed in this way by the Holy Spirit, listened to the happy impulse of his soul and raced towards a higher good now that he had trampled over the vanities of the world. On the other hand, he could no longer delay because the deadly disease had already become so widespread everywhere and had paralyzed the limbs of many people so severely that if the doctor delayed even just a bit longer, it would have claimed their lives.

He rose, made the sign of the cross, prepared a horse, bounded into the saddle and, taking scarlet fabric[13] with him to sell, he hastened to the city of Foligno. He sold the goods there, as was his custom and -- lucky merchant! -- he even put his horse up for sale. On his return, freed of his burden, he walked along thinking carefully about what he should do with that money.

Quickly and miraculously converted to God's service, he felt that the money would be too much of a hindrance to him even for an hour and since he gave any advantage it might offer the same consideration as he would sand, he hurried to get rid of it.

On his way back to Assisi, he noticed a church along the way that had been built long before in honor of St. Damian and that now threatened to fall into ruin within a short time.

9. When the new soldier of Christ drew near, he was moved to pity by the sight of such misery and went inside in awe and reverence. Finding a poor priest in there, Francis kissed his sacred hands with great faith, gave him all the money he had with him and explained his intentions. The priest, amazed by that incredible and sudden conversion, could not believe his ears and thinking that he was being made fun of, he refused to take the

---

[13] Scarlet fabric was also the most costly.

money being offered. In fact, he had seen Francis the day before, so to speak, living licentiously among his friends and relatives and surpassing them all in vanity. But with great insistence, the young man tried to convince him of the truth of his words, praying and begging him to let him live with him out of the love of God.

The priest finally agreed to Francis' request to lodge there, but fearing Francis' relatives, he wouldn't accept the money. Hence that true disparager of money threw it onto a window sill, caring as much about it as he would of dust. He desired to possess only wisdom, which is better than gold, and to acquire prudence, which is more precious than silver.[14]

CHAPTER V
How his father persecuted him and held him prisoner

10. While the servant of the Most High was staying in that place, his father went everywhere, investigating like a diligent explorer in order to find out what had happened to his son. As soon as he learned that Francis was living there in that way, saddened to the bottom of his heart and greatly disturbed by such an unthinkable occurrence, he assembled his friends and neighbors and hurried down to the place where the servant of God was staying. As soon as Francis, who was new to Christ's battles, heard about the threats of his persecutors, he anticipated their arrival and in order to escape their rage, he descended into a hidden cavern that he had excavated for this very purpose.

For one month, he remained hidden in that ditch, which was in his house and was known only to one person, and would only dare to come out for the bare necessities. When he was given food from time to time, he would eat in the dark pit and any service was given to him secretly. Tear-soaked, he begged God to deliver him from the hands of those who were persecuting his

---

[14] *Prov* 16, 16.

soul and to fulfill his vows through the mercy of grace. During his fasting and his weeping, he invoked the clemency of our Savior and, not trusting himself, he placed all his faith in God. Even though he was down in the dark pit, he was nevertheless filled with an unspeakable happiness that he had never felt before. Kindled by this fire, at last he abandoned his refuge and faced the insults of his persecutors.

11. He thus arose, prompt, impatient and ready, and taking up the shield of faith, he armed himself with great faith to fight the Lord's battles and started to walk towards the city, accusing himself, in his divine enthusiasm, of idleness and cowardice.

As soon they saw him, all those who knew him, comparing his present state with what he had been, began to insult him, calling him foolish and mad, and they threw mud and flung rocks at him from the street. They found him so changed from his usual behavior, exhausted by his self-mortification, that they thought his actions were due to fatigue and madness.

But since patience is worth more than arrogance[15], the servant of God turned a deaf ear and, without becoming unruffled or losing his temper over these insults, he gave thanks to God for those trials. It is useless for sinners to persecute those who want to do good, because the more embattled they are, then the greater the triumph of their fortitude will be. Someone once said that humiliation makes a generous spirit even stronger[16].

12. That noise and those shouts spread throughout the streets and squares of the city, together with the echoes of his mockery and since this had reached the ears of many people, it also reached his father's. When he heard his son's name being uttered, feeling as if all the slander of the townspeople were addressed directly to him, he moved quickly, not to save Francis but to ruin him. Losing all reserve, he rushed upon him like a wolf upon sheep and, glaring at him with grim and threatening scowl,

---

[15] *Ecc* 7, 8.
[16] This has been attributed to Seneca, *Moral Letters*, 1, IV, ep. 10, 2.

he brutally set his hands on him and dragged him into the house. There he pitilessly kept him locked away in a dark place[17] and tried to bend him to his will, first with words and then with beatings and chains.

But the young man, who through his very sufferings had become even stronger and more prepared to accomplish his holy intention, never lost his patience with either this harsh reproof or with his nerve-wracking imprisonment.

Indeed, the man who has been ordered to rejoice in his tribulations will not go back on his just intentions and feelings on account of whips and chains, nor can he be turned away from the flock of Christ. Truly, he who takes refuge in the Son of God during times of distress will not tremble when the flood waters rise because, in order to make our own troubles seem less harsh, He has shown us that He suffered much worse on our behalf.

CHAPTER VI

How his mother freed him,
and how he took his clothes off before the Bishop of Assisi

13. Now it happened that due to urgent family matters, for a certain amount of time Francis' father had to be away from his house, where the servant of God was kept imprisoned. Therefore, his mother, now left alone with him and disapproving of her husband's actions, spoke sweetly to her son, but seeing that it was impossible to dissuade him from his resolve, she was moved to the bottom of her maternal heart and broke his bonds to set him free.

So, thanking Almighty God, he quickly returned to the place he had been before.

---

[17] This was a small room in the wall of modern-day Chiesa Nuova, located just off the main square.

By this time, the experience of temptation had freed him even more and after the many hardships he had faced, he even looked more peaceful. His spirit had been strengthened under abuse and, going everywhere with great candor, he went ahead more boldly.

In the meantime, his father returned and when he couldn't find him, he heaped sin upon sin by covering his wife with rude insults. Then, quaking and shouting, he ran to St. Damian's to force Francis at least get out of the district, given that he was unable to bring him back to what he had been before. And this time, since the fear of God makes one trust in safety[18], as soon as Francis heard that his flesh-and-blood father was coming to look for him, the son of grace confidently and happily went forth to meet him, declaring that he was not afraid of chains or beatings, and he asserted moreover that he was prepared to submit joyfully to any evil, in the name of Christ.

14. Seeing that he would not be able to turn him back from his new path, his father then focused all his attention on taking his money away from him. The man of God had decided to spend it to feed the poor and restore the chapel. Nevertheless, since he did not love money, he would not allow himself to be deceived by the appearance of goodness and since he felt no sort of attachment to money, he felt no concern about losing it. Therefore, the discovery of the sum that the great disparager of earthly things and avid seeker of heavenly riches had tossed into the dust on a window sill, managed to soothe the anger of his father, whose thirsty greediness was somewhat appeased by the relief he felt over his discovery.

Nevertheless, Francis' father summoned him to appear before the bishop of the city[19] to force him to relinquish all his

---

[18] *Prov* 14, 26.

[19] The Bishop was Guido II, Bishop of Assisi from about 1204 until 1228. His father had requested that Francis appear before the consuls, but Francis refused to appear before government authorities, declaring that at this point he was servant only to the Most High, as he had been "converted" at St. Damian's.

property into the hands of the bishop and to give back everything that he still possessed. Not only did Francis fail to pose any resistance to this, but he joyfully hastened to accomplish what had been asked of him.

15. Therefore, called before the bishop, he did not stand for any delay or hesitate under any pretext. Indeed, without saying or awaiting a word, he immediately took off all his clothes and threw them onto the ground, returning them to his father. He did not even keep his underpants and he stood stark naked in front of everyone. The bishop, understanding his intentions and admiring his fervor and constancy, immediately stood up, took him into his arms and covered him with his own cloak. He understood clearly that divine inspiration was at work and that the act of the man of God, which he had witnessed, held a mysterious meaning. Thus, from that moment on, he became his protector and embraced him with the depths of charity, supporting and comforting him.

So there he was, struggling naked against the naked enemy, and having thrown aside all the world's vanities, he recalled only divine justice. He tried to keep his own life on a base level, abandoning all care for himself so that through poverty, he could achieve peace on such a perilous path and so that the thin shield of the flesh would now be the only thing keeping him from seeing God.

CHAPTER VII
How, seized by bandits, he was thrown into the snow,
and how he devoted himself to helping lepers

16. Wrapped in ragged clothing, he who had once dressed in scarlet was walking through the woods singing God's praise in French[20] when he was suddenly set upon by bandits, who

---

[20] This is a sign of the great joy Francis felt that day since, as Celano has often noted (particularly in the *Second Life,* 127), St. Francis would sing in French when he was particularly happy.

brusquely asked him who he was. Full of confidence, the man of God replied in a sure voice, "I am the herald of the great King. What is it to you?" At that, they beat him and tossed him into a ditch filled with snow, saying, "Then you sit there, villain herald of God!" As soon as they left, however, he rolled about to shake the snow off and bounded from the ditch. Overjoyed, he began to praise the Creator of all things and his lauds echoed loudly throughout the woods[21].

He arrived finally at a monastery where, dressed only in a rough work-shirt, he stayed in the kitchen for many days working as an errand boy, reduced to being satisfied with just a bit of thin soup! Then, however, since he had found no piety and didn't even manage to obtain an old habit, he left -- not out of scorn but out of need -- and went to the city of Gubbio where he was given a poor tunic by a man who had once been a friend of his[22]. Some time later, since the fame of the man of God was growing and spreading among the people, the prior of that monastery, recalling how Francis had been treated, went to beg forgiveness for himself and his men in the name of the Savior.

17. The saint who loved perfect humility then went among the lepers and stayed with them, helping them with all their needs out of the love of God. He washed their decaying bodies and cleaned the matter from their wounds, doing so, as he himself stated in his *Testament,* "because when I was in sin, the sight of lepers disturbed me, and the Lord brought me among them and I practiced piety with them."[23] He would recount that the sight of lepers had previously bothered him so much that, during his life of vanity, whenever he caught a glimpse of their hospices two miles away from him, he would pinch his nostrils shut. Nevertheless, since through the grace and virtue of the Most High he had already begun to think holy and salutary thoughts, while he was still a worldly person, one day he met a leper and, steeling himself,

---

[21] This event seems to have taken place at the beginning of 1207.
[22] Later documents have identified this man as Frederick Spadalunga.
[23] See *The Writings of St. Francis.*

he went up to him and kissed him[24]. From that moment on, he began to despise himself more and more until, through the mercy of the Redeemer, he succeeded in conquering himself completely. He also assisted other poor people, even while he was still living in the world, and would respect the maxims about them, stretching his hand out to the needy and lovingly sympathizing with the afflicted.

In fact, one day when, contrary to his usual custom -- for he was always very courteous -- he had rudely turned down a poor man who was begging him for alms, he regretted it and began to say to himself that it would be very rude and shameful not to satisfy a request made in the name of such a great King. Therefore, in his heart he decided that anything in his power would never be denied to anyone who asked for it in the name of God and he faithfully kept this promise, giving of his entire self and putting the advice of the Gospel into practice even before he taught it: "Give to the man who begs from you. Do not turn your back on the borrower."[25]

CHAPTER VIII
How he repaired the Church of St. Damian,
and about the way of life of the Ladies who lived there

18. The first work that blessed Francis set his hands to as soon as he had been freed from the yoke of his blood father, was to rebuild one of the Lord's temples. He did not attempt to build Him a new one, but repaired an old and dilapidated church instead. He did not undermine the foundations but built over them, thus reserving his privilege with Christ without even knowing it. In fact, no one can lay any other foundation than the one that has

---

24 *Second Life*, 9.
25 *Mt* 5, 42.

already been laid, namely Jesus Christ[26]. Thus, returning to the place where, as we have said, the church of St. Damian had been constructed long before, with the grace of the Most High he carefully restored it in a short time.

This is the blessed and holy place in which, through the work of Francis himself, the glorious religion and most excellent Order of the Poor Ladies and holy virgins was founded almost six years after the conversion of blessed Francis[27]. This was the place where lady Clare, a native of the city of Assisi, most precious and strong stone, was the foundation for the other stones that were laid over her. In fact, having been converted to the Lord through the Saint's encouragement following the beginning of the Order of the Friars Minor[28], she was the source of spiritual gain for many and was an example to countless people. She was noble by birth but even more noble in grace, virgin in body and purest of spirit, young in age but old in judgment, constant in her resolve and burning with the enthusiasm of divine love, rich in wisdom and humility, Clare by name, brighter in her life, brightest in virtue[29].

19. Erected above her was the noble edifice of those most precious pearls whose praises cannot be sung by men but only by God[30], because limited human thought cannot suffice to conceive of it, nor is meager human language enough to repeat it.

---

[26] *1 Cor* 3, 11.

[27] This undoubtedly means "initial conversion" between 1205 and 1206, rather than his full conversion, which took place when he renounced his father's property at the beginning of 1207.

[28] She took the veil on the night of Holy Monday, March 28, 1211. As soon as St. Francis gave her the habit of poverty at the Porziuncola, she was brought immediately to the Benedictine monastery of St. Paul near Bastia, and shortly thereafter to the monastery of Sant'Angelo di Panzo on Mount Subasio. Finally, together with her sister Agnes, within a matter of a few weeks or months at the most she went to St. Damian's.

[29] The name Clare is derived from the word "clarus" in Latin ("chiara" in Italian), an adjective meaning "bright, clear, unclouded, renowned". Here Celano's dual meaning of the word is unfortunately lost in the translation.

[30] *Rom* 2, 29.

In fact, what flourishes above all else in their lives is the supreme virtue of mutual and continuous charity, which so closely unites their will that even in a community of forty or fifty, as is the case in some places, their common will makes a single soul out of many.

In the second place, gleaming in each one of them is the gem of humility, which preserves heavenly goods so that they will earn the gift of all the other virtues.

Thirdly, the lily of virginity and chastity has given all of them such a marvelous fragrance that, forgetting all earthly thoughts, they wish only to meditate about heavenly things and this fragrance has generated such great love in their hearts for the eternal Groom that the fullness of this holy love keeps them away from any ties to their former lives.

In the fourth place, all of them have been invested with the title of most holy poverty, so that they are scarcely willing to satisfy the bare necessities of food and clothing.

20. Fifthly, they have attained the grace of silence and abstinence to such a degree that it is hardly any effort for them to repress the stirrings of the flesh and to hold their tongues. Some of them are so unaccustomed to conversation that when they are forced to speak, they can barely remember how to formulate words properly.

Sixthly, among all these merits, they are so adorned with the virtue of patience that no tribulation or nuisance can break or change their spirit.

Lastly, in the seventh place, they have earned the lofty heights of contemplation so that through this, they have learned what they must do or avoid and they are happily able to lose themselves in God, spending night and day in divine praise and prayer.

May the Eternal God, through His holy grace, deign to crown such a holy beginning with an even holier end[31]. And may

---

[31] Clare died many years later, on August 11, 1253, and was canonized in 1255.

these few words about the virgins consecrated to God, most devout handmaidens of Christ, suffice for the time being since their
marvelous life and glorious rules, which they received from lord
Pope Gregory, Bishop of Ostia[32] at that time, entails its own
book as well as the opportunity to write it[33].

CHAPTER IX

*How, having changed his life, he repaired the Church of St. Mary's in the
Porziuncola; and how, upon hearing a passage from the Gospel,
he left everything behind and invented the habit used by the friars*

21. In the meantime, having changed his lifestyle and repaired the church we mentioned before, the Saint of God moved
to another place near the city of Assisi. There, he began to rebuild
a church that was dilapidated and almost destroyed, but he did not
stop the good works he had started until everything had been
completed[34]. From there, he moved to another place called the
Porziuncola, where a church had been built during ancient times
in honor of the Blessed Virgin Mother of God. By this time, it
had been abandoned and no one took care of it. Upon seeing it in
such ruin, he took great pity, also because he was fervently devoted to the Mother of all goodness, and established his dwelling
there. He then finished restoring it during the third year of his
conversion. At that time, he wore a habit similar to the one used
by hermits: a leather belt, a rod in his hand and sandals on his
feet.

22. In that church one day, during the Gospel reading
about how the Lord had sent his apostles to preach, the Saint of

---

[32] The was the *Way of Life* that was given to the Poor Clares by Cardinal Hugolin
in 1218-19.

[33] This chapter is a rough draft for the biography that Celano later wrote in
around 1255 and that was entitled *The Life of St. Clare, Virgin*.

[34] This refers to the church of San Pietro della Spina, near San Petrignano, located between St. Damian's and the Porziuncola.

God, who was present and had roughly understood the meaning of those evangelical words, begged the priest to explain the passage to him once the celebration of the Mass was over. The priest agreed, explaining all the details to him, and when Francis heard that the disciples must not possess gold, nor silver, nor money, nor should they carry rucksacks, nor travel bags, nor bread, nor a walking staff, nor have sandals, nor two tunics[35], but that they must only preach the kingdom of God and penance, exulting with divine fervor, he suddenly exclaimed, "This is what I want and what I ask: this is what I wish to do with all my heart."

Thus the holy Father, overcome with happiness, hastened to carry out this salutary counsel and did not hesitate to put what he had heard into devout practice. He immediately untied his sandals, threw down his staff and, content with just one tunic, he got a rope to use in place of a belt. From that time on, he made his cowl in the shape of the cross so that it would keep all the devil's illusions away. He made it extremely rough in order to crucify the flesh, with all its sin and vice. Lastly, he made it very poor and coarse-looking so that the world would feel no envy for it. With the same transport, he also tried diligently to carry out all the other advice he had heard.

Because he never turned a deaf ear to the Gospel but committed what he heard to his sharp memory, he attempted to accomplish everything to the letter.

CHAPTER X
*Of his preaching of the Gospel and his announcement of peace;
and of the conversion of the first six brothers*

23. Then with great fervor of spirit and gladness of mind, he began to preach penance to everyone, edifying his listeners with his simple speech and generous heart. His words were like a

---

[35] *Mt* 10, 9-10.

blazing fire that penetrated to the depths of people's hearts, arousing everyone's admiration. Everything about him seemed different than before and, intent upon heaven, he disdained to gaze upon the earth. And another thing that is surely marvelous is that he began to preach in exactly the same place where he had learned to read as a boy and which would later become his first burial place, so that a happy beginning was crowned with an even happier ending. He taught where he had learned and he happily ended where he had begun[36].

In all his preaching, before explaining the word of God to the people who had gathered, he would wish them peace by saying, "May the Lord's peace be with you!" He always devoutly announced this peace to men and women when they came to him or when they left, so it happened that because of this wish, many people who hated both peace and salvation embraced peace wholeheartedly through the grace of God and they in turn became children of peace and yearned for eternal salvation.

24. Among them, a man from Assisi who was pious and simple in spirit was the first to follow the man of God in devotion[37]. Then brother Bernard, who wanted to join this mission of peace, readily pursued the Saint of God[38] to gain the kingdom of heaven. Since he had often extended his hospitality to the blessed Father, he was thus able to see and experience Francis' life and

---

[36] This was the church of St. George (the site over which the Basilica of St. Clare would later be built), which is where he first learned the basics of Latin and religious teachings and was the place in which he was buried the day after his death. After his canonization (July 16, 1228), in 1230 his body was translated to his permanent tomb beneath the basilica of the Hill of Paradise, site of the Basilica of St. Francis.

[37] There is quite a bit of mystery surrounding this first and anonymous companion. Some scholars have identified him as the friend who accompanied Francis to meditate prior to his conversion (*First Life*, 3).

[38] Dante expressed this as:

> *"... so first the venerable Bernard bared*
> *His feet, and to such great peace swiftly hied,*
> *And thought he went slow, though he ran so hard."*
> (Par. XI, 79-81)

customs and find comfort in the odor of his sanctity. In this way, he came to understand the fear of God and brought forth a salutary spirit. He had seen him sleep very little and spend the entire night in prayer, praising God and the glorious Virgin, His mother. Thus, filled with admiration, he had said to himself, "Truly this man comes from God!"

Accordingly, he hurried to sell all his possessions and distributed the proceeds to the poor rather than to his relatives. Committing himself to the way of perfection, he fulfilled the advice of the Gospel: *'If you seek perfection, go, sell your possessions, and give to the poor. You will then have treasure in heaven. Afterward, come back and follow me.'*[39]

After he had done this, he joined St. Francis, copying his habit, and he remained with him constantly until the number of brothers had grown and, in obedience to the pious father, he was sent to other regions[40]. His conversion to God continued to be an example to all those who were converted by selling their property and distributing it to the poor.

St. Francis was extraordinarily jubilant over the arrival and conversion of such a pious man, since it seemed to him that the Lord was taking care of him by giving him a needed companion and a faithful friend at the same time.

25. He was followed shortly by another Assisan, worthy of great praise because of his life, which ended even more piously than it had begun[41]. Following after him was Brother Giles, a simple and upright man full of the fear of God who, persevering for a long time in a holy, just and pious life, leaves us an example

---

[39] *Mt* 19, 21. These were the words that were read from the Gospel by the priest at the church of St. Nicholas on April 16, 1209 *(Chronica XXIV Generalium* in *Anal. Franc.* III).

[40] He also went to Spain with St. Francis, as indicated in *the Treatise of Miracles*, 33.

[41] This was Peter Catanii, lawyer and canon of San Rufino. He died at the Porziuncola in March of 1221.

of perfect obedience, manual toil, meditation and holy contemplation[42].

Yet another one joined them[43] and at last there were seven of them counting Brother Philip, whose lips God had touched with the stone of purification[44], so that he spoke about Him with marvelous anointing. Although he had not studied, he interpreted the Holy Scriptures and explained even the most recondite meanings, resembling those men whom the leaders of the Jews mocked as ignorant and unlettered.

CHAPTER XI
Of St. Francis' spirit of prophecy and of his predictions

26. Therefore, our blessed father Francis was filled with the consolation and grace of the Holy Spirit more and more each day and with careful consideration, he began to mold his new sons through a new method, teaching them to walk sure-footedly along the path of holy poverty and blessed simplicity.

Now one day, admiring the mercy of the Lord in all the good bestowed upon him and waiting for God to show him how he and his brothers should progress, he went to the place of prayer, as he did quite often. He remained there at length to pray in fear and trembling to the Master of the entire world and, frequently repeating the words, "O God, be gracious to me, a sinner!", he felt unspeakable happiness and immense sweetness filling him to the bottom of his heart. At that point, it was as if he were outside of himself and his anguish subsided, the darkness that had clouded his heart out of fear of sin dissipated and he was filled with the certainty that his sins would be remitted and took

---

[42] Giles long outlived Francis. His death has been dated to April 22, 1262.
[43] According to tradition, Giles was followed by Sabbatino, Morico, John of Cappella and Philip Longo (the Long), who was the well-known visitor to the convent of the Poor Clares, as stated in the *Life of St. Clare*, 37.
[44] *Is* 11, 6.

faith that he would live in grace. In rapture beyond his being and absorbed in divine illumination, by broadening the horizons of his mind he was able to contemplate the future at his leisure. Lastly, when that sweetness vanished with the light, it was as if he had a new soul and he now seemed to have become a new man.

27. So he joyously went back and said to his brothers, "Be comforted, dear brothers, and rejoice in the Lord. You should not be downhearted when you see that there are just a few of you. Do not upset my and your simplicity, for it has been revealed to me in truth that God will turn us into an immense multitude and will spread us to the ends of the earth. For your benefit, I must tell you what I saw, even though I would prefer to keep it to myself if it weren't for the love that is compelling me to speak. I saw a great multitude of men coming to us out of the desire to be united under the habit of our saintly life in common and the rule of the blessed Order and the noise of their comings and goings in the command of holy obedience is still ringing in my ears. I saw the roads filled with crowds of them converging here from almost every nation. The French are coming, the Spanish are hastening, the Germans and the English are gathering and a great crowd speaking other languages is coming in haste."

Upon hearing this, the brothers were filled with salutary joy, not only because of the grace that the Lord was granting his Saint, but also because they thirsted ardently for the good of others and hoped that every day other souls would arrive to increase their number in seeking salvation together.

28. And the Saint continued, "To thank the Lord our God for all his gifts faithfully and devoutly, o brothers, and so that you may be aware of how the brothers should live now and in the future, listen to the truth about future events. In the beginning of our life in common, we will find very sweet and pleasant fruit to eat, but shortly thereafter we will have other fruit that will not taste as good. Lastly, we will harvest still other fruit that is full of bitterness, which we will be unable to eat, for even though it is fragrant and beautiful on the outside, it will be so tart that no one

will be able to eat it. And truly, as I have said to you, the Lord will make us grow until we become a great people, but in the end we will be like a fisherman who tosses his nets into the sea or into some lake and takes in an abundance of fish but who, after he has put them all into his boat, not wanting to carry them since there are too many, chooses the best and biggest to put into his baskets and then tosses the rest out[45]."

What great truth shines from all these predictions made by the Saint, and how honest they have turned out to be, is quite evident to those who consider them in the spirit of truth. This is how the spirit of prophecy rested upon St. Francis[46].

CHAPTER XII

How he sent his brothers into the world two by two;
and how after a short time they were reunited

29. At that time, since another respectable man had entered the religion[47], there were now eight of them in number. So blessed Francis summoned all of them and after speaking about the kingdom of God, contempt for the world, the repudiation of one's own will and of how one's body must be subdued, he divided them into four groups and said to them, "Dear brothers, go forth two by two to the various parts of the world, announcing to men peace and penance in the remission of sin, and be patient in your trials, certain that the Lord will accomplish His design and keep His promises. Respond humbly to anyone who questions you, bless those who persecute you and thank those who insult

---

[45] *Mt* 13, 47-48.

[46] *Is* 11, 2 and *Rev* 19, 10.

[47] This appears to refer once again to Philip the Long, indicated previously; this would mean seven companions plus Francis. In any case, it is not easy to establish the order in which his first followers joined him.

and slander you[48], because the eternal kingdom is being prepared for us through them."

Now, since they had joyfully accepted the command of holy obedience, they prostrated themselves on the ground before St. Francis, who tenderly and devotedly embraced them and said to each one, "Trust in the Lord and He will take care of you."[49] This is what he said each time he sent one of his brothers out in obedience.

30. Thus, Brother Bernard and Brother Giles set off towards St. James[50]. Then St. Francis, together with another companion, chose a different direction. The other four, going two by two, went off in the two remaining directions.

But after just a short time had gone by, since St. Francis wished to see them all again, he prayed to the Lord who has always gathered the lost people of Israel[51], so that in His mercy He would deign to reunite them soon. Just as he had desired, in a short time and without having been summoned by anyone, they were able to meet again and give thanks to God. They expressed their joy over seeing their pious shepherd again and marveled that they had had the very same thought. They recounted the gifts that they received from the merciful Lord and for any faults of negligence or ingratitude, they requested and humbly accepted their chastisement and penance from the holy Father.

This, in fact, is what they were always accustomed to doing when they went to him and they did not hide their least thoughts or even the involuntary impulses of their souls. Moreover, when they had completed everything that they had been ordered to do, they considered themselves useless servants[52]. Indeed, that first family of blessed Francis was filled with the spirit of purity, so

---

[48] *Mt* 5, 44.
[49] *Ps* 55, 23.
[50] The famous sanctuary of St. James of Compostela in the Galizia area of Spain.
[51] *Is* 58, 8.
[52] *Lk* 18, 10-13.

that although they were able to accomplish useful, holy and just works, they would never take vain pleasure from them.

Having welcomed his sons in great charity, the blessed Father disclosed his intentions and told them what the Lord had revealed to him.

31. In the meantime, four other virtuous and worthy men came to join the followers of the Saint of God[53], whereby this caused a great stir among the people and his fame spread even further.

At that time, St. Francis and his brothers exulted with extraordinary cheerfulness when, led by the spirit of God, one of the faithful, no matter who he was or what his status might have been -- rich or poor, noble or lowly, contemptible or honorable, erudite cleric or ignorant layman -- would come from the population to take the habit of the holy Order.

All of them also aroused the great admiration of the men of the world and through the example of their humility, they urged them to lead a better life and to do penance for their sins. Neither a lowly condition nor base poverty could keep anyone from finding edification in holy works, whom that God, who delights in being with those the world finds despicable and with the simple, wished to edify.

CHAPTER XIII

How, having eleven brothers, he first wrote the Rule,
which was then approved by Pope Innocent;
and about the vision of the tree

32. Seeing that every day the Lord was increasing their number, simply and concisely Blessed Francis wrote a way of life

---

[53] They were John of San Costanzo, Barbaro, Bernard of Vigilante and Angelo Tancredi.

and rule[54] for himself and for his brothers, both present and future, making particular use of expressions from the holy Gospel, whose perfection was the only thing he desired. He nevertheless included a few other precepts required for the practice of good community life. Then he went to Rome with all the brothers we have cited, fervently wishing to have Pope Innocent III confirm what he had written so far.

The venerable bishop of Assisi, Guido, who honored and venerated St. Francis and all the brothers with special affection, happened to be in Rome at that time. Not knowing why they had come, he was greatly disturbed when he saw them, for he was afraid that they wanted to leave their town, in which the Lord had already begun to work immense good through His servants. He was extremely happy to have such holy men in his diocese, for he expected great things from them because of their way of life, but once he heard the reason for their trip and learned of their plan, he rejoiced greatly in the Lord and promise to advise and help them.

St. Francis was also introduced to the reverend bishop of Sabine, John of St. Paul[55], who had a reputation among the princes and prelates of the Roman Curia for despising worldly things and loving the heavenly ones. He welcomed him affectionately and highly praised his resolution and intentions.

33. Nevertheless, being a prudent and moderate man, he objected that there were many difficulties and tried to persuade him to embrace monastic or hermitic life[56]. However, St. Francis rejected his proposals as humbly as he could, not out of disdain but because a more sublime desire was driving him towards a dif-

---

[54] This refers to the "Regula prima" or Rule of 1221, which was replaced two years later with the "Regula secunda" or "bullata", which bore the written approval of Honorius III.

[55] A Benedictine at the monastery of St. Paul and later cardinal under the title of St. Prisca and lastly, bishop of Sabine. He died in 1215.

[56] In other words, to enter one of the existing religious orders, especially the Benedictines or the Augustinian hermits.

ferent goal. The bishop admired his fervor, but fearing that he would withdraw from such lofty intentions, he showed him an easier path. In the end, won over by his insistent entreaties, he consented and tried to promote the issue before the pope[57].

The head of the Church of God at that time was Innocent II, glorious pontiff who was very knowledgeable, famous for his eloquence and fervent in his zeal for justice wherever the Christian faith required it. When he learned of the vow made by the men of God, after deep reflection he agreed to their petition and once their experiment was completed, he ratified it. After numerous exhortations and instructions, he blessed St. Francis and his brothers saying, "Go with God, brother, and as He deigns to inspire you, so too must you preach penance to everyone. When Almighty God has helped you grow in number and in grace, you will return joyously to tell me about it and I will grant you even more numerous benefits and will entrust more important tasks to you with greater confidence[58]."

The Lord was truly with blessed Francis wherever he went, cheering him with revelations and encouraging him with His favor. One night as he was dozing off, he had a vision that he was walking along a road and on the side of the road stood a majestic, stout and beautiful tree that was quite big and tall. As he approached it and stood under it to observe its beauty and height, he suddenly found that he had grown so tall that he was able to touch the top of the tree. He took the treetop and with just one hand, he could quite easily bend it down to the ground. This is in fact what happened when Innocent, the tallest and loftiest tree in the world, bowed down so benevolently to his petition and will.

---

[57] St. Bonaventure (*Major Life*, III, 9) later made explicit reference to the opposition set forth by several cardinals.

[58] This recount indicates that there was a certain time lapse between Francis' petition and the approval of the Rule. The pope's hesitation is detailed by the numerous visions described in later texts such as the *Second Life*, 16-17, and St. Bonaventure's *Major Life*, III, 8.

CHAPTER XIV
Of his return from the city of Rome to the Spoleto valley
and of one of his stops along the way

34. Exulting over the gifts and the grace of this father and lord, St. Francis and his brothers gave thanks to almighty God, who elevates the humble and comforts the afflicted[59]. Shortly thereafter, he went to visit the basilica of blessed Peter and then, having completed his prayers, he and his companions set off for the Spoleto valley.

Along the way, they discussed the many great gifts the most clement God had bestowed upon them, the benevolent welcome given to them by the vicar of Christ, lord and father of all Christianity, how to accomplish his advice and commands, how exactly to observe the Rule that they had taken upon themselves and safeguard it without falling away from it, the path to follow in holiness before the Most High and lastly, how by enhancing their holy virtues they could be an example to their neighbors through their lives and their customs.

The new disciples of Christ had already discussed these matters at great length in this school of humility and it was late in the day, which was now drawing to an end. In the meantime, they had arrived at a deserted place where, rather tired and hungry, they were unable to find any food since that place was quite far from any inhabited areas. But through divine providence, there suddenly appeared a man bearing some bread, which he gave to them and then left. Since they didn't know him, they were quite astonished and they devoutly exhorted each other to place greater faith in divine mercy. Eating that food and feeling refreshed, they then went on to a place near the city of Orte and stopped there for about fifteen days.

Some of them went into the city to purchase the vital essentials and what little they were able to procure by begging from

---

[59] *Jb* 5, 11.

door to door they would bring back to the other brothers, eating together contentedly and giving thanks to the Lord. Then, if anything was left over and they were unable to donate it to some poor person, they would place it in a tomb, which had once held the dead, so that they could eat it later. That place was deserted and abandoned and precious few, indeed virtually no one, passed by there.

35. They were very happy, since they did not see or have anything that could give them vain or sensual delight. Thus, they began to enjoy holy poverty and, fully comforted even in their lack of all the things of this world, they decided to continue living united perpetually with poverty, just as they had done there. Moreover, since they had set aside all worldly cares and delighted only in divine consolation, they firmly resolved that they would not allow temptation to tear them away from its embrace. While the enchanting beauty of that region was no danger for them -- although it certainly did not lack the power to weaken spiritual strength -- they nevertheless left that place so that a longer stay would not give any semblance of ownership and, following the blessed Father, they then proceeded to the Spoleto valley.

Being true worshippers of justice, they asked if they should stay among men or go to solitary places, but St. Francis, who being mistrustful of himself made each decision through holy prayer, chose to live not for himself but for Him who died for all[60], fully aware that he had been sent to gain for God the souls that the devil had tried to tear away from Him.

CHAPTER XV

Of St. Francis' fame and of how many were converted to God;
how the Order came to be called the Order of the Friars Minor;
and how St. Francis educated those who entered the Order

---

[60] *2 Cor* 5, 14-15.

36. Thus, that most stalwart soldier of God traveled through cities and villages announcing the kingdom of God, doing so not with the cleverness of human knowledge but with the wisdom and virtue of the Spirit, preaching peace and teaching the way to salvation and penance through the remission of sin[61].

Because of the authority granted to him by the apostolic See, he acted with full confidence without resorting to adulation or soothing flattery[62]. He was unable to pamper vice but harmed it, did not approve of those who lived in sin but shook them up with sharp rebukes. Since he had brought himself, first of all, to do what he was instilling in other with his words and thus was not afraid of being caught in contradiction, he proclaimed the truth frankly, so that even very learned men who were illustrious in fame and rank admired his speeches and trembled in wholesome fear before him. Men and women gathered and clerics and religious hastened, so that they could see and hear the Saint of God, who appeared to everyone to be a man from another world.

People of all ages and both sexes hurried to gaze upon the marvels that the Lord was working once again in the world through his servant. Truly St. Francis' presence, or even his mere fame, seemed to be a new light sent from heaven to earth to drive away the haze of darkness that had already covered almost the entire region, to the point that hardly anyone knew which way to turn. In fact, everyone had fallen into such deep oblivion of the Lord and in such numb heedlessness of His commandments that they found it hard to free themselves, even just a little, from this ancient and ingrained evil.

37. He shone like a dazzling star in the dark night and like the morning light rising over the darkness[63], so that soon the entire region changed in appearance and became more pleasant,

---

[61] This entire section makes numerous allusions to passages from the four Evangelists and from the letters of St. Paul.

[62] Innocent III had entrusted him with moral preaching.

[63] This is also how the speech given by Pope Gregory during St. Francis' canonization rites began.

losing its horror. The previous aridity disappeared and the harvest immediately flourished in the once-dismal field, the uncultivated vines also began to give forth the seed of God's lovely fragrance and, blossoming in sweet flowers, they produced the fruits of honesty and goodness. Hymns of thanks and praise resounded everywhere, so that many, abandoning the cares of the world, came to know themselves through the life and teachings of the blessed father Francis and began to love and worship the Creator. Touched by divine inspiration, many people -- nobles and plebeians, clerics and laymen -- began to go to St. Francis, wanting to battle forever under his guidance and orders. Like a very abundant stream of heavenly grace, the Saint of God watered all of them with the waters of charism, making the flowers of virtue blossom in the garden of their hearts: the excellent Craftsman was the rule behind this example and its teachings -- solemn boast! -- renewed the Church of Christ among the faithful of both genders and the triple militia of the elect triumphed. He gave a way of life to everyone and showed the true path of salvation to each one according to his condition[64].

38. Above all, however, we must discuss the Order that he embraced and then kept forever through his love and vow, for he was the one who originally founded the Order of the Friars Minor. This is how he gave it its name. While it was being written in the Rule that "we are lesser,"[65] upon hearing this passage being read to him, he exclaimed, "I want this fraternity to be called the Order of the Friars Minor."

[HUMILITY]. And they were truly "lesser", since they were always subject to all and sought the lowliest place and the most vile occupations so that they might deserve to have a solid foundation in true humility, on which to build the edifice of all virtue.

---

[64] This section refers to the three great Franciscan orders: the first is the Order of the Friars Minor, while the second one is the Order of the Poor Clares. The Third Order Secular is for those who, while remaining in the world, want to profess the Franciscan gospel.

[65] *Rule*, I, chap. 7.

[CHARITY] And truly on this stable foundation there stood the noble structure of charity where, like living stones gathered from all parts of the world, they were used to erect the temple of the Holy Spirit. O, what great ardor burned in the new disciples of Christ! How great was the love of those in this pious community! When they met somewhere or if by chance they ran into each other along the way, spiritual affection, which is the beginning of all true love, would stand out above all other love. What else can I say? There were chaste embraces, gentle expressions, saintly kisses, pleasant words, modest laughter, a cheerful appearance, a simple gaze, mild spirit, courteous conversation, kind replies. They had the same desires, were prepared for obedience and were tirelessly active.

39. In fact, having spurned all earthly things and not nourishing any selfish love, they poured all the love in their hearts into the bosom of the community, endeavoring to give of themselves in helping their brothers' needs. They wished to be united and were happiest when they were together, whereas separation was painful, parting bitter, the sorrow of departure piercing.

[OBEDIENCE]. However, they dared to place nothing ahead of the command of holy obedience: before the word "obedience" was even out, those most obedient soldiers were already prepared to carry out the order. Without any discussion and overcoming every obstacle, they rushed to accomplish what had been assigned to them.

[POVERTY]. Disciples of most holy poverty, they possessed nothing and were not attached to anything and as a result, they were not afraid of losing anything. They were content with just one robe that, at times, was patched both inside and out and had no semblance of refinement but only of contempt and poverty, so that those clothes seemed to be true crucifixes to the world. They wore rough pants with a rope belted around their waists and they piously resolved to remain this way without owning anything else.

[SERENITY]. Consequently, they were always serene, not upset by any fear or distracted by any thought, and they had no anxiety over the future. They did not even worry about having a lodging in which to spend the night, even though they may have encountered great hardship during their journey. When they were unable to find the hospitality they needed during very cold weather, they would often curl up inside a hearth or would miserably take refuge at night in grottos or caves.

[WORK]. Then by day, those who were able to do so would dedicate themselves to manual labor or would stop at lepers' houses or at other honest places, waiting on everyone with humility and devotion. They did not want to perform any duty that could give rise to embarrassment but always kept themselves busy with things that were holy and just, honest and useful, setting an example of humility and patience for all those around them.

40. [PATIENCE]. They were so rich in the virtue of patience that they preferred to remain where they had suffered material persecution rather than where, since their holiness was known and praised, they could enjoy the favor of the world. Many times, insulted and ridiculed, naked, beaten, bound and imprisoned, without seeking the safety of anyone's protection, they bore everything so courageously that only songs of praise and thanks resounded in their mouths.

[SPIRIT OF PRAYER]. They hardly ever ceased in praising and praying to the Lord, but continuously examined each one of their actions, thanking God for the good that had been done and weeping and wailing over faults of neglect and error. They felt abandoned by God if, in their devout observances, they did not experience the usual sweetness of spirit. Moreover, since they wanted to stay awake for prayers, they used various means to keep sleep from overtaking them: some of them would hang suspended from ropes so that their prayers would not be interrupted by sleep creeping up on them, while others would wear instruments of penance made of iron or wood. If at times they had been less moderate than usual because they had had a sufficient amount of food and drink, or if due to the fatigue of their travels, they had gone beyond the limits of bare necessity, even by just a little, then they punished themselves harshly by fasting for many days. Lastly, they strived to repress the urgings of the flesh with such severity that they often did not hesitate to plunge themselves in ice stark naked and to prick their entire bodies with brambles until they were streaked with blood.

41. [SELF-CONTEMPT]. They disdained all earthly possessions so wholeheartedly that it was only with great difficulty that they could accept the bare essentials of life and, long unaccustomed to all bodily comfort by this time, they did not fear the harshest deprivation.

[PEACE]. They always used peaceful and polite ways with everyone. They were involved only in decent and peaceful works and very studiously avoided any scandal. Indeed, they spoke only when necessary and no impolite or vain words came from their mouths, so that in each of their actions and throughout their entire lives, nothing that was less than honest and modest could be found.

[HONESTY OF HABIT]. Every one of their actions was highly disciplined, their behavior was modest and their senses were so mortified that they did not see or hear anything except what required their attention. With their eyes fixed on the ground, their minds looked towards heaven. Neither envy, nor malice, nor rancor, nor contradiction, nor suspicion, nor bitterness had any place in them, but only great harmony, continuous tranquillity, songs of thanks and praise.

These are the lessons of the pious Father. This is how he went about teaching his new sons, not just with words but through his works and, above all, his example.

CHAPTER XVI
Of his dwelling in Rivotorto; and of the observance of poverty

42. Blessed Francis used to assemble with the others near
the city of Assisi, in a place called Rivotorto[66]. Those valiant be-
littlers of great and beautiful houses would stay in an abandoned
hovel there to take shelter from the storm, since according to the
Saint, you can get to heaven faster from a hovel than from a palace.

The sons and brothers stayed there with the blessed Father
in great hardship and utter want, quite often even deprived of the
refreshment of bread and contenting themselves with beets that
they had begged for up and down the Assisi plains. The place was
so narrow that you could barely sit or lie down, but no mumbling
or complaining could be heard about these straits for instead, with
peace of heart and cheerfulness of spirit, all patience was maintained[67]. Every day and, indeed, continuously, St. Francis kept
strict supervision over himself and his own, not tolerating that
anything mundane remain in them and driving all carelessness
from their hearts.

[STRICTNESS]. He was stern and ever vigilant with himself
and if he were overcome by some temptation of the flesh, which
is natural, during the winter he would plunge himself into a ditch
full of ice and stay there until the temptation had left him. This
extraordinary example of penance was followed very fervently by
the others.

43. He taught them not only to mortify vice and repress the
urgings of the flesh, but also to maintain the purity of their external senses, through which death enters the soul. It happened that
at that time the emperor Otto was passing through there, amidst
great pomp and circumstance, on his way to take the crown of the

---

[66] Its location, not far from Francis' father's land, corresponds to the modern-
day church of Rivotorto.
[67] Celano has set into prose three verses from the ancient hymn *Sanctorum meritis.*

terrestrial empire[68]. The most holy Father, who was with the others in this hovel that was along the road traveled by Otto, had no desire even to step outside to see him, nor did he allow any of his own to go, with the exception of one brother who was to announce firmly to the emperor that his glory would last but a short while.

Since the home of the glorious Saint was deep within his own spirit, wandering through the fullness of his heart, he prepared a worthy dwelling place for God there. Thus, his ears were not distracted by external clamor, nor could any voice shake him or interrupt the great work on which he was so intent. He felt that he had been invested with apostolic authority and thus he disdained to flatter kings and princes.

44. He always sought holy simplicity and did not allow poverty of place to restrain the outpourings of his heart[69].

Accordingly, he wrote the names of the brothers on the small beams in the hovel so that whenever one of them wanted to pray or sleep, each one would be able to recognize his place and the narrowness of that place would not disturb spiritual meditation.

[CONTEMPT FOR PROPERTY]. Now while they were lodging there, one day along came a man with a donkey, and since he was afraid that he would be sent away, the man pushed the donkey into the shelter with these words, "Go in, for we will do this place some good!". These words saddened St. Francis, for he guessed the intent of that man, who in fact believed that the brothers wanted to stay there and extend it, adding one house onto the

---

[68] In September of 1209, Otto IV came down from Bologna through the Spoleto valley on his way to Viterbo, where he met Innocent III. He was crowned emperor in Rome on October 4th. He went to Assisi on November 4, 1210 and on November 18th the title of emperor was taken away from him for having invaded the lands of the "heritage of St. Peter."

[69] What Celano says about material poverty can also be extended to refer to all spiritual limitations. This is the essence of the spirit of Franciscan simplicity.

next[70]. Because of the farmer's words[71], St. Francis immediately abandoned the hovel and he moved to another place not far away known as the Porziuncola where, as we have already said, he himself had repaired the church of St. Mary a long time before.

He did not wish to possess anything of his own so that he would more fully possess everything in the Lord.

CHAPTER XVII

How blessed Francis taught the brothers to pray;
and about the brothers' obedience and purity

45. During that time, the brothers begged him to teach them how to pray since, proceeding in simplicity of spirit, they did not know the liturgical Offices yet, and he replied, "When you pray, say: *Our father*, and *We adore You Christ, also in all Your churches throughout the entire world and we bless You, because through your holy cross, You have redeemed the world.*"

[TRUE OBEDIENCE]. The brothers, disciples of the pious Father, took care to put this suggestion into diligent practice, since they did their best to carry out not only the fraternal advice and paternal commands of their father, Francis, but also his secret thoughts, if they managed to guess them through some clue. In fact, the blessed Father would tell them that true obedience does not consist only in the external fulfillment of an order, but that it lies in one's innermost assent and in the very desire to receive the order. In other words, if before even hearing the voice of his superior, a brother perceives his intention, he must prepare himself to obey and carry out what he can comprehend at the least sign.

---

[70] *Is* 5, 8.
[71] Something in this episode seems to be missing. The *Legenda Antiqua* infers that the reason they abandoned Rivotorto was that there was no chapel. It is also possible that Francis' relatives, who owned land in that area, may have caused trouble.

Therefore, wherever there was a church, even if they did not go near it but could only catch a glimpse of it from afar, they would lower themselves to the ground facing in that direction and, prostrating themselves in body and spirits, they would worship the Almighty, saying, "We adore You, Christ, here and in all churches", since the holy Father had taught them to do this. In addition, something that is no less admirable is that they would also do the same thing wherever they saw a cross or the shape of a cross, either on the ground or on a wall, or in the trees or bushes along the road.

46. [HOLY SIMPLICITY]. They were so full of holy simplicity, so innocent and pure at heart, that they were completely unaware of duality[72], since just as faith is unique, likewise in them there was just one spirit, one will, one charity and a common identity of spirit, agreement of custom, adoration of virtue, conformity of thought and piety of action always reigned.

Indeed, they made their confessions to a secular priest who had deserved the infamy and contempt of all because of the enormity of his misdeeds, and even though they had heard many people talk about his bad conduct, they nevertheless did not want to give any credence to this, nor therefore did they stop confessing their sins to him as usual or paying him due reverence. Indeed, that same priest -- or perhaps it was a different one -- said to one of the brothers one day, "Be careful, brother, not to be a hypocrite." Soon, because of the priest's words, that brother truly came to consider himself a hypocrite and so he moaned day and night over this great sorrow. The others asked him the reason for such enormous sadness and unusual grief, and he replied, "A priest said this to me and I am so troubled by it that I can think of nothing else." To console him, the brothers urged him not to believe such words, but he replied, "But what are you saying, brothers? It was a priest who said this to me, or could it be instead that a priest can

---

[72] In his *Praises of the virtues*, St. Francis placed simplicity first and foremost, together with knowledge, its complement, commenting that simplicity confounds worldly and carnal knowledge.

tell a falsehood? Given that a priest cannot lie, then I must necessarily believe that what he said to me is true." And he persisted at length in this simplicity until he was reassured by the words of the most blessed Father, who explained the priest's sentence to him and wisely excused his intention.

There was no anxiety so great for a brother that Francis' fiery words couldn't soothe by driving all clouds away and restoring his serenity.

CHAPTER XVIII
Of the chariot of fire; and of the knowledge
that blessed Francis had about those far away

47. Walking in simplicity and confidence before God and men, the brothers then came to earn the joy of divine revelation. Kindled by the fire of the Holy Spirit, with a suppliant voice they would sing the *Our Father* in a spiritual melody, doing so not only at the established hours but at every hour since they were unconcerned with material cares and needs. Now one night, the very blessed father, Francis, left them in body[73]. At around midnight, while some of the brothers were sleeping and others were fervently praying in silence, through the little door of the house there came the most brilliant chariot of fire, on top of which was a large globe that, like the sun, lit up the darkness of night, and it went back and forth around the room two or three times. Those who were awake were amazed and those who slept were terrified, and all of them felt inundated by that light, not only in body but also in soul. Gathering together, they began to ask themselves what on earth it could be and by the virtue and grace of such great light, they were able to gaze into each other's minds. They finally understood that it was the soul of the holy Father that shone so

---

[73] He had gone to San Rufino because he had to preach there the next morning (St. Bonaventure, *Major Life*, IV, 4).

amazingly and that, thanks above all to his purity and the affectionate care he had for his sons, he had deserved to be blessed with that rare gift from the Lord.

48. Indeed, they had very often had clear proof that the secrets of their hearts did not remain hidden from the most holy Father. O, how many times, without anyone having told him but only through the revelation of the Holy Spirit, had he been aware of the actions of faraway brothers, penetrated their hearts' secrets and read their minds! O, how many did he counsel in their dreams, telling them what they should do and what instead they should avoid! O, to how many, who appeared to be living soundly at the present time, did he predict future ruin, and instead, to how many did he announce that they would receive the grace of salvation once they put an end to their iniquity!

Rather, if anyone deserved to be enlightened because of his spirit of purity and simplicity, he had the singular consolation of a vision of the Saint in a way that was never experienced by the others. Among the many events, I will recount one that was recounted to me by trustworthy witnesses.

Brother John of Florence, elected minister of the brothers in Provence by St. Francis and endowed by the Lord God with great eloquence that made all the brothers ready and open to listen to him, once celebrated a Chapter in that Province[74]. In their midst was a brother priest by the name of Monaldo, who was renowned because of his fame and even more so because of his life and whose virtue, based on humility and enhanced by frequent prayer, was protected by the shield of patience. Also present was brother Anthony[75], who was endowed by the Lord with acumen in understanding the Holy Scriptures and with his gift for preaching Jesus to the whole world with words that were sweeter

---

[74] This was the Chapter of Arles, held in 1224. The provincial minister was John Bonelli.

[75] When Thomas of Celano wrote the *First Life*, St. Anthony of Lisbon was still alive and was famous for his learning and eloquence. He died in 1231 near Padua, whence his more well-known denomination of St. Anthony of Padua.

than honey. Now, while Anthony was very fervently and piously preaching to the brothers on the subject of "Jesus of Nazareth, King of the Jews", this brother Monaldo glanced towards the door of the room in which the brothers had congregated and with his bodily eyes, he saw blessed Francis hovering in the air with his arms outstretched in the shape of a cross, in the act of blessing the brothers. All the others seemed to be filled with the consolation of the Holy Spirit[76] and because of the salutary joy that they themselves had experienced, they gave credence to the account of the vision of the most glorious Father.

49. With regard to the knowledge that he had of their hearts' secrets, out of the countless evidence I will relate one incident about which there can be no doubt whatsoever. A certain friar by the name of Riccerio, noble in birth and even more noble in morals, a man who loved God and despised himself, had the pious desire and the firm will to conquer father Francis' benevolence completely, but he greatly feared that the Saint abhorred him and secretly deemed him to be bad, thus depriving him of the grace of his affection. That brother, so full of scruples, thought that anyone who was loved by St. Francis with special affection would be worthy of receiving divine grace and thought that, instead, anyone towards whom he was not benevolent and polite would incur the wrath of the heavenly Judge. So he kept turning this over continuously in his mind, without ever revealing his hidden thoughts to anyone.

50. One day, however, when this brother troubled by his usual doubt was approaching, the blessed Father, who was in his cell praying, sensed his arrival and understood what was in his soul. Therefore, he had him summoned at once and said to him, "Son, let no temptation trouble you, let no doubt upset you, for you are very dear to me and are among those who are dearest to me. And know that you are most worthy of my love and my friendship. Come to me without any fear whenever you want, and

---

[76] *Acts* 9, 31.

talk freely to me as to a friend." The brother was quite astonished and from then on, becoming even more reverent, he began to abandon himself to divine mercy even more confidently.

Holy Father, how painful must your absence be to those who despair of ever finding another one like you on this earth! We beg you to intercede for those you see involved in the harmful disgrace of sin. Although you were already filled with the spirit of all the just, foreseeing the future and knowing things present, you showed yourself to be cloaked in holy simplicity so that you would always flee from pride

But let us return to following our story in its proper order.

CHAPTER XIX

Of his vigilance over the brothers,
of his self-contempt and of true humility

51. Most blessed Francis returned bodily among his brothers[77] whom, as we said, he had never left in spirit.

He carefully examined the conduct of each one, sacredly curious to know the spirit of those under him, and he never left the least voluntary fault unpunished. He would focus first of all on faults deep within the spirit, then he judged the exterior ones, eliminating lastly all the occasions that will usually lead to sin.

He guarded holy lady poverty with the greatest zeal and to such a degree that, fearing that they would end up with a surplus, he would not tolerate having even the smallest tool in the shelter if they thought they could do without it even in case of need, because he would say that it is impossible to satisfy need without serving pleasure.

Only rarely would he consent to eating cooked food and he would either sprinkle it with ashes or add cold water to make it insipid. As he was going about the world to preach the Gospel of

---

[77] Here the stories goes back to the episode recounted in n° 47.

the Lord, how many times when invited to dinner by great princes, who worshipped him with extraordinary affection, would he taste just a bit of meat in observance of the holy Gospel[78] and, pretending to eat it, would put the rest in his lap while he kept bringing his hand to his mouth so that no one would realize what he was doing! What should I say then about wine, since he didn't even want to drink enough water when he was thirsty?[79]

52. Then, wherever he received hospitality for the night, he would not allow anyone to put mattresses or covers on his pallet but, putting his cowl in between, he would lay his naked limbs on the naked ground and when he would comfort his weak body with the benefit of sleep, he would usually remain seated rather than stretched out, using a piece of wood or a rock as a pillow.

If he hungered for something to eat, as would happen, he then could barely bring himself to taste it.

It happened once that he had eaten a bit of chicken because he was ill and as soon as he had regained his strength, he decided to go into the city of Assisi. Upon reaching the city gates, he ordered a brother who was with him to tie a rope around his neck and to drag him through the city as if he were a thief, shouting like the town crier, "Look here at this glutton who, unbeknownst to you, has fattened himself on chicken!" Many hastened to see such a sight and, weeping and sighing, said, "Woe to us wretches, who have brought our entire lives down to satisfying our instincts and to nourishing our hearts and bodies in lasciviousness and gluttony!". Thus filled with remorse, they were brought to lead better lives by that extraordinary example.

---

[78] In his original Rule, St. Francis had repeated to his brothers the instructions given by Christ to the apostles: *"eat and drink what they have"* (*Lk* 10, 7). Subsequently, some of the friars who were more given to exterior practice than they were to interior spiritual perfection felt that these instructions were too broad and tried to have them abrogated. However, the Saint confirmed this in the *Rule of 1223*, chap. 3.

[79] At the Hermitage of St. Urban, however, he changed water into wine. See *First Life*, 61 and *Treatise of Miracles*, 17.

53. He quite often did many other things of this kind in complete self-contempt, but also in order to bring others to gain him perpetual honor. In his own mind, he was like a broken dish[80] and, free of all fear and care for his body, he heroically covered it with insults in order to prevent love for it to induce him into desiring any temporal things.

As a true despiser of himself, through his words and deeds he also taught others to have little consideration for themselves. What else can I say? Everyone exalted and praised him and he was the only one who looked upon himself in profound contempt. He often grieved at seeing himself being honored by everyone and, fleeing from human honor, he would have someone rebuke him to counterbalance this. He would therefore summon a brother and say, "In obedience I order you to insult me harshly and to tell the truth against their falsehoods." And while the brother reluctantly called him a villain and a useless mercenary, he would smile and reply approvingly, "God bless you, because you say very true things that the son of Peter Bernardone should rightfully hear," and through these words he wanted to recall the humble origins of his birth.

54. In order to demonstrate that he was truly worthy of contempt and to give the others an example of sincere confession, when he preached before an entire congregation, he was not ashamed to confess that he had fallen into some error. So if he happened to think badly about someone or were too sharp in his reproof, in all humbleness he would soon confess his sin to the person of whom he had thought badly or who he had reproached, asking his forgiveness. Although a witness to his innocence, given the power his conscience exerted over him, it would not let him rest until he had soothingly healed the wound in his soul. He wanted to progress in every type of virtue, but he didn't want to be noticed and so he fled from admiration using every possible means to avoid falling into conceit.

---

[80] *Ps* 30, 13.

Woe are we who have lost you, holy Father, the model of all good and humility! Through just punishment we have lost you, for we did not take the care to know you while we had you among us!

CHAPTER XX

Of his desire for martyrdom that led him first to Spain and then to Syria; and how by multiplying the supplies through him, God saved the crew from death[81]

55. Burning with divine love, the most blessed father Francis always attempted substantial undertakings and walking wholeheartedly along the path of God's commands, he yearned to reach the peak of perfection. During the sixth year of his conversion[82], kindled by his desire for sacred martyrdom, he wanted to go to Syria to preach the faith of Christ and penance to the Saracens and other infidels. He boarded a ship that was headed there, but since adverse winds were blowing, he and the other crew members found themselves in Slavonia[83]. Since he had been disappointed in his desire, a short time later he begged some of the sailors who were going to Ancona to take him with them, since it was unlikely that another ship would be leaving for Syria that year, but when those men obstinately refused to put him up due to the lack of supplies, the Saint of God, trustful of the Lord's goodness, sneaked aboard with his companion. Then, through the work of Divine Providence, a stranger bearing supplies arrived unbeknownst to anyone and, calling aside one of the God-fearing crew

---

[81] The title does not take into consideration Francis' first and unsuccessful trip to Syria, or in other words the Middle East, but it refers instead to his second one to Egypt. Between these two voyages, Francis also tried to go to Morocco through Spain.

[82] From his definitive conversion in 1207, so that this event took place towards the end of 1212.

[83] Modern-day Dalmatia.

members, he said to him, "Take all this and distribute it accordingly to those poor ones hidden aboard the ship whenever they may need it." Now it happened that since a frightful squall had come up, the sailors, exhausted by their many days of rowing, ate all their victuals and all that was left was poor Francis' food. Through divine grace and virtue, however, it had multiplied so much that even though there were still many days of sailing left, it was enough to satisfy everyone's needs as far as the port of Ancona. Acknowledging that they had been saved from danger at sea thanks to God's servant, Francis, the sailors then thanked the Almighty Lord who, through his servants, always reveals Himself to be marvelous and beloved.

56. After he left the sea behind, the servant of the Most High, Francis, began to travel over land and, furrowing it with the plowshare of the Gospel, he sowed the seed of life that produces blessed fruits. In fact, many good and worthy men, clerics and laymen alike, fled from the world and bravely avoided the devil's temptations, following Francis devoutly in his resolution and life through the grace and will of the Most High.

However, even though he, the evangelical vine branch, produced an abundance of the finest fruit, his lofty resolution and ardent desire for martyrdom could not be cooled in him at all. Therefore, after a short time[84] he set off for Morocco to preach the Gospel of Christ to the Miramolin[85] and his fellow worshippers. So strong was Francis' desire that, in spiritual elation, every so often he would leave one of his traveling companions behind, hastening to fulfill his resolution. Thus, praise be to our good Lord who, through His goodness alone, was willing to remember me and many others. In fact, after Francis got to Spain, He countered him and in order to keep him from proceeding any further,

---

[84] It has not been established if this took place in 1213 or in 1214.

[85] Name drawn from the Arabic Emir-el-mumenin, which means "leader of the believers". The Sultan at that time was Mohammed-ben-Nasser, who had been driven back into Africa from Spain in 1212, following his defeat at Las Navas de Tolosa.

He pulled him away from the path he had undertaken and struck him down with disease.

57. A short time after Francis had thus returned to St. Mary's of the Porziuncola, he was joined by several men of letters and some noblemen[86], and he who was most noble in spirit and quite modest treated them with fitting honor, giving each one of them his due. Blessed with rare tact, he bore each one's status in mind.

But he still could not set his mind at rest unless he followed the blessed impulse of his soul even more fervently. In the thirteenth year after his conversion, he went to Syria, where hard battles were being fought every day between Christians and pagans and, together with a companion[87], he unhesitatingly presented himself before the Sultan of the Saracens[88].

But who can relate how staunchly he stood before him, how courageously he spoke to him, how very eloquently and confidently he responded to those who insulted the Christian law? Before he got to the Sultan, he was snatched by his bodyguards, slandered and flogged, yet he was not frightened, nor did he fear the threat of the torture or imminent death. And even though he was made the target of the malice and brutal hatred by many, he was received with great honor by the Sultan himself. He gave Francis signs of his honor and tried to bend his spirit to worldly riches by offering him many gifts, but noting that he spurned everything as if it were dung, the Sultan was filled with great wonder, seeing him almost as if he were different from the rest. He was moved by his words and listened to him very willingly.

---

[86] It is possible that Celano may also have been a nobleman.

[87] Brother Illuminatus of Arce, not to be confused with Illuminatus of Chieti, who later became Bishop of Assisi.

[88] St. Francis probably arrived at the court of Sultan Melek-el-Kamel (who had succeeded the brother of the famous Saladin in 1218) during the truce that took place between the end of August and the end of September, 1219.

In all these circumstances, the Lord accomplished the Saint's desire, to whom He reserved the prerogative of rare grace[89].

CHAPTER XXI
About how he preached to the birds and about the
obedience of the creatures

58. In the meantime, while the number of brothers was increasing as we have said, the most blessed father Francis was traveling through the Spoleto valley[90]. He came to a place near Bevagna, where he was welcomed by an enormous number of birds of all species, doves, crows and the so-called jackdaws. When he saw them, the Servant of God, who was filled with such great fervor that he even felt compassion and love for lesser and unreasoning creatures, hurried over to them and left his companions behind on the road. As he approached them and saw that they were waiting for him, he greeted them as was his custom, but amazed by the fact that the birds had not flown off as they usually do, he was filled with joy and humbly begged them to listen to the word of God.

Among other things, he told them, "My winged brothers, you should give your Creator great praise and love Him always, because he has given you down to cover you, feathers to fly and everything that you need. God made you noble among all other creatures and allowed you to live in the clear sky. You do not sow or reap, yet He Himself protects you and feeds you without any care on your part." At these words, the birds -- as he himself and

---

[89] This is a reference to the idea that the miracle of the Stigmata was given to Francis to compensate for the martyrdom he did not achieve. Dante also closely connected these two motifs (*Par* XI, 100-108), despite the five-year interval between the two events.

[90] Based on Celano's indications in N° 62 below, the episode in Bevagna probably took place between 1212 and 1213.

the brothers who were with him recounted -- wondrously gave signs of exultation according to their nature, stretching out their necks, spreading their wings, opening their beaks and looking at him. He went back and forth among them, grazing their little heads and bodies with his tunic. Then he blessed them at last and making the sign of the cross, he gave them permission to fly away. The blessed Father then set off again on his journey with his companions, rejoicing and giving thanks to God, whom all the creatures worship in devout belief.

Francis, who was not simple by nature but through grace, then began to accuse himself of negligence for never having preached to the birds before then, given that they had listened to the word of God so reverently. From that day on, he promptly began to exhort all birds, all animals, all reptiles and even unfeeling creatures to praise and love the Creator[91], for every day he experienced their obedience when the name of the Savior was invoked.

59. One day, in fact, when he had gone to a town named Alviano[92] to announce the divine word, he climbed up to the highest spot so that everyone could see him and began to motion for silence. However, while everyone else quieted down and prepared to listen to him with devotion, a number of swallows who had their nests there continued to chirp and make noise.

Thus, since the people could not hear blessed Francis because of this chirping, he addressed the birds, saying, "My sister swallows, now it's my turn to speak, since you have spoken quite enough until now. Listen to the word of God, and keep quiet and still until my speech is over!" And to the wonder and marvel of all the bystanders, the swallows immediately fell silent and did not move from there until the sermon was finished. Then the listeners began to say in amazement, "Truly this man is a saint and a friend of the Most High!" and with great devotion they tried to

---

[91] This is a reference to the inspiration that is evident in the *Canticle of the Creatures*.
[92] Between Orte and Orvieto.

touch at least his clothes, praising and blessing God. It is certainly a marvelous thing that even unreasoning creatures should know and have a sense of the mercy and very sweet affection that he felt for them.

60. Once when he was near Greccio, a brother brought him a leveret that had been taken out of the trap alive and upon seeing it, the most blessed man said emotionally, "Brother leveret, come to me. Why did you let yourself get caught?". And soon the little animal, set free by the friar who was holding it, took refuge with the Saint and without anyone urging it to do so, it sat on his lap as if it were in a very safe place. After it had stayed there a while, the holy Father stroked it with maternal affection and let it go so it could return freely to the woods, but after it had been set down on the ground several times, it kept going back to the Saint's arms, who finally had the brothers carry it into the woods nearby.

On the island in the lake of Perugia, something similar happened with a rabbit, which is a difficult animal to tame.

61. He also had the same tender compassion for fish and whenever he could, he would put them back in the water still alive after they had been caught, cautioning them to make sure not to get caught again.

Once while he was on a small boat near a port on the lake of Rieti[93], a fisherman who had caught a large fish commonly called a tench, devoutly offered it to him, and when he solicitously and happily accepted it, he began to call it "brother". Then he put it back out of the boat into the water, devoutly blessing the name of the Lord. While he was praying, the fish played in the water near the little boat for a little while and would not leave until the Saint of God had given it permission to go after the prayer was over.

In this way, the glorious father Francis, following the path of obedience and fully accepting the yoke of divine submission,

---

[93] Lake Piediluco is a small lake in central Italy.

received from God the great honor of being obeyed by His creatures.

Indeed, even water turned to wine for him once when he was seriously ill while he was staying in the hermitage of St. Urban[94]. As soon as he had tasted it, he was healed so quickly that everyone believed it was a miracle of God, as truly it was, and he whom the creatures obey in this way and at whose mere word the very elements transform their attributes, must surely be a saint.

CHAPTER XXII

Of his sermon in Ascoli; and how the ill were cured through the objects touched by the Saint

62. At the time that, as we have said[95], he was preaching to the birds, going through cities and villages to sow the seeds of blessing everywhere, the venerable father Francis also went to the city of Ascoli. There, he preached very passionately, as usual, and it can be said that through the work of the Most High, the entire population was so filled with grace and devotion that everyone, yearning to listen to him and to see him, crowded on top of each other. Over thirty clergy and laymen took the habit of the holy religion from him at that time, and so great was the faith and devotion of men and women for the saint of God that anyone who had managed to touch his garments considered himself blessed.

Whenever he went to some city, the clergy rejoiced, the bells were rung, men exulted, women were delighted, the children clapped their hands and, holding branches, they would often go out singing to meet him. The perversity of heresy was mortified and the faith of the Church was magnified and as the faithful rejoiced, heretics would hide, for the signs of holiness were so

---

[94] The hermitage is near Narni.
[95] See n° 58 above and *Treatise of Miracles*, 17.

manifest in him that no one would dare dispute him and the crowd had eyes only for him. He believed that in everything and above all, he had to observe, worship and follow the faith of the holy Roman Church, which is the sole path to salvation. He venerated priests and nourished great love for the entire ecclesiastical hierarchy.

63. They brought him loaves of bread to bless, which they would then preserve for a long time since they were cured of various illnesses by eating it[96]. Out of great faith, they would often cut pieces of his cowl so that sometimes he would almost be left naked and, something that is even more marvelous, some of the objects touched by the hand of the holy Father restored some ill people to health.

A pregnant woman who lived in a small village in the area of Arezzo had been in labor for a number of days when it came time for her to deliver and she was prey to terrible spasms, hanging between life and death. Her neighbors and relatives had heard that blessed Francis was to pass nearby on his way to a hermitage. It happened, however, that as they were waiting for him, the Saint took another road on horseback because he was weak and ill. Halfway along, however, he sent another brother by the name of Peter to return the horse to the person who had charitably lent it to him and as Brother Peter was leading the horse along, he went through the street where the suffering woman lived. Consequently, as soon as the men in the neighborhood saw him, they ran to him thinking he was blessed Francis, but as soon as they realized it wasn't he, they became very downcast. In the end, they looked to see if they could have something that the Saint had touched and after searching at length, they came up with the reins from the bit that Francis himself had held as he rode. Taking the bit from the mouth of the horse the Saint had ridden, they took the reins he had gripped in his hands and placed them on the

---

[96] See *Treatise of Miracles*, 19 and other passages.

women who, all danger now thwarted, happily gave birth at once[97].

64. Gualfreduccio, a resident of Città della Pieve and a religious and God-fearing man who, together with his entire family, honored the Lord, owned a piece of rope that blessed Francis had used to tie around his waist. Now it happened that in that neighborhood, many men and women were struck with fever and various other illnesses. He went to the houses of the sick people, put the rope or a strand of rope in water, then gave that water to the patients to drink, and all of them regained their health in the name of the Christ.

These miracles took place in blessed Francis' absence and there were many more that we cannot recount even with a lengthy dissertation. Therefore, with regard to the miracles that the Lord our God deigned to work while Francis was present, we will briefly include a few of them in this part of the work.

CHAPTER XXIII
How he cured a lame boy in Toscanella and a paralytic in Narni

65. One time while he was traveling extensively through various regions to announce the kingdom of God, Francis, the Saint of God, came to a city called Toscanella. There, as he was sowing the seed of life as was his custom, he was the guest of a knight whose only son was lame and weakened throughout his entire body and who, still a youngster, had already been weaned yet was still in a cradle. Upon seeing the holiness of the man of God, the boy's father threw himself humbly at his feet, asking him to cure his little son. The Saint, considering himself unworthy of possessing so much virtue and grace and incapable of working such a miracle, was reluctant to agree, but finally, won over by the

---

[97] Also in the *Treatise of Miracles*, 108.

man's insistent pleas, he placed one hand on the boy and after saying a prayer, he blessed him and ordered him to get up. As everyone looked on in delight, in the name of our Lord Jesus Christ the boy arose healthy and began to walk here and there throughout the house[98].

66. On another occasion, Francis, the man of God, had gone to Narni and stayed there for many days. A man from the city, who was called Peter, was paralyzed and bedridden. He had lost the use of all his limbs for five months so that he was unable to get up at all and could not even move a little bit, managing only to move his tongue and open his eyes, but unable to use either his feet or hands or to turn his head. Now upon hearing that St. Francis had arrived in Narni, he sent word to the bishop of the city to ask that in the name of divine mercy, he deign to send him the servant of the Most High, because he was confident that he would be cured of his illness through the sight and presence of the Saint. And truly it happened that, as soon as blessed Francis was at his side and made the sign of the cross over him from head to toe, the illness ceased at once and he was restored to health.

CHAPTER XXIV

*How he restored a blind woman's eyesight
and cured a paralyzed woman in Gubbio*

67. A woman from the above-mentioned city[99] who had been struck with blindness immediately regained the eyesight she desired after blessed Francis made the sign of the cross over her eyes.

In Gubbio, there was a woman, both of whose hands were so paralyzed that she was unable to do anything. As soon as she learned that St. Francis had come to the city, she ran to him and,

---

[98] See *Treatise of Miracles*, 175.
[99] Narni, see *Treatise of Miracles*, 121.

her face full of suffering and her appearance pitiable, she showed him her twisted hands and began to beg him to touch them. Moved to compassion, he touched her hands and healed them. Then the woman went home gladly and made some cheese[100] with her own two hands and offered it to the Saint, who accepted some to please her and then told the woman to eat the rest of it with her family.

CHAPTER XXV

How he freed one of the brothers from falling sickness[101] or from the devil,
whatever the case may be;
and how he cured a possessed woman in Sangemini

68. A brother was suffering from a very serious illness that was horrible to see and that I don't know what to call, since some people think it should be attributed to the presence of the malignant devil. He was often overcome with convulsions and with his features set gruesomely, he would roll around foaming at the mouth and his limbs would contract and then relax, becoming twisted and contorted and then hard and rigid. At times, completely contracted and stiff with his feet up to his head, he would get up to a man's height and then fall down again. Taking pity on his very serious illness, holy father Francis went to him and after saying a prayer, he made the sign of the cross over him and blessed him. He was cured immediately and no longer suffered the least disturbance thereafter on account of this illness.

69. One day, as most blessed Francis was passing through the diocese of Narni, he came to a town called Sangemini. Preaching the kingdom of God there, he and three brothers were the guests of a God-fearing and devout man who enjoyed a very good reputation in that place. As the inhabitants of the area were well aware, however, the host's wife was tormented by the devil,

---

[100] Or cheese bread.
[101] Epilepsy.

and the husband prayed to blessed Francis for her, believing that she would be healed through the merits of the Saint. Nevertheless, the Saint who, in his simplicity, preferred to be despised rather than receive the world's honors by proving his saintliness, refused to work the miracle. At last, since it was the glory of God that was involved and many people begged him to do so, won over by their insistence, he finally agreed. Therefore, he summoned the three brothers who were with him and sending each one into a corner of the room, he said, "Let us pray to the Lord for this woman, brothers, so that God might free her of the yoke of the devil to His praise and glory. Each one of us should stay in a corner so that this evil will not escape from us and trick us by hiding there." Upon finishing this prayer, through the virtue of the Holy Spirit, blessed Francis went up to the woman, who was twisting and writhing miserably and was screaming horribly, and said to her, "In the name of our Lord Jesus Christ, in obedience I order you, O demon, to leave her[102] and not to torment her any longer!". As soon as these words were out, the demon promptly came out with such great fury and clamor that because woman was healed so quickly and the devil had obeyed so readily, the holy Father thought he had been tricked. Red-faced, he rushed off immediately through the intervention of divine Providence, so that he would not be tempted by vainglory in any way.

It then happened that when blessed Francis went through that same place again (and Brother Elias was with him), as soon as this woman heard about his arrival, she got up and began to run through the square, calling after him so that he would deign to speak to her. He was unwilling to do so because he knew that she was the woman from whom, by divine virtue, he had cast out the devil, but she kissed the ground he walked on, thanking God and his servant, Francis, who had freed her from the power of death. Brother Elias finally convinced the Saint to speak to her and

---

[102] *Acts* 16, 18 and 4, 10.

Francis was reassured by many about both the sickness, as has been said, as well as the cure[103].

CHAPTER XXVI
How he also cast out a devil in Città di Castello

70. There was a possessed woman in Città di Castello as well and while the most blessed father Francis was in that city, the woman was brought to the house where he was staying. While she was standing outside, she began to gnash her teeth grotesquely and shout wretchedly as unclean spirits are wont to do. Thus, many people from the city, both men and women, went to pray to St. Francis for her since she had long been tormented by evil and, in turn, had disturbed many people with her cries. The holy Father, wishing to test whether it was the demon or if it was trickery on the woman's part, first sent one of the brothers who was with him to see her. As soon as she saw him, she began to jeer at him, knowing that he was not St. Francis. The holy Father, who had stayed inside to pray, came out when the prayers were over and soon the woman began to tremble and to roll around on the ground, since she could not bear his virtue. However, he summoned her, saying, "By virtue of obedience I order you, unclean spirit, to leave her," and it departed at once without doing her any harm, going off indignantly[104].

Thanks be to Almighty God, who works all things in everyone.

Nevertheless, since we have not been engaged to demonstrate his miracles, which prove his saintliness yet do not constitute it, but the excellence of his life and his exemplary conduct, let us go back to describing his holy works and leave his innumerable miracles behind.

---

[103] See *Treatise of Miracles*, 155.
[104] *Mk* 5, 8; *Treatise of Miracles*, 156.

CHAPTER XXVII

Of the purity and constancy of his spirit and of his speech
to Pope Honorius; and how he entrusted himself and
his brothers to Cardinal Hugolin, Bishop of Ostia

71. Francis, the man of God, could seek not his own profit, but what he felt was useful for the good of others. Above all else, however, he wanted to be released from his body to be with Christ[105]. Therefore, he went to great pains to keep himself free of all worldly cares so that his peace of mind would not be darkened by any speck of earthly dust even for an instant. He knew how to ignore all exterior clamor and, guarding his external senses with the greatest care and curbing the impulses of his spirit, he lived absorbed only in God. He had made his nest among the cliffs and his home was in the clefts[106]. With truly saintly devotion, he looked for solitary places so that he could trustingly abandon himself longer in the wounds of the Savior.

Thus he often chose solitude so that he could turn his soul completely to God, yet when the need arose, he did not hesitate to take a willing interest in anything that could help the good of other souls.

His safe haven was prayer, not just a few minutes' worth or empty and presumptuous prayer, but long prayers that were full of devotion and serenely humble. If he began at night, he would barely be done by morning and regardless of whether he was walking or seated, eating or drinking, he was intent on prayer. He would go off all alone at night to pray in abandoned and secluded churches and there, through the help of divine grace, he would vanquish much of his fear and spiritual anguish.

72. In those places, he had to fight hand-to-hand with the devil who, not content with disturbing him on the inside with temptation, would also frighten him externally with noise and

---

[105] *Phil* 1, 23.
[106] *Sg* 2, 14.

ruin. But that most stalwart soldier of God, knowing full well that God can do everything everywhere, would not allow himself to be frightened, saying deep in his heart, "O evil one, you cannot hurt me any more than you would if we were among other people."

He was truly steadfast and waited to find only what belonged to God. In fact, even when he was preaching the divine word to many thousands of people, as often happened, he would be as calm and confident as if he were speaking to a close friend. He regarded the biggest crowd of people as a single man and preached to the single man the way he would have done for a great multitude. Within the purity of his spirit, he found the confidence to preach and, without any preparation, he was able to say marvelous things that no one had ever heard before. Instead, if he would think about the speech he was to give, at times it happened that when he was in front of the audience, forgetting what he had thought about and unable immediately to find something else to say, he would candidly confess that he had prepared a long speech that he could not remember in the least and soon he would become so eloquent that he would charm the souls of his listeners. Instead, at other times, unable to speak he would bid the crowds farewell with a blessing, and this would be worth the best of sermons.

73. Indeed, one time, when he had gone to Rome about matters concerning the Order, he ardently desired to preach before the lord pope, Honorius, and the cardinals. As soon as Hugolin, the glorious bishop of Ostia who particularly loved the Saint of God, heard about this, he felt both fear and joy, for he admired the Saint's fervor but was also aware of his simplicity. Yet, trusting in the mercy of the Almighty, who never fails the faithful when they are in need, he brought him before the pope and the reverend cardinals. When he had been given their permission and blessing, he began to speak fearlessly in the presence of such great princes. He talked with such great ardor that he was unable to contain his joy, so that as he uttered his words, he moved about on his feet so that he was practically jumping, not

like a jester but like one who is burning with the flame of divine love and not bringing people to laughter but drawing tears of remorse. Indeed, many of those he moved in this way admired the grace of God and the confidence of his servant. In the meantime, the venerable bishop of Ostia was awestruck and he prayed to the Lord with all his might that the simplicity of that blessed soul would not be scorned, because the glory or discredit of the Saint would fall upon him as well, since he had been made the father of that family.

74. In fact, St. Francis was as close to him as a son to his father or rather, like an only child to his mother, and he slept and rested peacefully in the bosom of his clemency. In truth, the bishop exercised the role of shepherd and carried out this duty, whereas he had left the title of shepherd to the Saint. The blessed Father provided the bare necessities, but it was that kind lord who put all this into effect. O, how many set traps for the new plantings of the Order to ruin it, especially in the beginning! How many tried to suffocate the chosen vineyard that the hand of the Lord was lovingly planting in the world! How many tried to disturb and destroy its first and most beautiful fruits, and all of them were destroyed by the sword of this reverend father and lord. He was indeed a river of eloquence, a wall of the Church, champion of truth and lover of the humble.

Thus, blessed was that memorable day in which the Saint of God placed his trust in such a venerable lord. Once when the latter held the office of papal legate in Tuscany, as was often the case, blessed Francis, who at that time had only a few brothers and wanted to go to France, arrived at the bishop's residence in Florence. They were not bound yet by deep friendship, but the fame of their saintly lives united them in a bond of mutual and kindly affection.

75. Moreover, it was blessed Francis' custom to pay a visit to the bishops or priests whenever he went to some city or territory. Thus, upon hearing that this illustrious prelate was there, he went to him in great reverence. As soon as he saw Francis, the

lord bishop welcomed him humbly and devoutly, which was always the practice with all religious and especially with those who wore the noble uniform of blessed poverty and holy simplicity. Then, since he was always ready to help the poor and take singular interest in their needs, he diligently questioned Francis about the reason for his visit and kindly welcomed his resolution. Thus, seeing that Francis despised all earthly possessions more than anyone else and that he burned with the love that Jesus had brought to this earth, from that moment on, his soul merged with the other man's and he asked for the charity of his prayer, very willingly offering Francis his own protection in everything. Then he advised Francis not to continue his voyage but to watch carefully over those whom the Lord God had entrusted to him. St. Francis rejoiced greatly over the compassionate spirit, sweet love and effective words of such a reverend lord and prostrating himself at his feet, he committed and entrusted himself and his brothers to him.

CHAPTER XXVIII

About his spirit of charity and of his burning compassion towards the poor; and how he treated a ewe and some lambs

76. Poor Francis, father of the poor and imitator of the poor in everything, would suffer when he saw someone poorer than he, not out of self-pride but through true compassion, and even though he settled for a miserable rough tunic, quite often he yearned to share it with some needy person. Driven by great pity, he, very rich poor man, would ask the wealthy of the world for a cape or fur when the cold weather was very intense so that he could come to the aid of the poor. When they would give these things to him even more enthusiastically than he had requested them, he would say, "I accept them as long as you never expect to get them back again." Then, in complete delight and happiness, he would clothe the first poor person he happened to meet.

It was very upsetting for him to see some wretch being insulted or to hear curses flung at some creature. Now it happened that a brother offended a poor man who was begging him for alms by saying to him, "Look, I would hate for you to be a rich man who is feigning poverty!". As soon as he heard this, blessed Francis, father of the poor, was deeply saddened and harshly reproached the brother who had uttered those words, ordering him to strip before the poor man and to beg his forgiveness by kissing his feet. Indeed, he used to say, "Anyone who says rude things to a poor person is insulting Christ, whose noble uniform that person is wearing and who became poor on earth for us." Then often, if he encountered poor people loaded down with wood or with other burdens, although he was quite weak, he would take the load on his own shoulders in order to help them.

77. He abounded in charity and compassion not only towards indigent men, but also towards dumb and brutish animals, reptiles, birds and all feeling and unfeeling creatures. But above all other animals, he felt special love and tenderness towards lambs since, on account of His humility, our Lord Jesus Christ is often rightly compared to the lamb in the Holy Scriptures. Thus, he more dearly loved and more willingly protected all those things that particularly offered some allegory or image of the Son of God.

One time, he was traveling from the March of Ancona after he had announced the word of God in that city and was on his way to Osimo with lord Paul, whom he had named minister of the brothers in that same Province, when he came across a pastor who had a herd of goats and rams grazing in the countryside. There was a single lamb in the middle of this large flock and it was humbly and quietly nibbling grass. As soon as he saw it, blessed Francis stopped and, saddened to the bottom of his heart, he cried to his brother companion, "Do you see that ewe going about so meekly in the middle of that herd of goats and billy goats? I say to you, that is exactly how our Lord Jesus Christ had to walk meekly and humbly among the Pharisees and the priestly leaders. Therefore, my son, I beg that you too be moved to compassion for this little lamb out of love for Him. Let's buy it and take it away from these goats and these billy goats."

78. Observing his piety, Brother Paul began to feel compassion too. While they were thinking about how they could buy it, for they possessed nothing except for the two rough robes they were wearing, along came a merchant who offered them the sum they desired.

Thanking God, they went to Osimo with the little lamb and went before the bishop of the city, who honorably received them. At first, he marveled that the man of God should bring a ewe before him and that he should be so affectionate towards it, but after the servant of Christ had told him a long parable about the little ewe, with a contrite heart, he thanked God for the Saint's simplicity. As he was leaving the city the following day, Francis was reflecting about what to do with the little lamb, until upon the advice of his brother companion, he entrusted it to the care of the maidservants of Christ at a cloister near San Severino. The venerable sisters joyfully welcomed the lamb like a great gift of the Lord and attentively took care of it for a long time. Afterwards, they wove a cowl with its wool and sent it blessed father Francis at the Porziuncola when a Chapter was being held, and the Saint accepted it with great devotion and celebration, clasping it to his chest and kissing it and inviting all those who were present to rejoice with him.

79. Another time, when he was going through the same Marches again accompanied happily by the same brother, he encountered a man carrying two little lambs tied from the shoulders hanging head down, for he was on his way to the market to sell them. Blessed Francis was deeply moved when he heard them bleating and went up to them, stroking them the way a mother would do with a crying child and showing his compassion. So he asked the owner, "Why are you tormenting my little brother lambs, keeping them bound and hanging like that?" The man replied, "I am bringing them to the market to sell them because I

need the money," to which the Saint asked, "What will happen to them?" The other man replied, "The buyers will kill them and eat them." "That mustn't happen!" replicated the Saint, "so here is my cloak to pay for them and now you give me the lambs." The man was more than happy to give the little animals away and to take the cloak that the Saint had just received that very day to protect himself from the cold, for it was worth much more. In the meantime, Francis, who had taken the lambs, was thinking carefully about how to provide for them and upon the advice of his brother companion, he entrusted them once again to their owner, ordering him never to sell them nor to harm them in any way, but to feed them and watch over them with care.

CHAPTER XXIX
Of his love towards all creatures on account of the Creator;
and a physical and moral portrait of him

80. It would take too long and, indeed, it would be impossible to recount all the deeds and teachings accomplished by the glorious father Francis during his mortal lifetime.

Who can express his extraordinary love for all of God's creatures? Who could possibly relate all the sweetness he felt by gazing upon the knowledge, power and goodness of the Creator in His creatures? This contemplation would fill him with marvelous and unspeakable joy whenever he looked at the sun or the moon or the stars in the firmament. O simple piety and pious simplicity! He even felt great love for worms, since he had read that the Savior had said *I am a worm and not a man*[107]. Hence he would pick them up from the road and shelter them in a safe place so that they would not be crushed by the feet of passersby. What then of the other lesser creatures, if he went so far as to prepare honey and wine for the bees during the winter so that

---

[107] *Ps* 27, 7.

they wouldn't die of the biting cold? For the glory of God, he exalted their clever industriousness and keen instinct so much that he spent an entire day praising them and other creatures.

Just as the three young men in the furnace invited all the elements to praise and glorify the Creator of the universe[108], so too this man, filled with the spirit of God, never ceased to glorify, praise and bless the Creator and Ruler of all things in all His elements and creatures.

81. And what about the pleasure he drew from the elegance of flowers when he admired their gracious shape or took in their sweet perfume? This would immediately turn his mind's eye to the beauty of the flower that, sprouting forth in purity from the root of Jesse during the spring, raised uncountable thousands from the dead with its fragrance[109]. And when he found flowers in great abundance, he preached to them and invited them to praise Lord as if they were endowed with reason. Likewise, with simplicity and purity of heart, he invited the corn and the vines, the rocks and the forests, the beautiful countryside, running water, green gardens, earth and fire, air and wind, to love God and give Him their homage spontaneously. Lastly, he called all creatures brother or sister and in an extraordinary and unusual manner, through the penetrating intuition of his heart he could understand the secrets of these creatures because he had conquered the glorious freedom of the children of God[110]. O good Jesus, he who on earth preached your love to all creatures is now in heaven with the angels singing your praises.

82. Indeed, he would be moved beyond human imagination whenever he uttered your name, o holy God, and he was so full of chaste joy that he seemed like a new man, a man from another world. Thus, wherever he would find something written about a divine subject or even a human one, either along the road or at home or on the ground, he would very reverently pick it up and

---

[108] From canticles 3, 17 and 51 in the *Book of Daniel*.
[109] *Is* 11, 1 and *2 Cor* 2, 14-16.
[110] *Rm* 8, 21.

put it in a holy place, or at least in a decent place so that the name of the Lord or anything else that pertained to Him would not remain there. One time, when a brother had asked him why on earth he so diligently picked up even pagan writings and writings that did not have God's name on them, he answered, "My son, because they contain the letters from which the most glorious name of the Lord God is composed. Moreover, whatever good there may be does not pertain to pagans or other men, but to God himself, who possesses all good!" And no less admirably, whenever he would have a message of greeting or counsel written for him, he would not allow any letter or syllable to be erased, even if one of them was superfluous or wrong.

83. How beautiful, splendid and glorious he was in his innocence, the simplicity of his words, the purity of his heart, his love for God, his charity towards his brothers, his ready obedience, his kind acquiescence, his angelic appearance!

Lovable in appearance, placid by nature, affable in his way of speaking, timely in his exhortations, most faithful in fulfilling the duties entrusted to him, discerning in his advice, effective in his actions, gracious in everything. Serene in spirit, sweet at heart, sensitive, absorbed in contemplation, assiduous in prayer, ever fervent, constant in his resolutions, steadfast in virtue, persevering in grace and always true to himself. Quick to pardon, slow to anger, perspicacious, endowed with a sharp memory, subtle in his discussions, cautious in his decisions and simple in everything. Severe with himself, indulgent towards others, always discreet.

Highly eloquent, with a cheerful face and benign features, neither lazy nor haughty. He was of ordinary height, tending on the short side; he had a regularly-shaped round head, a rather long protruding face, a small flat forehead; his black eyes were of normal size and his gaze was full of simplicity; black hair; straight eyebrows; a normal, thin and straight nose; small and detached ears; flat temples and a persuasive, ardent and sharp tongue; a vibrant, sweet, clear, sonorous voice; small white and even teeth; small thin lips; a thin black beard; a slender neck; straight shoulders; short arms; lean hands; long fingers; protruding nails; slender legs; small feet, delicate skin. Lean, roughly dressed, one who didn't need much sleep, very open-handed. In his great humility, he acted meekly with everyone, sagely suiting himself to each one's habits. More than saintly among saints, yet like a sinner among sinners.

O lover of sinners, most holy father, help all sinners and through your most glorious merits, mercifully deign to elevate those you see lying wretchedly in the degradation of sin!

CHAPTER XXX

Of the crèche prepared on Christmas night

84. His greatest care, his most vivid desire, his supreme resolution was to observe the holy Gospel always and in everything[111] and with all vigilance and care, with all of his mind's desire and his heart's fervor, he wanted to follow the teachings and imitate the examples of our Lord Jesus Christ to perfection. He continuously recalled and meditated over His words and with very keen contemplation, he kept His works before his eyes.

The humility of the Incarnation and the charity of the Passion were foremost in his mind, so that he rarely wanted to think of anything else.

On this subject, it is worthwhile to remember and celebrate reverently what he did three years before his death on the birthday of our Lord Jesus Christ in the area around Greccio[112].

In that territory, there lived a man named John who had a good reputation and an even better life, and he was very beloved by blessed Francis because although he came from a noble family and was highly esteemed, he disdained the nobility of birth and

---

[111] St. Francis expressly indicated that this was the basis of the *Rules of 1221* and *1223*, and also stressed this in the instructions that St. Clare later included in her own *Rule*.

[112] Thus the night of December 25, 1223.

aspired only to nobility of the spirit[113]. About fifteen days before Christmas, blessed Francis had him summoned, as he often did, and said to him, "If you would like us to celebrate this feast day of the Lord in Greccio, then go there ahead of me and prepare what I tell you. I would like to portray the Child born in Bethlehem and to see somehow with my bodily eyes the hardship he underwent because he lacked all a newborn's needs, the way he was placed in a manger and how he lay on the hay between the ox and the ass." Upon hearing this, that good and pious man hastened off and had everything that the Saint had told him prepared in the designated place.

85. The day of gladness, the time of exultation, arrived. The brothers were summoned from many places and, each according to his means, the men and women of the area festively brought candles and torches to brighten the night that, with its gleaming star, has brightened everyone's days and years. At length, the Saint of God arrived, saw that everything was ready and was delighted by it. The manger was prepared, the hay was brought and the ox and ass were led in. There, simplicity was honored, poverty exalted, humility praised, and Greccio was virtually transformed into a new Bethlehem. The night, a delightful night for men and beasts, was as bright as broad daylight[114]. The crowds who hastened there were gladdened with new joy over the renewed mystery. The woods resounded with their voices and the cliffs echoed their hymns of joy. The brothers sang the Lord's praise and the entire night was spent in celebration. Sighing, the Saint of God stood before the crèche, filled with sighs, contrite in piety and overcome with ineffable joy.

---

[113] According to tradition, this was John of Velita, but nothing else is known about him. Moreover, based on this passage it is not clear if this event took place in Greccio itself or in another town in the Sabine area.

[114] *Ps* 37, 6.

The solemn rite of the Mass was celebrated over the crèche[115] and the priest felt unusual solace.

86. The Saint of God was dressed as a Levite, for he was a deacon, and he sang the holy Gospel in a resonant voice. That strong, sweet, clear, melodious voice invited everyone to the highest reward. Then he preached to the people and said the sweetest things about the birth of the poor King and about the little city of Bethlehem.

Moreover, many times when he wanted to refer to Christ by the name of Jesus, burning with immense love, he would call him *the Child of Bethlehem* and like a bleating sheep, when he pronounced the word *Bethlehem* his voice, or rather, the sweetness of his emotion would fill his mouth, and in saying the name *Jesus* or *Child of Bethlehem*, he would lick his lips, tasting all the sweetness of that word even on his tongue.

The gifts of the Almighty were multiplied there and a very virtuous man had a marvelous vision. He saw that a lifeless child was lying in the crèche and that the Saint went alongside him and roused him from a sort of deep sleep. Indeed, this vision was not contrary to reality, for through His grace, His holy servant Francis brought Baby Jesus back to life in the hearts of many where He had been forgotten and his memory became etched deeply in their minds.

At last, when the solemn vigil was over, each one went home in joy.

87. The hay placed in the manger was saved so that through it the Lord could heal the beasts of burden and other animals, increasing this mercy. Truly, it happened that many animals in the surrounding area that had been struck with various illnesses were healed after having eaten some of that hay. Indeed, even some women who were in the midst of a long and difficult labor delivered happily after a bit of this hay had been placed on

---

[115] In his *Major Life* X, 7, St. Bonaventure mentions that permission was obtained from the Holy See.

them, and many men and women were cured of a variety of diseases through this means.

That place has now been consecrated to the Lord and an altar has been built there in honor of St. Francis and a Church has been dedicated to him[116], so that in the place where the animals once ate hay, for the health of their soul and body, men can now eat of the flesh of the immaculate and unblemished Lamb, our Lord Jesus Christ, who gave Himself for us with infinite and inexpressible love and who now lives and reigns with the Father and the Holy Spirit, eternally glorious God, world without end, amen. Alleluia. Alleluia.

Here ends the first book of the life and acts of
Blessed Francis

---

[116] In the year 1228.

PART TWO

Here begins the second book, which recounts only the last two years of the life of our most blessed Father Francis and his happy death

CHAPTER I
About St. Francis' happy death
and of his exceptional merits

In the previous section, which we were able to conclude through the grace of our Savior, we described to the best of our ability the life and actions of our most blessed father Francis, up to the eighteenth year of his conversion[1]. With this small work, we will now add the other deeds about which we have been able to obtain reliable information, starting from the second-to-last year of his life[2], and it is our intention to report only the essential facts here, leaving some material for anyone who may later wish to add something else.

Thus, in the year of our Lord's Incarnation twelve-hundred and twenty-six, in the fourteenth indiction, on Sunday the fourth of October[3], in the city of Assisi where he was born, at St. Mary's of the Porziuncola where he had founded the Order of the Friars Minor, our most blessed father Francis departed from the prison of the flesh twenty years after the time in which he had united

---

[1] That is, until Christmas of 1223, if we calculate that his definitive conversion took place in February 1207.

[2] Celano begins this section with the mystery of the Stigmata (September 1224).

[3] Based on our modern system, in which days are counted from midnight to midnight, this would correspond to the 3rd of October and, more precisely, to Saturday at around sunset. Celano followed the medieval practice, which was still used for liturgical purposes, of calculating the day from sunset to sunset. In fact, in his *Encyclical Letter*, Brother Elias specifies, "the fourth day before the Nones of October, of Sunday...".

himself perfectly with Christ[4], following the life and the footsteps of the Apostles and, having completed the work of perfection that he had begun, he ascended happily to reside among the heavenly spirits. With hymns and songs, his sacred and holy body was brought and honorably safeguarded in that city where, to the glory of the Almighty, it shone through many miracles. Amen.

89. In the bloom of his youth and with little or no instruction in the way and knowledge of God, he spent much time in natural freedom and ardent passion, but forgiven of sin[5] through the transformation worked by the right hand of God[6], through the grace and virtue of the Most High he was filled with wisdom far beyond anyone else who lived during his times. In fact, in the debased state into which evangelical doctrine everywhere had fallen -- not in particular but in general -- he was send by God to bear the whole world universal witness to the truth, just as the Apostles had done. Through his teachings he pointed out the stupidity of all worldly knowledge and in a short time, with Christ's help he led the world to the true knowledge of God through the stupidity of his preaching since, a new evangelist in these recent times, like one of the rivers of paradise he flooded the whole world with the flowing waters of the Gospel and with his works he preached the way of the Son of God and the doctrine of truth. Thus, in him and through him, an unhoped-for reawakening of fervor took place on earth and this holy renewal rejuvenated very old and hardened branches with the seed of the ancient religion. New vigor was instilled in the hearts of the elect and salutary anointment was spread in their midst as soon as the holy servant of Christ, like a heavenly light, spread his light through a new form of sanctity and with new miracles. Through him, the ancient miracles were repeated when, in the old way but with a new method, the fruitful vine that produces the sweet blos-

---

[4] Although in N° 119, Celano says, "during the twentieth year".

[5] *Rm* 6, 7.

[6] *Ps* 77, 11.

soms of holy virtue was planted in the desert of the world, extending the shoots of the holy religion everywhere.

90. Although, like us, he was subject to the miseries of the flesh[7], he nevertheless was not content with observing common precepts: abounding in most fervent love, he set out on the path of perfection, touched the summits of saintliness and succeeded in fulfilling everything to the letter[8]. In him, therefore, all kinds of people of both sexes and all ages have the clear teachings of the doctrine of salvation and splendid examples of holy works. Anyone who resolves to undertake good endeavors and tries to conquer the excellent charisms of a better life should thus look at the mirror of Francis' life and there he shall learn all perfection[9]. On the other hand, anyone who has devoted himself to humble and plain practices and is afraid of walking through arduous places and climbing to the top of the mountain will find fitting lessons in him about this level of spiritual life as well. Lastly, anyone who wants signs and miracles should examine his sanctity and he shall find what he is seeking.

It is precisely his glorious life that reflects clearer light onto the perfection of the early saints. This is proven by the Passion of Jesus Christ and His cross fully manifests this. In fact, the venerable Father was marked with the sign of the Passion and cross on five parts of his body, as if he had been crucified together with the Son of God. This is a great mystery[10] and it indicates the sublimity of the prerogative of this love, yet it also hides an arcane plan and conceals a venerable mystery that we believe is known to God alone and that the Saint himself revealed, only in part, to one per-

---

[7] *Jas* 5, 13-15.

[8] *Ps* 119.

[9] This concept of Francis as the "mirror of perfection" is discussed further ahead. This is also the title of a well-known Franciscan work.

[10] *Eph* 5, 32.

son[11]. Thus, it is not fitting to test oneself much against the praise of the Saint who was glorified by the One who is the laud, the source and highest honor of all and who gives the reward of eternal light. Thus offering this blessing to the holy, true and glorious God, let us return to our story.

CHAPTER II

Of blessed Francis' greatest desire; and how he learned of the Lord's will for him when he opened the book of the Gospel

91. One time, leaving behind the crowds that hastened devoutly every day to hear and see him, the blessed and venerable father Francis went off to a place of tranquillity and solitary meditation, yearning to devote himself only to God there and to shake off any of the worldly dust that may have settled over his spirit. He was accustomed to dividing the time that was allotted to him for gaining grace and, as he deemed fit, he would spend part of it for the good of his neighbor and the other part in the blessed solitude of contemplation.

Thus he took with him just a few companions who were more familiar with his saintly habits than the others were, so that they would guard him from meeting people and from distraction and lovingly protect his retreat.

After remaining there for quite some time and achieving an extraordinary unity with God through continuous prayer and frequent contemplation, he began to want to know what it was about him and in him that was or could be most pleasing to the eternal King. Insistently and piously, he tried to find out how, through which means or through which desire, he could become united more perfectly with the Lord God, according to the design and decision of His will. As long as he lived, this was always the es-

---

[11] To whom is Celano referring? If it had been Brother Elias, he would have named him. Could it be Brother Leo? In his *Major Life* XIII, 4, St. Bonaventure named Brother Illuminatus.

sence of his philosophy, his most ardent desire: to ask the simple as well as the learned, the perfect as well as the imperfect, how to achieve the way of the truth and arrive at the highest goal.

92. Indeed, even though he was most perfect among the perfect, he refused to acknowledge his own perfection and truly considered himself imperfect. He had tasted and seen how sweet, gentle and good the God of Israel acts towards those who are clean of heart[12] and seek Him with pure simplicity and true purity. In fact, the inspired and gentle sweetness -- given rarely and to very few -- that he felt radiating within him from heaven forced him to step completely outside himself, so that when he was filled with such great joy, he was fully consumed by the desire to proceed completely to the place where he had already ascended in part by rising beyond himself[13]. This man, who had the spirit of God within him, was prepared to suffer all torture, to tolerate all bodily pain, as long as, in the end, he would be allowed to have the will of the heavenly Father clemently accomplished in him.

Because of this, one day he approached the sacred altar built in the hermitage where he was staying and, picking up the book of the holy Gospel, he reverently placed it there. Then, prostrating himself in prayer as much in his heart as in his body, he humbly implored the benevolent Lord, Father of mercy and God of all consolation[14], to deign to show him His will. And in order to complete to perfection what he had begun in simplicity and devotion, he begged that He reveal to him what he should do the very first time he opened the book. He was led by the spirit of those saints and most perfect men who, driven by the pious desire to be sanctified, had done likewise, as it has been written[15].

93. Then, getting up from his prayer, humble in spirit and with a contrite heart[16], he made the sign of the holy cross, took

---

[12] *Ps* 73, 1.
[13] Celano uses the Latin term *excedendo*, which means mystical ecstasy.
[14] *2 Cor* 1, 3.
[15] St. Anthony, St. Augustine, St. Gregory of Tours, St. Martin.
[16] *Dn* 3, 39.

the book from the altar and opened it in reverence and awe. It so happened that when the book was opened, the first thing to present itself was the Passion of our Lord Jesus Christ and, more precisely, only the passage that announced that He was to face an agonizing passion. Nevertheless, in order to eliminate any suspicion that this had happened purely by chance, he opened the book a second time and then a third, and he found the same passage or a similar one. The man filled with God's spirit understood then that it was through many trials, much torment and many struggles that he was to gain entry to the kingdom of God[17].

But that valiant knight was not troubled by these imminent battles, nor did he lose heart when he was about to fight the Lord's battles on the field of this world. He who had not surrendered even to himself during the long efforts he had sustained beyond human endurance was not afraid of succumbing to the enemy. He was truly filled with fervor and even though he had had a predecessor in his intentions during bygone centuries, no one more fervent with desire than he can found. It was easier for him to do good than to say it and so, instead of using words, which can demonstrate good but do not accomplish it, he turned all his energy to doing holy works, so that he could remain peaceful and happy and sing hymns of joy in his heart for himself and for God. Because of this, he who was so happy over the smallest revelation was found worthy of even greater revelation and since he had been faithful in smaller things, he was borne to much greater heights[18].

---

[17] *Acts* 14, 22.
[18] *Mt* 25, 21.

CHAPTER III
Of the vision of the Crucified in the figure of a Seraph

94. Two years before he died[19], while he was staying in the hermitage that is named La Verna[20] after the place in which it is located, in a divine vision[21] he saw above him a man with six wings like a seraph whose hands were outstretched and whose feet were joined together, and who was nailed to the cross. Two wings rose from his head, two were outstretched out to fly and the last two covered his whole body. When he saw this, the blessed servant of the Most High was filled with admiration, but he was unable to understand the meaning of the vision. He was inflamed with joy by the loving sweetness of the Seraph's glance, which was immeasurably beautiful, yet he was terrified by the consideration of that cross to which he was nailed and the bitterness of his passion. He got up feeling sad yet happy at the same time, if this is what we can call it, and joy and sorrow were intermingled in him. In the meantime, he tried to understand the meaning of the vision and his whole spirit was troubled by this effort. He could not understand anything specific and was engrossed with the uniqueness of the vision, when the signs of the nails began to appear on his hands and feet, just like the ones on the man he had seen crucified above him just a short time before.

95. His hands and feet were pierced right through the middle by nails and the heads of these nails could be seen in the palms of his hands and on the upper part of his feet, whereas the ends came out on the opposite side. The seals were round on his palms and long on the backs of his hands, and a bit of flesh, like a twisted and riveted end of a nail, stuck out from the rest of his skin. Likewise, the signs of the nails were impressed on his feet and were raised with respect to the rest of his skin. Moreover, his

---

[19] In other words, in 1224. St. Bonaventure specifies, "around the feast of the Holy Cross", that is, around September 14th.

[20] On the slopes of Mount Penna in the Tuscan province of Arezzo.

[21] *Is* 6, 1-2 and *Ez* 8, 3.

right side looked as if it had been pierced by a lance and had a long scar that bled frequently so that his robe and his underpants would often get wet. How few merited seeing the sacred wound in his side while that crucified servant of the crucified Lord was alive! Lucky Elias who, while the Saint was still alive, was deserving of a small glimpse and Rufino, who touched it with his very hands, was no less fortunate! In fact, one time, when he had put his hand on the Saint's chest to give him a rub, his hand slipped to his right side, as can easily happen, and he touched the precious wound. At his touch, the Saint felt a sharp pain and moved that hand out of the way, crying out to the Lord to forgive him, for not only did he want to hide that miracle from strangers, but he also kept it carefully concealed from friends, so that even his closest brothers and most devout followers were unaware of it for a long time.

Although this servant and friend of the Most High found himself adorned with these pearls, like most precious gems, and was more wonderfully rich in honor and glory than any other man, he nevertheless did not become haughty about it deep within himself and never attempted to boast about it with anyone out of the desire for vainglory. Instead, in order to prevent the favor of men from stealing heavenly grace from him, he tried to hide it in every way possible[22].

96. Rarely -- indeed to no one -- was he accustomed to revealing this extraordinary secret, out of the fear that, as friends are wont to do out of their great affection, they would spread the word and his grace would diminish because of this. Thus, he always had that saying of the prophet in his heart and often on his lips as well: "Within my heart I treasure your promise, that I may not sin against you[23]." In fact, he had agreed with the brothers and sons who were with him to recite this little verse whenever he wanted to stop conversing with the people of the world who

---

[22] *Mt* 6, 18-20.
[23] *Ps* 119, 1.

would go to talk to him. At that signal, they were to dismiss the visitors courteously.

He had learned through experience that it is a great evil to tell everyone everything, and that anyone whose innermost secrets are no deeper or more numerous than the spiritual things that can be read on his face and can be judged fully by men, cannot be a spiritual man. In fact, he had seen that some people made a show of sharing his ideas, whereas deep inside they held a different opinion. They would approve of him to his face and deride him behind his back. They would claim the right to judge and instill suspicion in him towards those with good intentions[24]. In fact, malicious people often try to denigrate the simple and since lying is a common vice, the few honest people are not believed.

CHAPTER IV
Of Blessed Francis' fervor;
and of his eye disease

97. At around that time, he began to be afflicted with various physical ills that were worse than usual and that were caused by the mortification with which he had punished and subdued his body for many years. Over the course of the eighteen years that had just ended, his flesh had gotten little or no rest during his travels to the various and far-flung regions in which that ready, devout and fervent spirit that pervaded him went to sow the seed of the divine word. He filled each land with the Gospel of Christ, to the point that he had even managed to travel to four or five villages or cities in just one day to announce the kingdom of God to each of them, and it could be said that he had made a single tongue of his whole body, since he preached as much through example as with words. And so great was the harmony between

---

[24] Celano's argumentative tone is obvious, but it is not clear to whom he is referring.

his flesh and his spirit, so great was the obedience of the former
to the latter, that as he was striving to reach the summit of holiness, not only did it fail to offer any resistance but indeed, it sur-
passed him, just as it has been written: "For you my flesh pines
and my soul thirsts!"[25] Constancy had made this very subjection
voluntary and through daily obedience he had achieved the
steadiness of such great virtue, since habit often becomes second
nature.

98. Also, since it is the law of nature and of the human
condition that, insofar as his body is concerned, man wastes away
day by day even though he is renewed in spirit, that precious case
that contained this heavenly treasure began to decay and lose its
strength. However, since it is once man has been consumed that
he will truly begin to live, and he will start producing right when
he has come to the end[26], so also in that weak flesh his spirit further readied itself. Moreover, he so greatly loved the salvation of
souls and thirsted to gain his neighbor for God that when he was
unable to walk on his own, he went through the towns seated on
the back of a donkey.

The brothers often suggested and begged him insistently to
restore his ill and weakened body through medical care but Francis, whose his noble spirit was turned towards heaven and who
yearned only to be engrossed with and to be with Christ[27], utterly
refused.

Nevertheless, since what was needed to fulfill Christ's Passion had not yet been completed in his flesh[28], even though he
bore the Stigmata on his body, he developed a very serious eye
disease as a multiplication of divine mercy towards him. Since his
illness got worse by the day and seemed to be aggravated by lack
of care, Brother Elias, whom Francis had chosen to act as his own

---

[25] *Ps* 63, 2.
[26] *Sir* 18, 5-6.
[27] *Phil* 1, 23.
[28] *Col* 1, 24 and *Gal* 6, 27.

mother and as a father for the other sons[29], forced him not to refuse the medical remedies but to accept them in the name of the Son of God, by whom they have been created, since it is written that "God makes the earth yield healing herbs which the wise man should not neglect."[30] And so the holy Father agreed and humbly obeyed.

CHAPTER V

How he was received in Rieti by Cardinal Hugolin,
Bishop of Ostia, and how the Saint foretold
that he would become Bishop of the whole world

99. However, since he was unable to find any effective remedies although many people offered them to him, he went to the city of Rieti, where a doctor very expert in curing that illness was said to live. Upon his arrival, he was received very kindly and with honor by the entire Roman Curia, which was in the city at that time[31], and in particular by Hugolin, Bishop of Ostia, who was renowned for his integrity and saintly life. Blessed Francis had chosen him as father and lord of entire Order of his brothers, with the consent and approval of Pope Honorius, precisely because blessed poverty pleased him very much and he greatly honored holy simplicity.

This bishop imitated the life of the brothers and in his desire to sanctify himself, he was simple among the simple, humble among the humble, poor among the poor; he was a brother among the brothers and he was even the least among the Friars Minor and, insofar as he was allowed to do so, he tried to behave like one of them in his every action. It was his concern to estab-

---

[29] Brother Elias had been named Vicar General after the death of Peter Catanii in 1221.

[30] *Sir* 38, 4.

[31] Honorius III and the entire Curia stayed in Rieti from June 23, 1225 until January 31, 1226. The Saint's ophthalmia was well advanced by this time.

lish the holy order of the Friars Minor everywhere and the fame of his life gave even greater prestige to our Order in far-off places. The Lord gave him wisdom of speech through which he shamed adversaries of the truth, and he confuted the enemies of the Cross of Christ, brought the erring back to the straight path, reconciled discord and strengthened the bond of charity among those who were already living in peace. In the Church of God he was a lamp set aflame and burning bright, the chosen arrow set aside for the right moment[32].

How many times, having set aside his rich garments to don rough ones, would he go forth barefoot like a brother, seeking what brings peace and trying, whenever he was given the opportunity, to reestablish peace between man and his neighbor, between man and God! Consequently, a short time later God chose him as the shepherd of his holy Church and exalted him among all peoples[33].

100. And the fact that this truly took place through divine inspiration and through the will of Jesus Christ is proven by the fact that long before then, the blessed father Francis had foretold it with words and symbolized it in deed. Thus, through the work of divine grace, the Order of the Friars Minor began to grow, and just as the cypress in the garden of God raised the height of its worth towards heaven, and just as the chosen vine extended its holy branches along the ground, St. Francis went before Pope Honorius, head of the Church of Rome at that time, and begged that he be granted Hugolin, Bishop of Ostia, as father and lord for him and his brothers[34]. The supreme pontiff satisfied these prayers and benevolently delegated to the bishop his jurisdiction over the Order. Hugolin received it with reverence and devotion and, as a faithful and cautious servant, elected to such a high position, he tried in every way to distribute the food of life properly to all those entrusted to his care. Therefore, the Saint for his own

---

[32] *Jn* 5, 35; *Is* 49, 2 and *Ps* 31, 6.

[33] Hugolin was elected pope on March 19, 1227.

[34] *Ez* 31,8.

part remained subject to him and venerated him with affectionate devotion.

Guided by the Spirit of God that filled him, Francis had sensed long before what would take place before everyone's eyes. Each time that he wrote to him on account of the Order or because he was driven by the love he bore for Christ, in his letters he was never content with referring to him as Bishop of Ostia or of Velletri, as the other were accustomed to greeting him, but going even further he would say, "To the most reverent father, o lord, Hugolin, bishop of the whole world"[35]. Also, he often greeted him with odd blessings and even though he was subject to him like a devout son, again through the inspiration of the Holy Spirit, at times he would comfort him by speaking to him as a father so that he would gain the desire for the eternal hills[36].

101. The most excellent lord dearly loved the Saint as well, and therefore he approved of his every word and his every action, and just looking at him comforted him fully. He himself declared that he never suffered any disturbance or anxiety in his heart so great that the sight and words of St. Francis could not dispel, scattering the clouds over his spirit and restoring serenity, dissipating sadness and making joy stir once again in his heart. He attended to blessed Francis as a servant would his master. Each time he saw him, he would pay him homage as if he were one of Christ's Apostles and bowing down in body and in spirit, he often kissed his hands with his holy lips.

Now, this solicitous and devout bishop addressed his thoughts to having the blessed Father's eyesight restored, for he knew that he was holy and just and that he was necessary and most useful to the Church of God. He felt compassion for him as well as for the entire congregation of brothers and in his role as their Father he felt pity for his sons. Therefore, he urged him to get treatment and not to refuse the remedies necessary for his

---

[35] Unfortunately, these letters that St. Francis wrote to Hugolin have never been found.

[36] *Gn* 49, 26.

illness, admonishing him that neglecting them could be ascribed to him as sin rather than merit. And in order to observe humbly the advice of such a reverend and very dear father, St. Francis became less scrupulous and began to have some regard for his illness. By now, however, it was so serious that in order to cure it somewhat, a physician's deep knowledge and very painful treatment were required. Thus his head was cauterized in various spots, his veins were cut, poultices were applied and collyria was injected, but there was no improvement and, indeed, you could say that he kept getting worse.

CHAPTER VI

Of the virtues of the friars who assisted
St. Francis, and how he would have liked to live

105. For almost two years he had to endure this suffering with patience and humility, offering thanks to God for all of it. Nevertheless, in order to turn his attention more freely to God and to roam frequently through the blessed heavenly abode in ecstasy and virtually enter there, and to live always in an abundance of grace with the sweet and most serene Lord of the Universe, he had entrusted the care of his own person to several brothers who, rightly so, had become his favorites.

These were men of virtue, devoted to God, dear to the saints and acceptable to men, and the blessed father Francis leaned on them like a house on four columns[37].

I will keep my silence about their names out of respect for their modesty, which was a friend to them as it is to all truly spiritual men. Modesty is in fact the ornament of every age, the witness of innocence, evidence of a chaste spirit, rod of discipline, special glory of conscience, guardian of a good reputation and the merit of all honesty. This virtue adorned them, making them ami-

---

[37] *Jgs* 16, 29.

able and gentle among men, and while it was a grace common to all of them, each one of them was also adorned with a singular virtue. One was extraordinarily discreet, the second one was singularly patient, the third had glorious simplicity, the last was stout in body and meek at heart[38]. With assiduous watchfulness, constant care and all good will, they protected the tranquillity of the blessed Father's spirit. They treated his bodily illness without saving themselves from boredom or fatigue while they devoted themselves entirely to serving the Saint.

103. Although the glorious Father was already perfect in grace in the eyes of God and shone before men on account of his glorious works, he nevertheless always thought about undertaking a path of even higher perfection and, like a highly skillful soldier in the divine army, about inciting his adversary into new battles. He resolved to do extraordinary things under Christ's guidance and although his limbs were wasting away and his body was exhausted, he hoped to achieve new victories in the new battle. In fact, true virtue knows no time limit since it hopes for eternal reward.

Thus, he burned with the desire to return to his initial humility and, through the strength of the love that was gladdened by new hope, he resolved to bring that body back under its ancient bondage, even though it had reached its limit. He withdrew from the obstacle of treatment and silenced the din of human considerations, and although he was necessarily forced to moderate his initial severity because of illness, he would say, "Brothers, let us begin to serve the Lord God because so far we have gained little or nothing." He did not believe he had achieved his goal and, indefatigable in his resolution for holy renewal, he always hoped to begin.

---

[38] It is traditionally thought that the four companions who took care of Francis during his final illness were Angelo, Leo, Rufino and Bernard. However, the passage in *Mirror of Perfection* in which St. Francis describes the ideal Friar Minor, also includes Masseus.

He wanted to assist the lepers again, to become the object of disdain that he once had been. He resolved to flee from the company of men and to retreat to secluded spots so that, stripped of all care and of all anxiety for others, only the shield of the flesh would divide him from his God.

104. He saw many who were avid to spring to a commanding role and, detesting their temerity, he tried to turn them away from this plague through his example. He said governing others was a good thing that was acceptable to God, but that the care of souls should be assumed only by those who seek nothing for themselves but who always look only to divine will in everything. In other words, it is for those who place nothing ahead of their spiritual health and who take no heed of their subjects' applause but of their gain, for those who do not aspire to the prelacy but who fear it and lastly, for those who, when they have it, feel humiliated by it rather than glorified and who, when it is revoked, are not discouraged but are pleased. However, it is especially during this age of malice and sin, he declared, that governing is a danger and that it is better to be governed. He grieved that some of them, leaving their initial works behind, would forget ancient simplicity for new discoveries. Thus, he mourned that some who had once been lit by the highest spiritual desires should stoop to such lowly and worthless things and that after having abandoned the true joys of the soul they should go forth amidst frivolity and vanity wandering in a field of freedom that is devoid of blessing. He therefore implored divine mercy to redeem his sons and most devoutly beseeched that they be kept in the grace that had already been bestowed.

CHAPTER VII

*How he returned to Assisi from Siena; and of the
church of St. Mary's of the Porziuncola and of
his blessing of the brothers*

105. Six months before he died[39], he began to be seriously
ill throughout his whole body while he was in Siena for his eye
treatment. Since his stomach had been weakened by his lengthy
illness and he had lost a great deal of blood because of a liver attack, he seemed to be near death[40]. As soon as he heard this
news, Brother Elias quickly rushed to his side from far away and
upon his arrival the holy Father improved to the point that he was
able to leave Siena with him and go to Le Celle near Cortona.
However, after he had stayed there for just a short while, his belly,
legs and feet became swollen and his stomach ailment got so bad
that he was practically unable to eat any more.

He thus begged Brother Elias to bring him back to Assisi
and the good son agreed, making all the arrangements and accompanying him there himself. Upon the arrival of the blessed
Father, the entire city exulted and praises to God resounded on
the lips of the people, for everyone thought that the Saint of God
would die there and this was the reason for their rejoicing[41].

And through divine will, it so happened that this sainted
soul, freed from the yoke of the flesh, ascended to the kingdom
of heaven right there where, while still alive, he had had his first
revelation of supernatural truth and was first imparted with saving
grace.

He was well aware that the kingdom of heaven is in every
corner of the earth and that the elect can receive divine grace
anywhere. Nevertheless, he had also found that the place near the

---

[39] Therefore, around April of 1226.

[40] The loss of blood, together with Celano's indication of stomach and liver
problems, could also be diagnosed as carcinoma or cirrhosis of the liver.

[41] The reason for this strange joy was that the people were thus convinced that
they would be able to keep Francis' holy body in Assisi.

little church of the Porziuncola was more filled grace and was honored by the frequent visits of angelic spirits.[42] Therefore, he often repeated to the brothers, "My sons, be sure that you never leave this place, so that if you are kicked out from one door, go back in from the other, for this place is truly holy[43] and it is the house of God. Here, when there were just a few of us, the Most High multiplied us; here, with the light of His wisdom, he illuminated the hearts of his poor ones; here, He kindled our will with the flame of His love; here, anyone who prays with devotion will obtain what he asks[44], but anyone who desecrates it shall be severely punished. Therefore, my sons, consider this place the house of God, worthy of all honor and in a voice of exultation and praise, sing to the Lord here with all your heart."

107. In the meantime, since his illness was getting worse, all the strength was ebbing from his body and he was so exhausted that he was completely unable to move. Yet, questioned by a brother as to whether he preferred the suffering of constant and long illness or martyrdom at the hands of an executioner, he replied, "O child, what always has been and still is the sweetest, the dearest and the most welcome thing for me is what the Lord God shall most wish should happen in me and to me, for my sole desire is to be found fully compliant and obedient to His will. But if I were not to consider the reward but only the spasms of this suffering, tolerating this illness even for only three days would be more atrocious for me than any martyrdom!"

O martyr twice over who, smiling happily, bore what was so painful and anguishing for anyone even to watch! In fact, there was no part of him that was not racked with pain any more and each day, gradually losing his natural warmth, he was approaching his limit. The doctors were astonished and the brothers were amazed that the spirit could keep living in that flesh that was al-

---

[42] *Second Life*, 19.

[43] *Ez* 42, 13.

[44] This could also be a reference to the famous "Assisi Pardon".

ready dead, so that because his flesh was so wasted away, all that was left was skin and bones.

108. When he saw that his last day was approaching, as had also been indicated to him through divine revelation two years before, he summoned to his side the brothers he wished to see again. As he had been instructed by heaven, just as the patriarch Jacob had once done with his sons, he gave each one his blessing[45] and like a latter-day Moses about to climb the mountain shown to him by God, he bestowed his blessing upon the sons of Israel[46]. Since Brother Elias was on his left side and the other sons stood all around him, crossing his arms he placed his right hand on him. Being blind, he asked, "Upon whom," he asked, "have I placed my right hand?" They answered, "Upon Brother Elias." "This is what I want too," he said, adding, "O son, I bless you in all and for all, and since under your direction the Most High has multiplied my brothers and sons, so upon you and in you I bless them all. In heaven and on earth, may the Lord, king of all things, bless you. I bless you as I can and more than I can, and let anything that I cannot do, be done in you by Him who can do all things. May God remember your works and your toil and may your fate hold the rewards of the just in store for you. May you find every blessing you desire and let any just request of yours be fulfilled. Farewell, all my sons, live in fear of the Lord and remain in Him always, since a terrible temptation will come upon you and tribulations are already at hand. Happy are those who will persevere in the work they have begun, for many will part because of future scandals. As for me, I am hastening to the Lord, with the faith of joining my God, whom I have served devoutly in spirit."

He was staying in the palace of the Bishop of Assisi at that time and he begged the brothers to bring him to the Porziuncola in great haste, since he wanted to render his soul to God in the

[45] *Gn* 49, 1.
[46] *Dt* 33, 1.

place where, as we have already said, he had first gained perfect knowledge of the way of the truth.

CHAPTER VIII
What he said and did when he died blessedly

109. The twenty-year cycle following his conversion, meaning the time that divine will had been shown to him, had already come to an end. In fact, once when the blessed Father was in Foligno with Brother Elias, one night while he was sleeping Brother Elias had a vision of a priest dressed in white who was well on in years and venerable in appearance, who said to him, "Get up, brother, and tell brother Francis that eighteen years have already gone by since he renounced the world to follow Christ and that he will remain in this life for only two more years. Then, called by the Lord, he will pass on to the next life."

Accordingly, at the established time, the divine prophecy made two years before was being fulfilled here. He had been resting for just a few days in the place he had so greatly desired when, realizing that death was imminent, he called two of his favorite brothers and sons to his side and ordered them to sing aloud with a joyful spirit to praise the Lord for his imminent death, or rather, for the true life that was approaching. Then he intoned that song of David as well as he could: "With a loud voice I cry out to the Lord, with a loud voice I beseech the Lord"[47]. One of the brothers who was present and was greatly beloved by the Saint, was very solicitous of all the brothers. Upon seeing this, knowing that the end was near he said to Francis, "Loving Father, your sons are already to remain fatherless and deprived of the light of their eyes! So remember the orphans you are about to leave behind, forgive all their faults and comfort those present as well as those who are absent with your holy blessing." And the

---

[47] *Ps* 142, 1.

Saint said, "Here, I am summoned by God, o son. I pardon all the offenses and sins of my brothers, present and absent, and I absolve them insofar as I am able. In announcing this, you should bless all of them for me."

110. Then he had the book of the Gospel brought to him and asked that the Gospel according to John be read to him, at the point starting, "Six days before Passover, Jesus realized that the hour had come for him to pass from this world to the Father..."[48]. Even before receiving these instructions, the minister had already stepped forward to read this very passage, and this was the first passage he came to when the book was first opened, even though the book from which he was to read this Gospel contained the whole Bible. After this, he ordered them to put his hair shirt upon him and sprinkle ashes over him, since he would soon be dirt and ash.

While many brothers, whose father and guide he was, were gathered together there in reverence to await his blessed passing and sacred end, that most holy soul was released from the flesh to be taken into the abyss of eternal light and his body fell asleep in the Lord. One of his brothers and disciples, who was quite famous and whose name I have omitted for now since he is still alive and does not wish to boast about such immense grace[49], saw the soul of the most holy father going straight up to heaven, rising above many waters, and he was like a star yet as big as the moon and as brilliant as the sun, borne up on a small white cloud[50].

111. Let me thus exclaim, "O how glorious is this Saint whose soul was seen by one of his disciples as it ascended into heaven: beautiful as the moon and noble as the sun, ascending on a white cloud, beaming with a glorious light![51] O true light of the world who shines more brightly than the sun in the Church of

---

[48] This is a combination of *Jn* 12, 1 and 13,1.

[49] In his *Liber de Laudibus*, Bernard of Bessa indicates the name of Brother James. The *Treatise of Miracles,* 116, also discusses this.

[50] This description is based on passages from St. Paul, Revelation, etc.

[51] *Sg* 6, 10 and 3, 6; *Rev* 14, 14.

Christ, lo! you have already concealed the rays of your light and, passing on to that lucent homeland, you have exchanged the company of us wretches for the company of angels and saints. O glorious fountain of such illustrious merit, even though you have already been released from your mortal flesh, do not relinquish the care of your sons. You know -- how well you know -- the danger in which you have left them, now that your benevolent presence no longer restores them in their innumerable efforts and constant woes! O truly merciful, most holy Father, who was always ready to be compassionate and to forgive your errant sons! Thus, holy Father, we bless you who were blessed by the Most High, ever our blessed God over all things. Amen."[52]

CHAPTER IX

*Of the weeping and joy of the brothers when they
saw that he bore the signs of the crucifixion;
and of the wings of the Seraph*

112. Then there gathered a multitude of people who were praising God, saying, "Praise and blessed be the Lord our God, who has entrusted such precious custody to us unworthy beings. Praise and glory to you, ineffable Trinity!" The entire population of Assisi came in droves and the citizens of the entire district hastened to see the divine marvels that the God of majesty had manifested in his holy Servant. Spurred on by the happiness in his heart, each one of them chanted a song of joy, blessing the omnipotence of the Savior who had fulfilled their desire[53].

But the sons grieved that they had been left without such a Father and weeping and sighing, they poured forth the sorrow in their hearts. Yet an inexplicable joy tempered their spirits and

---

[52] *Rm* 9, 5.
[53] That is, the desire that Francis die in his city, which could then keep his sacred remains.

their sadness and the novelty of the miracle turned their minds to the extraordinary marvel. Mourning was transformed into song and weeping into joy.

Indeed, never had they heard nor read in any writings about what was displayed before their eyes and about which they would have been difficult to convince if they had not had such evident testimony of it. There appeared in him the image of the cross and passion of the immaculate Lamb who washed away the sins of the world[54]. He looked as if he had just been taken down from the cross, with his hands and feet pierced by the nails and his right side as if it had been wounded by a sword. They could also see his flesh, originally swarthy, now shining whitely and its beauty bore witness to the reward of blessed resurrection. They saw that his face looked almost like the face of an angel[55], as if he were alive rather than dead, and they saw that the other parts of his body had gained the softness and suppleness of the limbs of an innocent baby. His nerves had not contracted as they usually do in the dead, nor had his skin gotten hard. His limbs were not stiff but could still be bent back and forth at will[56].

113. In such extraordinarily beautiful splendor, in everyone's sight and within the flesh that had become snowy white, it was marvelous to see in the center of his hands and feet, not nail holes, but the nails themselves made of flesh the brown color of iron, whereas his right side was red with blood. Rather than arousing horror in those who contemplated them, instead those signs of martyrdom bestowed dignity and beauty, like little black flecks on a white floor.

The brothers, his sons, hastened to him and wept as they kissed the hands and feet of the pious Father who had left them, as well as his right side, whose wound brought to mind the mem-

---

[54] *I Pt* 1, 19; *Rev* 1,5; *Jn* 1, 29.

[55] *Acts* 6, 15.

[56] In his *Encyclical Letter*, Brother Elias wrote that *rigor mortis* did actually set in but that Francis' limbs soon became supple again.

ory of the One who, shedding both blood and water from that same place, had reconciled the world to His Father[57].

Among the people, anyone who, not permitted to kiss the sacred Stigmata of Jesus that St. Francis bore on his body, was merely allowed to see it, considered this to be a sublime gift[58]. Who would have been capable of abandoning himself to tears rather than joy or, in weeping, to shed tears of sorrow rather than happiness?

What heart of stone would have been left unmoved by that sighing? What heart would have been so hardened that it would fail to open itself up in compassion, be kindled with divine love and fail to arm itself with good will? Who could have been so obtuse and insensitive as to fail to understand with manifest certainty that just as the Saint had been honored with this singular gift on earth, so too must he have been magnified with ineffable glory in heaven?

114. Singular gift, evidence of special love, this, that the soldier should be decorated with the same glorious arms that are so excellent that they are fit only for the king! A miracle worthy of eternal memory, a sacrament to be remembered with unceasing wonder and reverence, representing in an arcanum of faith that mystery in which the blood of the immaculate Lamb, flowing so copiously from five wounds, washed away the sins of the world! Sublime beauty of the life-giving cross that restores the dead to life, whose weight is so gentle and which inflicts wounds so sweet that it revives flesh that has already died and restores the weakened spirit! Greatly were you loved by him, whom you so gloriously decorated! Glory and benediction to the one and knowing God, who renews signs and various omens[59] to comfort the minds of the weak with new revelations and to steal their hearts away to the love of things invisible through a visible marvel. Marvelous and lovable disposition of God who, to avoid any suspi-

---

[57] *Rom* 5, 10; *2 Cor 5*, 19-20.

[58] *Gal* 6, 17.

[59] *Lk* 7, 47; *Rev* 5, 13; *Rom* 16, 17; *Sir* 36, 6.

cion over the newness of the miracle, first clemently showed in Him who came down from Heaven what he would later miraculously accomplish in the man living on earth! And truly, the true Father of mercy wanted to show the great reward for which anyone who strives to love Him with all his heart will make himself worthy, and that reward is to be placed among the ranks of the heavenly spirits that are highest and closest to God.

And we would certainly be able to achieve this prize if, like the seraphim[60], we too were to keep two wings outstretched over our heads, or in other words if, following the example of blessed Francis in each good work, we are pure in intention and upright in deed and, turning this towards God, we unceasingly attempt to please Him alone in everything. These wings must necessarily come together to cover our heads because the Father of light would not accept any good work that was accomplished without purity of action and indeed, as He Himself said, the opposite is true: if your eyes are good, your body will be filled with light, but if your eyes are bad, your body will be in darkness[61]. Indeed, the simple eyes are not the ones that fail to see what must be seen or in other words, that have no knowledge of the truth, nor are they the ones that peer intently at what is not meant to be seen that is, with intentions that are not pure. In the former case, they are judged not to be simple but blind, whereas in the latter they are malicious. So the feathers of these wings are the love of the Father who mercifully saves and the fear of the Lord[62] who terribly judges, and these feathers must lift the spirit of the elect above the things of the earth, repressing bad impulses and governing chaste affection.

The second pair of wings is to fly in order to fulfill the dual duty of loving our neighbor and that is, of comforting the soul with the word of God and of sustaining the body with material aid. These wings rarely come together because it is difficult for a

---

[60] *Ez* 1, 5-14 and 22-25.

[61] *Mt* 6, 22-23.

[62] *Sir* 1 and 2.

single person to accomplish the two duties. The feathers on these wings are the works needed to offer counsel and help to one's neighbor.

Lastly, the last two wings must cover the naked body with merit and this can be accomplished properly if each time it is left naked by sin, it is then clothed again with the innocence that is regained through contrition and confession. Their feathers are the various kinds of love generated through the execration of sin and the desire for justice.

115. All this was perfectly accomplished by the most blessed father Francis, who bore the image and shape of a seraph and who, by persevering in the cross, deserved to soar to the heights of the sublime spirits. In fact, he always remained on the cross, never avoiding any effort or pain, so that he would be able to fulfill the Lord's will in him and for him.

The brothers who lived with him know this: they know how every day and in every moment the subject of Jesus came to his tongue and of the very sweet, gentle and loving tenderness with which he spoke to Him. His mouth spoke from his heart's abundance[63] and that font of illuminated love that filled him inside overflowed to the outside, for surely he was intimately united with Jesus. He always bore Jesus in his heart, Jesus on his lips, Jesus in his ears, Jesus in his eyes, Jesus in his hands, Jesus in all his other limbs. How many times, as he was seated at dinner, would he forget bodily food upon hearing or naming or thinking of Jesus and, as we can read about a saint[64], he would look but not see, listen but not hear! Indeed, often when he was traveling, meditating and thinking of Jesus, he would forget about his journey and would begin to invite all creatures to praise Jesus. And since he always bore and kept Jesus Christ and this crucifix in his heart with marvelous love,[65] above anyone else he was gloriously marked with the sign of Christ whom, in ecstasy, he contemplated

---

[63] *Mt* 12, 34; *Lk* 6, 45.

[64] St. Bernard, *Major Life*, chap. 4.

[65] *1 Cor* 2,2.

in His unutterable and incomprehensible glory, seated at the right hand of the Father with whom He, the Most High and Son of the Most High, in unity with the Holy Spirit, lives and rules, conquers and reigns, eternally glorious God, world without end. Amen.

CHAPTER X

Of the grief of the Poor Ladies at St. Damian's;
and of how he was buried with praise and glory

116. The brothers and sons, assembled with the multitude of people who had hastened from the nearby cities to participate in the solemn funeral, spent the entire night after the death of the holy Father in divine praise so that because of the sweetness of their psalmodies and the brightness of the lights, it seemed like a wake of angels.

When morning came, a crowd from the city of Assisi gathered with the entire clergy and, lifting up the sacred body from the place where he had died, they carried it to the city with hymns, canticles and the sound of trumpets[66]. Everyone brought branches from olive trees and from other types of trees, and followed the sacred obsequies in a solemn cortege, carrying numerous torches and loudly singing praise.

Then, when the sons who were bearing their Father and the flock that was following its shepherd, who had gone to meet the Shepherd of all men, reached the place where he had founded the order of the sacred virgins, the Poor Ladies, they set him down in the church of St. Damian, where the daughters he had conquered for the Lord lived and the small grating that Christ's maidens used to receive the Sacrament of the Body of Christ in communion on set days was opened. The ark enclosing that treasure of heavenly virtues was also opened and he who was accustomed to bringing many was brought in there by a few. To-

---

[66] *Jn* 21, 4; *Acts* 2, 5; *Jos* 6, 20.

gether with her other daughters, in came lady Clare, truly pure[67] through the sanctity of her merits, mother of all the others and first plant of this holy Order, to see the departure of their Father, who could no longer speak and would no longer return in their midst.

117. Gazing at him with their tear-swollen eyes, they sobbed even more and wailing from the bottom of their hearts, they began to exclaim in a choked voice, "Father, Father, what will we do? Why are you abandoning us wretches? O, to whom are you leaving us so desolately? Why didn't you let us precede you joyfully to your destination, instead of leaving us behind in sorrow? What do you expect us to do, locked away in this prison, if you no longer come to visit us as you used to? All our solace has left with you and there is no consolation left for us, buried to the world! Who will help us in such great poverty, no less of merit than of material goods? O father of the poor, lover of poverty! Who will come to our aid during temptation, you who experienced so much and knew so well how to recognize it? Who will console us in times of trial, o comfort in the tribulations that have already been brought upon us in such abundance[68]. Such bitter separation, such terrible parting! O death most cruel, you are killing thousands of sons and daughters by depriving them of such a Father and you hasten inexorably to tear away from us the one through whose work our zeal, if indeed we have any, achieved its greatest strength!" However, virginal modesty kept a rein on great weeping, for it was not fitting to weep over one whose death had been accompanied by an army of angels and in which the citizens of the kingdom of saints and members of the house of God rejoiced![69] Therefore, torn between anguish and joy, they kissed his resplendent hands adorned with the precious and dazzling gems. Then he was taken away and that door, which would never

---

[67] The play on words is lost in the translation: as an adjective "chiara" also means light, clear and pure.

[68] *Ps* 45, 2.

[69] *Eph* 2, 19.

again be opened to such a deep sorrow, was closed[70]. How sharp was everyone's pain over the heart-felt and piteous grief of those virgins; how great the sorrow of his anguished sons above all! The grief felt by each one of them was common to them all and while those angels of peace were weeping so bitterly, they could barely hold back their tears!

118. Everyone reached the city at last and placed that most holy body in the place that was already sacred but that is now even more sacred, where to the glory of the Most High, God Almighty, he has illuminated the world with his frequent miracles, just as before he had illuminated it through the teachings of his holy sermons. Thanks be to God. Amen!

Thus, most holy and blessed Father, with my tribute of praise, inadequate as it may be, I have tried to honor you and have recounted your gestures as well as I could. Therefore, grant that this wretch may follow your example in this life so that, through divine mercy, I may deserve to join you in the next. O pious one, remember your poor sons, to whom almost no other consolation remains now that you, their sole and singular comfort, have gone. While you, their greatest and principal part, are already among the choirs of Angels at the glorious throne of the Apostles, instead they wallow in the mire, locked away in a dark prison, and so they cry out to you in a suffering voice, "Father, offer your Holy Stigmata to Jesus Christ, Son of the Father Most High, and uncover the signs of His cross in your side, on your feet and on your hands, so that He will mercifully deign to show His own wounds to the Father who, because of these merits, will surely always be benevolent to us wretches!"

Amen. So be it, so be it.

Here ends the second book

---

[70] This historic grating was later brought to the monastery of St. Clare and placed in the sisters' choir. They received Communion through the little door in the middle of the grating.

PART THREE

*Here begins the third book, which discusses the
canonization of our blessed father Francis and his miracles*

119. During the twentieth year of his conversion[1], putting a
fitting ending to a happy beginning, the most glorious father
Francis very gladly entrusted his spirit to heaven where, crowned
in glory and honor, set among stones as splendid as fire[2] and interceding before the throne of Divinity, he takes up the causes of
those he has left behind on earth. Truly, what could be denied to
him whose sacred Stigmata depicts the One who, like the Father,
sits on the right hand of the divine Majesty in the heavens, splendor of glory and image of God's essence, expiator of sin?[3]   How
can he help but be answered, for he was made similar to Jesus
Christ in the unity of his Passion and death, present in the holy
wounds on his hands, feet and side?

Surely, with new joy he has already gladdened the entire
world that is protected by him and offers everyone the way to true
salvation. Through the most dazzling light of his miracles, he illuminates the world and lights it with the brilliance of a true star.
The world wept that it had been deprived of his presence and felt
it was being enveloped by an enormous abyss of darkness when
he waned, but because of the rising of this new light, like the
noonday sun, the world feels that all the darkness has dissipated
and that it has been brightened by more brilliant rays.

Thanks be to God! The grief over his death has ceased,
now that in a rebirth of joy every day and everywhere the treas-
ures of holy virtue are being accumulated through his merit.
Those who, helped by his patronage, can testify to the veracity of
this statement are coming from the east and the west, from the

---

[1] This calculation appears to start with Francis' renunciation of worldly goods in
February of 1207.

[2] *Ez* 28, 14.

[3] *Heb* 1, 3; *Phil* 3, 9-10.

south and the north[4]. While he was alive, this singular lover of things divine did not want to have anything of his own so that he could fully and cheerfully possess the highest Good. He who did not want any portion whatsoever now shares in everything and he exchanged time for eternity. He has come to the aid of each one everywhere, assists everyone everywhere, and the fault of division is unknown to this lover of unity.

120. While he was still living among sinners, he crossed the entire earth to evangelize it. Now, reigning among the angels in heaven, like the herald of the great King he soars faster than thought and bestows glorious benefaction to all people. Thus, the whole world honors him, venerates him, glorifies him and praises him and all of them delight in the common good. Who could possibly say how many and which miracles the Lord has deigned to work through him? For example, how many miracles did Francis work in France alone, where the king, the queen[5] and all the magnates hastened to kiss the pillow used by St. Francis during his illness! There, even the scholars of the earth as well as men of letters, with whom Paris is richer than any other city, humbly and devoutly venerate, admire and honor Francis, unlettered man and friend of true simplicity and absolute sincerity. Truly he was Francis, who had a franker and nobler heart than anyone else[6]! Those who have experienced it know full well how free and generous, how sure and tranquil he was on every occasion and how ardently he deplored all earthly goods! And what should we say then about all the other parts of the world, where by virtue of his poor garments illness is driven away and where great numbers of men and women have been freed of their ills simply by invoking his name?

---

[4] *Mt* 8, 11; *Gen* 13, 14; *Ez* 48, 31.

[5] St. Louis IX, who was a child at that time, and his mother, Blanche of Castille.

[6] Note the word play between "France", "Francis" and "frank".

121. Miracles continue to occur at his tomb as well[7] and glorious benefaction is sought there for soul and body. Sight is restored to the blind and hearing to the deaf, the lame walk again, the mute speak, the gouty become agile again, lepers are cleansed, the swelling of those with dropsy goes down and those afflicted with various serious diseases regain desired health, so that the living are healed by that dead body, just as he brought dead souls back to life while he was alive.

The Roman pontiff, highest among all priests, leader of Christians, master of the world, shepherd of the Church, the Lord's anointed and vicar of Christ, came to know of these marvels. Pleased over this, he exulted, rejoiced and was gladdened by it, for he saw that during his own time the Church of God was renewed by new mysteries similar to the ancient ones and that this had taken place through the word of his son, whom he had carried in his holy womb, warmed at his breast, fed with the milk of the word and educated with the food of life. The venerable cardinals, who are the other guardians of the church, shepherds of the flock, defenders of the faith, friends and family of the Groom and cornerstones of the world, also heard about this and they congratulated the Church, were gladdened with the pope and glorified the Savior who, in His supreme and ineffable wisdom, supreme and incomprehensible grace, supreme and inestimable goodness, chose the world's foolish and despised[8] to bring Himself all that is great. The whole world has heard and applauds and the entire kingdom of the Catholic faith has exulted and is suffused with holy consolation.

122. Yet a sudden upheaval began, a new impulse arose in the world. The merry peace was disturbed, the torch of envy was lit once again and the Church was lacerated by an internal struggle. The Romans, a proud and rebellious people, raged as usual against their neighbors and rashly placed their hands on sacred

---

[7] When Celano wrote this, the tomb was still in the church of St. George, now the site of the basilica of St. Clare.

[8] *1 Cor 1*, 26-27.

things. The great pope Gregory tried to suffocate the growing evil, repress its cruelty, moderate this violence and, like a fortified tower, he tried to defend the Church. There were many impending perils, the great damage was becoming more frequent and in other regions the heads of sinners were rising up against God. What could be done? The Pontiff, wisely reflecting over present circumstances and future possibilities, abandoned the Eternal City to the rebels in order to defend the world from turmoil[9]. He thus headed to Rieti, where he was welcomed with due honor[10]. He then went to Spoleto, amidst signs of great respect. He stayed there for a few days, handling the cause of the Church and, accompanied by the venerable cardinals, he affectionately went to visit Christ's handmaidens, dead and buried to the world[11]. Their holy life, supreme poverty and glorious institution moved him and the others to tears, driving him to despise the times, kindling in him the desire for a simple and pure life. O humility that nourishes all virtues worthy of love! The prince of the whole world, the successor of the prince of the Apostles, visited the poor women, making himself like these wretched and humble prisoners, and this humility of his, while fitting if considered according to Christian criteria, was unprecedented and had never been seen before in bygone centuries!

123. By this time, he was hastening towards Assisi, where the glorious deposit was reserved for him so that he could drive out the suffering of the tribulations impending over him. As he entered there, the entire city rejoiced, a throng of people celebrated and the cloudless day was lit up with new light. Everyone

---

[9] This took place in St. Peter's Basilica on Easter Monday of 1228, following the assault by the Roman supporters of Frederick II, who had been excommunicated due to his ambiguous leadership during the Crusades.

[10] The pope arrived there sometime between April 20th and April 25th, 1228. He then went to Spoleto in May and, as indicated in historical documents, arrived in Assisi between May 26th and June 10th.

[11] He went to visit the *Pauperes Dominae* (they were not known yet by the name of "Poor Clares") at the monastery of St. Paul near Spoleto.

went forth to meet him and formed a solemn cortege. The pious company of the poor friars went forward to greet him, singing sweet canticles to the Lord's Anointed. When he reached the church, the first thing the Vicar of Christ did was to go down to pay homage to St. Francis' tomb reverently and fervently. He sobbed and beat his breast, weeping and bowing his head in great devotion.

The cause for the canonization of the Saint was thus initiated and the illustrious assembly of the cardinals convened often for this purpose. Many who had been delivered of their afflictions through the work of the Saint of God gathered there from all over and a great number of miracles were brought to light here and there. Testimony was discussed, verified, heard and approved.

In the meantime, for official reasons as well as because of the novel event that had come to pass, the pope had to go to Perugia[12], but only so that he would return to Assisi for the even greater and most singular grace in the interest of this very important cause. Another meeting was held at last in Perugia and the holy consistory of the venerable cardinals was celebrated in the Pontiff's room. Everyone agreed unanimously, read the miracle with profound veneration and then elevated the life of the blessed Father to heaven with highest praise.

124. "Because of the great saintliness of this most saintly man," they said, "his miracle doesn't require any testimonials, for we have seen it with our very eyes, touched it with our hands and examined it in light of the truth." Everyone rejoiced as they wept and all those tears were a blessing. They finally established the blessed day in which the whole world would be filled with holy bliss.

The solemn day finally arrived, "venerable through all time"[13] and bringer of joy to the earth and to the heavenly abodes. Bishops, abbots and prelates were convened and they

---

12 Between June 13th and July 13th.
13 From the Easter hymn by Venanzio Fortunato.

came from the most faraway places. Royalty was present[14] and a noble group of counts and grandees arrived. All of them escorted Lord of the entire earth and with him, they made their triumphant entrance into the city of Assisi.

They reached the place that had already been prepared for the ceremony and all the cardinals, bishops and abbots gathered around the pope. There gathered the illustrious assembly of priests and clerics, the happy and holy ranks of religious and the modest college of those who had taken the holy veil, and the immense throng of people of both sexes. With great enthusiasm, people of all ages hastened from all parts to join such an impressive gathering and the lowly were there with the great and the servant with his master[15].

125. Surrounded by the vast array of his sons, the supreme Pontiff, the groom of the Church of Christ, was there wearing the crown of glory on his head as a sign of holiness. There he was adorned with the pontifical infula[16] and dressed in the holy vestments, which were fastened with golden buckles in magnificent glory and covered with glittering and symbolic gems that attracted everyone's attention[17]. Circled around him were the cardinals and bishops who, bejeweled and cloaked in white vestments as bright as snow, were the image of celestial beauty and of the joy of the elect.

Everyone awaited the voice of joy, the voice of gladness, the new voice full of all sweetness, the voice of praise[18] and perpetual blessing. Pope Gregory first preached to all those people, announcing the Word of God with sweet love and in a resonant

---

[14] John of Brienne, crowned king of Jerusalem in 1210. When his right to rule was usurped by his son-in-law, Frederick II, he went into the service of the pope. Shortly before his death (1237) he took the Minorite habit.

[15] *Jb* 3, 19.

[16] These are the ribbons that hang from the pope's miter.

[17] This description borrows phases from Isaiah, Revelation, Ecclesiastes, Exodus, 1 Kings and the *Offices of St. Agnes*.

[18] *Jer* 25, 10; *Ps* 26, 7 and 66, 8.

voice. After that, he gave holy father Francis the most noble eulogy and, bathed in tears, he recalled the purity of his life. His speech began, "Like the morning star amidst the fog, like the full moon and like the bright sun: thus did he shine in the temple of God." At the end of his sermon, truthful and worthy of full acceptance,[19] one of the Pontiff's deacons by the name of Octavian read the Saint's miracles before the assembly in a very loud voice and the cardinal deacon Raynerius[20], a sharp-witted man renowned for his piety and morals, eloquently commented on them in tears. The Shepherd of the Church rejoiced and, sighing deeply from the depths of his being and sobbing repeatedly, shed copious tears. All the other prelates shed many tears too and this great weeping bedewed the sacred vestments. Lastly, all the people wept as well and became even more impatient because their suspense was filled with anticipation.

126. At this point, with his hands outstretched towards heaven, the Pope proclaimed in a loud voice, "To the praise and glory of Almighty God, Father, Son and Holy Spirit, of the Virgin Mary, of the blessed apostles Peter and Paul, and to the honor of the glorious Roman Church, now that our Brothers and other Prelates have conferred, we hereby ordain that the most blessed father Francis, whom the Lord has glorified in the heavens, be venerated on earth. May his name be inscribed in the catalogue of the saints and his feast be celebrated on the day of his death."

Once these words were out, the reverend cardinals began to sing *Te Deum laudamus* in a loud voice, together with the pope. The clamor of God's praises soon rose up from the crowd, the earth resounded with cheers, the air was filled with cries of rejoicing and the ground was bathed in tears. New canticles were sung and God's servants exulted in the melody of the Spirit. The organs played sweetly and spiritual hymns were sung with voices that were modulated in counterpoint by the sweetest of fragrances

---

[19] *I Tim* 1, 15.
[20] These two men were Octavian degli Ubaldini of Mugello and Raynerius Capocci of Viterbo.

and the melody that moved all these hearts became even merrier and more resonant. The day shone, lit by even more dazzling rays, and green olive branches and freshly-cut fronds of other trees swayed to and fro. The festive air of this luminous display shone over everyone and the blessing of peace gladdened the minds of all those who had gathered there.

In the end, blessed pope Gregory descended from the lofty throne and went down the subterranean steps to enter the sanctuary and make votive offerings and sacrifices, jubilantly kissing the tomb holding the holy body consecrated to God. He offers up many prayers and celebrated the sacred mysteries. The brothers, praising, adoring and blessing Almighty God, who has done great works throughout the world, circled around him and the people magnified their divine praise, offering holy thanks to St. Francis in honor of the highest Trinity. Amen.

These events took place in the city of Assisi during the second year of the pontificate of His Honor Gregory IX, on the sixteenth day of July.

In the name of Christ, here begin the miracles of our most holy father Francis

127. Invoking the grace of our Lord Jesus Christ, in order to stir the rightful devotion of those now present and to strengthen the faith of those to come, briefly but truthfully we shall transcribe the miracles that were read and announced to the people in the presence of the lord pope Gregory, as we have already recounted.

I. - *The cripples who were healed*

On the day that the sacred body of the most blessed father Francis was deposited like a precious treasure, embalmed more with heavenly perfume than with earthly fragrances, a girl was brought to the tomb. For over a year, her neck had been twisted monstrously, her head touching her shoulder so that she had to look sideways in order to look up. She was placed for a short time with her head under the sarcophagus holding the body of the Saint and through the merits of that most holy man, her neck promptly straightened out and her head returned to its proper posture so that the girl, frightened by this sudden transformation, fled in tears. A sort of hollow area could be seen on her shoulder, caused by the strain that her lengthy illness had produced.

128. In .the territory of Narni[21], there was a boy whose shinbone was twisted so that he was unable to walk without crutches. He was a beggar who had known neither his father or his mother and he had been in this unhappy condition for many years. Thanks to our most blessed father Francis, he was ridden of this illness and was able to walk on his own without a cane, praising and blessing God and his Saint.

129. A certain Nicholas, a citizen of Foligno, whose left leg had become stiff and tortured by sharp spasms, had spent so much on doctors in order to regain his health that he was indebted beyond what he wanted or could afford. Finally, since he had obtained no improvement through their cures, he was wracked by such sharp pain that his constant wailing kept his neighbors awake at night. Therefore, he consecrated himself to God and to St. Francis and had himself brought to the Saint's tomb, and after he had spent a night there in prayer, he was able to return home in jubilation, with his leg outstretched and without a cane.

---

[21] Between Rome and Assisi.

130. A boy whose leg was contracted so that his knee touched his chest and his heel touched his thigh, also went to the tomb of blessed Francis, whereas his father mortified his flesh with a hair shirt and his mother did harsh penance for him. He was immediately restored completely to health and could run through the squares happily, thanking God and St. Francis.

131. In the city of Fano[22], there was a cripple whose ulcerated shinbones were bent back and stuck to his body and the stench of the sores was so great that no one would take him in and keep him in the hospital. Thanks to our most blessed father Francis, whose mercy he invoked, he recovered after a short time.

132. A little girl in Gubbio, whose hands were crippled and who had lost the use of all her limbs for a year, was brought to the tomb of the most blessed Father by her nurse, together with a waxen image, in order to obtain the grace of healing. After she had stayed there for eight days, all her limbs were healed and they became even more capable than usual.

133. Another boy, who was from Montenero[23], had been lying for several days in front of the church in which the Saint's body rests, for the boy could neither walk nor sit because he had no strength from the waist down and was unable to use his limbs. One day he got into the church and after touching the tomb, he left healthy and sound. This boy said that while he was lying before the grave of the glorious Saint, there appeared a young man dressed in a friar's habit who was holding some pears in his hand. He had called to him, urging him to get up and offering him one of the pears. As the boy was taking it, he answered, "You see, I am paralyzed and cannot get up." He then ate the pear and began to stretch his hand out towards the other pear that was being offered to him, but when the young man asked him again to get up, he did not move for he could feel that he was paralyzed. However, as he stretched his hand out, the young man took it, led him

[22] On the Adriatic coast.
[23] There are several towns with this same name in the areas of Perugia, Todi, Rieti and elsewhere.

outside and disappeared. When the boy saw that he had been healed, he began to tell everyone in a loud voice what had happened.

134. A woman from a town called Coccorano[24] was carried to the tomb of the blessed Father on straw mats, since she was unable to use any part of her body except her tongue. After she had stayed there for a while, she got up perfectly healed.

Another citizen of Gubbio carried one his sons, a cripple, in a basket to the tomb of the holy Father, where he regained his health. The boy had been contracted so greatly that his shinbones, pulled up to his thighs, had atrophied completely.

135. Bartholomew of the city of Narni, who was extremely poor, had slept for a while under the shade of a walnut tree, but he awoke to find he was paralyzed and no longer able to walk. The illness got progressively worse and his leg and foot shrunk and became bent and withered so that he was unable to feel cuts or burns. However, most holy Francis, true lover of the poor and father of all the wretched, appeared to him in a dream one night and ordered him to go to a bath where, moved to pity by such misery, he wanted to heal him. When he awoke, not knowing what to do, he recounted his vision to the bishop of the city, who exhorted him to go to the bath and blessed him. Therefore, leaning on his cane he went to the specified place as well as he could and as he was going along, aching and fatigued, he heard a voice saying to him, "Go in the peace of the Lord; I am the one to whom you have made your vow." When he was near the baths, since it was nighttime, he went down the wrong road and again, he heard the voice warning him that he was not on the right path and indicating the right direction. When he arrived and went into the bath, he felt a hand being placed on his foot and another one on his leg, slowly stretching it out. As soon as the hand let him go, he jumped out of the water, praising and blessing the omnipotence of the Creator and of His servant, blessed Francis, who had

---

[24] Between Gubbio and Assisi.

granted him such enormous grace, for he had been greatly crippled for six years and was also poor and quite elderly.

II. - *The blind who regained their sight*

136. A woman by the name of Sibyl who had been blind for many years was brought in pain to the tomb of the man of God. Regaining her sight, she happily and merrily went home.

In front of the tomb, a blind man from Spello regained the eyesight that he had lost many years before.

With another woman from Camerino, who was blind in her right eye, her relatives placed a cloth touched by blessed Francis over the injured eye and made a vow. Together with her, they were able to thank God and the Saint for the sight she regained.

Something similar happened to a women from Gubbio, who regained her sight after making a vow.

A citizen of Assisi, who had been blind for five years and had been one of Francis' friends while he was alive, always recalled their old friendship when he prayed to the Saint and he was healed as soon as he touched the tomb.

A certain Albertino of Narni had lost the use of his eyes almost a year before because his eyelids had sagged down to his cheeks. He entrusted himself to blessed Francis and, immediately regaining his sight, he set out to visit his glorious tomb and did indeed go there.

III. - *The possessed*

137. In Foligno there was a man named Peter and during the trip he had undertaken to visit the sanctuary of blessed Michael the Archangel[25] on account of a vow he had made as well as

---

[25] On Mount Gargano in the region of Apulia in southern Italy.

the penance that he had been given, he arrived at a spring. Parched by the fatigue of his journey, he drank some water, but he immediately felt as if he had swallowed demons. He remained possessed in this way for three years and did things that were horrible to see and to relate. When he arrived at the tomb of the most holy Father, he could feel the enraged demons torturing him cruelly, but upon touching the tomb, he was wondrously liberated through a clear and manifest miracle.

138. Blessed Francis appeared in a vision to a woman from Narni who, raging mad, did and said horrendous things, and he said to her, "Make the sign of the cross." Since she replied that she was unable to do this, he made the sign of the cross over her himself and thus drove out her madness and demoniac passion.

Many other men and women, tormented by demons through numerous tortures and deceived by sorcery, were released from their bondage through the exceptional merits of the glorious Father, but since the men of our species are often prey to illusion, now that we have briefly mentioned these miracles, let us move on to more important ones.

IV. - The sick who were saved from death and ridden of dropsy, arthritis, paralysis and other diseases

139. A boy named Matthew from the city of Todi had been lying in bed for eight days as if he were dead, his mouth closed and his eyes dull, and with the skin on his face, hands and feet as black as a pot hanging over the fire. Given up for dead by everyone, he quickly recovered after his mother had made a vow. He had been spewing rotten blood from his mouth and it seemed as if he would vomit all his innards, but as soon as his mother, who had knelt down and invoked the name of St. Francis, got up from her prayers, the little boy began to open his eyes to see and started suckling milk. A short time later, once the black skin had fallen away, his flesh returned to its natural complexion and he recov-

ered his health and strength. As soon as he began to feel better, his mother asked him "Who delivered you, my son?". Stuttering, he replied, "Ciccu, Ciccu."[26] Again he was asked, "Whose servant are you?" and again he replied, "Ciccu, Ciccu," for indeed, he still couldn't speak well because he was so little and so this was how he mumbled the name of blessed Francis.

140. A young man who fell from a great height lost the power of speech and the use of all his limbs, and for three days he went without eating or drinking and gave no sign of sensitivity, so that he was thought to be dead. Instead of resorting to doctors for help, his mother asked blessed Francis to heal him and making a vow, she got her son back alive and well and began to praise the Savior's omnipotence.

Another man named Mancino, who was so deathly ill that no one held out any hope for him, was cured by invoking the name of blessed Francis.

A child from Arezzo named Walter, who was constantly feverish and suffering from two abscesses and whom the doctors had given up on, regained the health that had been hoped for, thanks to a vow that his parents made to blessed Francis.

Another child, near death, was cured of all disease even before a wax image, which had been started as a votive offering, had been completed.

141. A woman who had been lying in bed for many years and was unable to turn over or move, consecrated herself to God and to blessed Francis. Thus, she was cured and was able to do everything she needed to do.

In the city of Narni, there was a woman whose hand had been so withered for eight years that she couldn't use it to do anything. At last, most blessed father Francis appeared to her and, pulling at her hand, gave it back to her as fit and useful as the other one.

---

[26] "Cecco" is an Italian nickname for Francis.

A young man from this same city had been completely swollen for ten years due to a very serious illness. Through blessed Francis, he regained the blessing of health following a votive offering made by his mother.

In the city of Fano, there was a man suffering from dropsy and his limbs were horribly swollen. He was completed cured of this illness by blessed Francis.

A citizen from Todi was so afflicted with arthritic gout that he could not sit down or rest at all and his pain was so violent that it gave him constant shivers, so that he seemed to be on the verge of death. He called doctors, increased the number of baths and used a variety of medications, but there was no improvement until one day, in the presence of a priest, he made a vow asking St. Francis to restore him to his former state of health. After he had finished praying, he promptly found that he had been healed.

142. Upon invoking the name of blessed Francis three times, a paralytic woman from the city of Gubbio was cured of her disease.

A certain Bontadoso was suffering from very sharp pains in his hands and feet and, unable either to walk or move, he had lost his appetite and could not sleep. One day, a woman went to him and exhorted him to devote himself to blessed Francis if he wanted to be freed from his illness as quickly as possible. The man, who was beside himself because of the spasms, replied, "I don't believe he's a saint!". But since the woman kept suggesting that he consecrate himself, he finally made the following proposition: "I'll consecrate myself to St. Francis and will consider him a saint if he rids me of my illness within three days." He was immediately cured through the merit of the Saint of God and, giving praise to almighty God, he was able to walk, eat and sleep.

143. A man had received a serious head injury from an iron arrow that had gone through his eye socket and remained stuck in his head. Since his doctors' remedies gave him no relief, he consecrated himself devoutly to Francis, the Saint of God, hoping to be delivered through his help. Calming down and resting a bit, in his

sleep he was told by St. Francis to have the arrow pulled out through the nape of his neck. The next day, doing what he had seen in his dream, he was ridden of it without any great difficulty.

144. In the town of Spello, a man named Imperatore had been suffering from hernias for two years so that his intestines would make his lower abdomen swell. For a long time, he was unable to get them to go back into place and was forced to wear a cushion to hold them in. He turned to doctors, who asked him for a fee that he could not afford to pay, because he barely had enough money for food and expenses for one day, and as a result he could not count on their help. He finally turned to divine help and began to invoke blessed Francis on his way home and anywhere else he went. In a short time, through the grace of God and the merits of the Saint, he was restored completely to health.

145. In the March of Ancona, a friar from our Order was seriously ill because of a fistula in the iliac area, or in other words, on his hip, and due to the gravity of his illness, there was no longer any hope that the doctors could cure him. Thus, he asked the minister under whose authority he was bound to be given permission to visit the tomb of the most blessed Father, certain that he would be given the grace of healing through the merits of the Saint. However, the minister would not grant him permission to leave out of fear that the snow and frequent rain during that season, as well as the fatigue of the journey, would make his condition even worse. Although the friar was quite upset over that refusal, one night father Francis appeared to him and told him, "Son, do not torment yourself any more. Take off that fur you are wearing, throw away the poultice and the bandage, observe your Rule and you will be delivered." When he got up the next morning, the friar did what he had been ordered to and was immediately able to give thanks to God for curing him.

V. - *The lepers who were cleansed*

146. In San Severino, in the March of Ancona, there was a young man named Atto who was completely covered with leprosy and because of the doctors' diagnosis, everyone treated him like a leper. In fact, all his limbs were swollen and enlarged and because his veins had become relaxed and swollen, he looked deformed. To his parents' great sorrow, this wretch was unable to walk and was forced instead to lie on his bed of pain. Deeply anguished, his father no longer knew what to do. Finally, he got the idea of consecrating him to blessed Francis in every way and he said to his son, "My son, do you wish to devote yourself to St. Francis, who now shines everywhere through his numerous miracles, so that he might deign to rid you of your disease?". He answered, "I do, father." The father had some papyrus reed brought to him and measured his son's height and girth. Then he said to him, "Get up, consecrate yourself to blessed Francis and if you are healed, every year for as long as you live you must bring him a candle as tall as you are." At his father's instructions, the young man got up to the best of his ability and, folding his hands together, he began to plead for blessed Francis' mercy. After his measurements had been taken with the papyrus, as soon as he had finished praying he was cured of leprosy and was jubilantly able to get up and walk about, glorifying God and blessed Francis.

In the city of Fano a young man named Bonomo, whom all the doctors had diagnosed as a leper and paralytic, was offered up to blessed Francis by his parents: he was cleansed of leprosy and cured of paralysis, fully regaining his health.

VI. - *The dumb who spoke and the deaf who heard*

147. In Castel della Pieve, there was a very poor beggar boy who was completely deaf and dumb from birth. In fact, he had a very short tongue and many people who had examined it believed it had been cut off. One evening, he went to the house of a fellow townsman named Mark and with the signs that mutes are accustomed to using, he asked for hospitality. He tilted his head to one side, resting his cheek in his hand in order to let the man know that he wanted to sleep there that night. The man welcomed him lovingly and willingly kept him at his house because he knew that he was a very capable servant. The boy was good-natured and, although he had been deaf and dumb since he was a baby, he understood orders through gestures. One evening, as he was dining with his wife in the boy's presence, the man said to his wife, "It would be such a great miracle if the Blessed One were to grant him hearing and speech!"

148. Then he added, "I will make a votive offering to the Lord God, so that if blessed Francis deigns to work this wonder, out of love for him I will love this boy very dearly and will maintain him for the rest of his life." Miracle! As soon as the vow was out, the boy spoke, saying, "I can see St. Francis up there and he came to give me the power of speech." Then he added, "Now what will I tell people?". The man answered, "You will praise the Lord and will save many men." Then he got up happily and exultantly announced to everyone what had happened. All those who had seen the boy while he was still unable to speak hastened there and, filled with marvel and wonder, they praised God and blessed Francis. In the meantime, the boy's tongue grew and he was no longer tongue-tied, and he began to utter highly articulate words as if he had always been able to speak.

149. Yet another boy, by the name of Villa, was unable to speak or walk. On his behalf, his mother brought a waxen image she had had made as a votive offering to blessed father Francis'

resting place. When she got home, she discovered that her son was speaking and walking about.

A man in the diocese of Perugia, who was unable to speak, always kept his mouth open and he would pant horribly because his throat was very thick and swollen. However, when he came to the place where that most holy body rests and climbed the stairs to touch the tomb, he vomited blood and, completely cured, he began to speak and was able to open and close his mouth normally.

150. A woman was tormented by a sharp pain in her throat and because of the burning feeling in her throat, her tongue was parched and stuck to the roof of her mouth. She was unable to speak, eat or drink, nor could she find any relief through the poultices and other medicines she used. At last, she consecrated herself to St. Francis in her heart, for she could not speak, and suddenly her skin burst open and out of her throat came a round stone, which she showed everyone, and in this way she was cured at once.

In the town of Greccio, a young man had lost his hearing, memory and the power of speech and he could not understand or feel anything. His parents, who had great faith in St. Francis, consecrated the young man to him with devout prayers. As soon as they had made their vow, through the abundant grace of the most glorious Father the young man regained all the senses he had lost.

To the praise, glory and honor of Jesus Christ our Lord, whose sure and steadfast sovereignty will last world without end. Amen.

The End

(Epilogue)

151. We have said little about the miracles of our most blessed father Francis and have omitted even more, leaving the task of finding the grace of new blessings to anyone who may wish to trace it. Just as He has gloriously renewed the whole world with His words and example and with His life and teachings, so may He also deign to make the minds of those who love God's name fertile through the fresh rains of heavenly charism.

Out of love for the poor Crucified One and for His holy Stigmata, which blessed father Francis bore on his body, I pray that all those who read, see and hear my story will remember me, a sinner, before God. Amen.

All blessing, honor and praise to the one omniscient God who, in His glory, has always knowingly worked all things in everyone. Amen. Amen. Amen.

Here ends the First Life

SECOND LIFE

In the name of our Lord Jesus Christ. Amen

To the Minister General of the Order of the Friars Minor

***

Here begins the prologue

It has pleased the holy assembly of the General Chapter and you, most reverend father[1], to instruct that, with the guidance of divine counsel, our insignificance should write down the acts and the words of our glorious father Francis towards those of us who, more than the others, knew him personally through constant community life and mutual intimacy, for the solace of those present and the memory of our descendants.

Thus, we have reverently hastened to obey these saintly instructions, which cannot be ignored in any way. However, when we reflect more carefully on the weakness of our efforts, we are rightly struck by the fear that if not handled properly, a subject of such enormous worth could become unpalatable to others through our own fault. In fact, we fear that this food, fitting of the sweetest of taste, will be rendered insipid by the inability of the one who is preparing it and that we will thus be reproached that we dared to do so out of presumptuousness rather than obedience.

Thus, if the fruit of this effort were to be examined only by your benevolence, most blessed father, without reaching the ears of the public, we would gratefully welcome either the enlightenment of correction or the joy of approval. In fact, given such a diversity of words and deeds, who would be capable of weighing

---

[1] The prologue presenting this work is addressed by the Saint's "Companions" to the Minister General Crescentius of Jesi, following the General Chapter held in Genoa in 1244.

each thing on a scale of precision so that all listeners will reach identical conclusions about each individual point? Since it is with simplicity that we are seeking to benefit each and every person, we thus beg the reader to interpret this kindly and either to bear with the narrator's simplicity or to remedy it, so that the reverence due to the one of whom we are speaking will be left intact.

Like the memories of men who are uncultured or weakened by old age, our memory cannot reach His soaring thoughts and expressions or the wonders of his deeds, which could barely be understood by ready and practiced minds who were present at that time. Thus may the authority of the one who has repeated these instructions several times count towards excusing us with everyone for our inexperience.

2. First of all, this book contains some of the marvelous episodes of St. Francis' conversion that have not been reported in the other *Lives* that have been compiled so far, because their authors had no information about them. It is thus our intention to set forth and accurately state the good, benevolent and perfect will of the most holy Father in his own regard as well as for his own, in putting the divine teachings into practice and in seeking higher perfection, which was always the goal of his sacred transports towards God and of the examples he set for man. Several miracles have also been included whenever the occasion arose.

We have written in an unrefined style, as the subjects came up, wanting to adapt to those who are less discerning while pleasing scholars as well, if possible.

Thus, most benevolent father, we beg you to bless this small gift, no mean fruit of considerable labor, correcting its errors and eliminating what is superfluous, so that anything that, in your learned judgment, seems to have been well-said may grow everywhere and be multiplied in Christ through your name, truly Crescentius[2]. Amen.

---

[2] Another one of Celano's word plays that is lost in the translation: the Latin root "crescens" means "growing".

PART ONE

Here begin the memories "in the desire of our souls" [3]
*about the words and deeds of our most
blessed father Francis*

Of his conversion

CHAPTER I

*How he was first called John and then Francis;
of his mother's prophecies and of his own predictions;
of his patience during his imprisonment*

3. Francis, servant and friend of the Most High who was given this name through Divine Providence so that through its uniqueness and novelty[4] the fame of his ministry would spread more quickly throughout the world, had been named John by his mother so that, reborn by virtue of the baptismal waters and of the Holy Spirit, the child of wrath would become the child of grace[5]. That woman, the friend of supreme honesty, bore an almost visible sign of her virtue in her habits, having had the privilege of somewhat resembling the early saint, Elizabeth, both in the name she had given her son and in her gift of prophecy[6].

Indeed, when her neighbors expressed their marvel over the breadth and refinement of Francis' features, almost as if it were being suggested to her by divine oracle, she would reply,

---

[3] *Is* 26, 8.

[4] When Francis was born, his father, Peter Bernardone, was in France on business and upon his return, he had the baby's baptismal name changed from John to Francis, supposedly in honor of his successful business dealings in France. Although this name was not completely unheard of, it was nevertheless quite rare at that time.

[5] *Eph* 2, 3.

[6] *Lk* 1, 41-43.

"What do you think my son will be?[7] You'll see that, because of his merits, he will become a child of God."

This was also the opinion held by others, who found Francis, who had grown by now, likable because of his wonderful disposition. He always kept away from anything that could sound offensive to anyone and, as he reached adolescence, because of his urbane manner, it seemed to everyone that he did not come from the same stock as his parents.

The name John was fitting for the ministry to which he dedicated himself[8] and the name Francis for propagating his fame, which immediately spread everywhere as soon as he was fully converted to God. Therefore, he considered the feast day of John the Baptist more solemn than any other one, for the dignity of his name had marked him with a sign of mystical virtue. No man born of woman was greater than he[9] and no one was more perfect. This is a coincidence that deserves to be proclaimed.

4. John prophesied while still enveloped in his mother's womb; Francis predicted the future while in a worldly prison and still unaware of God's designs,.

In fact, since a disastrous battle was fought during the war between the Perugines and the Assisans[10], Francis, who was taken prisoner with many others, had to endure the torments of prison. His companions, overcome with sadness, complained about the disgrace of imprisonment. Instead, Francis rejoiced in the Lord and made fun of his chains. Those sufferers upbraided him for being happy even in prison and they thought he was either foolish or mad, but Francis answered prophetically, "What do you think I'm rejoicing about? One of the things is my idea that I will be

---

[7] *Lk* 1, 68.

[8] In other words, to preaching the word of Christ, since John the Baptist preached about the Lord and because it was customary to interpret his name as "grace of the Lord".

[9] *Mt* 11, 11; *Lk* 7, 28.

[10] During the war fought from 1202 to 1209, and more specifically, during the battle of Collestrada in 1202.

venerated as a saint throughout the world." In fact, this is precisely what happened, for his prediction has come true.

Among the prisoners, there was a proud and rather troublesome knight. Everyone tried to stay away from him except Francis, who did not lose his patience: he put up with the insufferable man and succeeded in getting everyone to make his peace with him.

That chosen vessel, capable of holding all grace, was already beginning to overflow with the charism of his virtue[11].

CHAPTER II

Of the poor knight he clothed, and of the vision he had about his own vocation while he was still in the world

5. Released from prison a short time later[12], he became more compassionate towards the poor. Indeed, he decided not to turn away any beggars[13] who ask him for charity out of the love of God. One day, encountering a poor knight who was practically naked, he took pity and, out of love for Christ, generously gave him the refined garments he was wearing. Did he perhaps do any less than the great and most holy Martin? The only difference was in how it was done, but the intention was the same and so was the deed, for Francis gave away his clothing first and then everything else, whereas Martin donated every possession and then lastly his garments: both of them were poor and modest on earth yet were rich when they went to heaven. The former, who was a knight but poor, cut his cloak in half to clothe a poor man, whereas the latter, who was not a knight but wealthy, dressed a poor knight in his garments. Because they fulfilled Christ's command, both of them were worthy of being visited by Christ in a vision, the for-

---

[11] *Sir* 24, 15; *Acts* 9, 15.
[12] Presumably, towards the end of 1203, together will other sick prisoners.
[13] *Tb* 4, 7.

mer receiving praise for his perfection and the latter the benevolent request to complete what he lacked to achieve perfection.

6. In fact, there immediately appeared to him a magnificent palace in which he could see various machines of war and a beautiful bride and in the dream Francis was called by name and was enticed by the promise of all these goods. He then arranged to go to Apulia to embark on a military career and made elaborate preparations in the hope of achieving the honorary title of knight. His human spirit led him to a totally human interpretation of the vision he had had, whereas another far more sublime interpretation was hidden in the treasure of divine wisdom.

And so another night as he was sleeping, a voice spoke to him again in a vision and asked him insistently where he wanted to go. In reply, he explained his plan of going to fight in Apulia and the voice then asked him whom it was better to serve, the servant or the master. Francis said, "The master!" and the other voice replied, "Then why are you seeking the servant instead of the master?" Then Francis asked, "What do you want me to do, Lord?"[14] And the Lord told him, "Go back to the land of your birth[15], because through my work your vision will achieve spiritual fulfillment."

He returned without delay, becoming a model of obedience, and by renouncing his own will he was transformed from Saul into Paul. Saul was flung to the ground and harsh blows produced sweet words. Francis exchanged physical arms for spiritual ones and instead of military glory, he was given the divine investiture of sovereignty. And since many people wondered about his strange happiness, he told them that he would become a great prince.

---

[14] *Acts* 9, 6-18: the conversion of St. Paul.
[15] *Gn* 31, 13; 32, 10.

CHAPTER III

How a company of young men chose their leader for a banquet; and of how he changed

7. He thus began to be transformed into a perfect man[16], completely different from the former one. As soon as he returned to his homeland, the sons of Babylon[17] began to follow him again and drag him, albeit reluctantly, on the path in the opposite direction from the goal towards which he was aiming. A company of young men of Assisi, whom he had originally led in their vanity, once again began to invite him to their banquets, which always indulged in laxity and vulgarity. They elected him king because, knowing his generosity through experience, they were sure that he would pay for everyone. They acted obediently in order to fill their bellies and agreed to be his subjects in order to be sate their appetites. He did not turn down the honor offered to him, for he did not want to be considered stingy and even in the middle of sacred meditation he did not forget courtesy. He had a sumptuous banquet prepared with plenty of exquisite food and they stuffed themselves until they were full. Then, inebriated, they sullied the city squares with unseemly songs. Francis followed them, bearing a rod in his hands as king of the party, but little by little he stepped back from them in body too, for in his mind he had already become deaf to those voices and in his heart he sang to the Lord instead. As he himself later recounted, he then felt such divine sweetness washing over him that he couldn't even speak or move. He was pervaded with such spiritual emotion that, by elevating him to the vision of things invisible, it made him judge all earthly things as unimportant, if not entirely useless.

What a marvelous thing for Christ to bestow -- to give the greatest gifts to those who do the smallest works and to save and advance those who belong to him, even amidst the flood of

---

[16] *Eph* 4, 24.
[17] *Ez* 23, 17.

abundant waters[18]. Christ fed the throngs with loaves and fishes and did not turn sinners away from his table, but when they sought him as their king, He fled and went up the mountain to pray.

These are the mysteries of God that Francis imitated, and without knowing it, he allowed himself to be led to perfect wisdom[19].

CHAPTER V

How, as he was praying, the devil showed him a woman, and of the answer God gave him; and how he acted towards lepers

9. Thus, hidden this way beneath worldly clothing was the spirit of a religious and he was often visited and taught by the Holy Spirit during his solitary retreats from inhabited areas. It was as if he had been abducted from himself and he was enticed by that sovereign sweetness that pervaded him so deeply right from the very beginning that it never left him again as long as he lived.

However, when he went to secluded places since they were more suited to prayer, the devil tried to turn him away from these beginnings with evil ruses. He showed him a woman from his city who was so monstrously deformed by a hunchback that she filled everyone with horror and he threatened to make Francis look like her unless he abandoned the work he has started. Comforted by the Lord, however, he rejoiced when he heard this response of salvation and grace. "Francis," said the Lord in his heart, "reject vain and bodily possessions for spiritual ones and learn to prefer the bitter to the sweet and to despise yourself if you want to know me, for things will be reversed and you will find what I am telling you pleasing." He immediately felt compelled to obey the divine instructions and was led to experiencing them.

---

[18] *Ps* 32, 6; *Mt* 14, 15-23; *Jn* 6, 16.
[19] *Jb* 22, 2.

In fact, while of all the wretched deformities in the world he instinctively abhorred lepers, one day while he was riding on horseback near Assisi, he encountered one. Now, although he was more than just a little disturbed and horrified, in order to keep from disobeying the command and violating the oath he had given, he leapt from his horse and ran over to kiss him. The leper, who was holding his hand out to him for alms, received both his money as well as a kiss from him. Immediately remounting his horse, he looked around -- for he was in the middle of a field and there was nothing to block his view -- and the leper could no longer be seen[20]. Thus, filled with wonder and joy, a few days later he wanted to do the same thing again: he went to the lepers' lodgings and distributing alms, he kissed each one on the hand and mouth.

He thus took bitter things instead of the sweet[21] and courageously prepared to observe the other commandments.

CHAPTER VI

Of the image of the Crucifix that spoke to him;
and of how he honored it

10. Already perfectly changed within his heart and about to be changed on the outside as well, one day he was passing by the church of St. Damian, which was practically in ruins and forgotten by everyone. On a spiritual impulse, he went inside to pray, and prostrated himself before the Crucifix[22] in devotion. Touched by unusual grace, he discovered that he was different than he had been when he had entered. Even though its lips were only painted, the image of Christ crucified spoke to this man who had

---

[20] See *Life of St. Martin,* Chap. 18, for a similar episode.

[21] *Prv* 27, 7.

[22] This historic Crucifix, a Byzantine-style *tavola* by the Spoleto school that dates to the 12th century, is now located in the monastery of St. Clare in Assisi. It was brought there by the sisters between 1257 and 1260 and was restored in 1939.

been moved in this way -- something unheard of over the centuries! -- and called him by name. "Francis," it said to him, "go and repair my house which, as you can easily see, is in ruins." The trembling young man was dumbfounded and felt faint, but he was immediately prepared to obey and everything became focused on that order.

Nevertheless, it would be best for us not to say anything about the ineffable change that he felt being worked within him, since not even he was able to express it.

From that point on, compassion for the Cross was driven into this saintly soul and as we can devoutly imagine, the venerable Stigmata of the Passion were etched deeply into his heart, although not yet in the flesh.

11. What a wonderful event, unheard of in our day and age! Who can help but marvel over it, and who has ever heard of anything like it? Who can doubt that Francis appeared to be crucified when he was about to return to his homeland, given the fact that through a new miracle, from the wood of the cross Christ spoke to Francis who, on the outside, had not fully withdrawn yet from the world? It was precisely from that moment that his soul began to torture itself when the Beloved was discussed[23]. The love in his heart was later shown through the wounds on his body.

He could no longer hold back his tears and he wept aloud over Christ's Passion, which was constantly present with him. He filled the streets with his grief and could not be consoled over the memory of Christ's wounds. When Francis encountered a friend and explained the reason for his sorrow, he moved him to tears.

In the meantime, he did not forget the sacred image, nor did he fail to fulfill the command. At once he offered a priest the money to buy a lamp and some oil so that the sacred image would never remain without the devotion of a light for even moment. Then he promptly hastened to carry out the rest, dedicating himself to repairing the church.

---

[23] *Sg* 5, 6.

In fact, although the divine command involved the Church that Christ had gained through His blood[24], he did not dare to reach for the highest level all at once and was elevated from the flesh to the spirit just a little at a time.

CHAPTER VII
Of the persecution by his father and brother

12. By this time, seeing that he was persevering in his works of mercy, his father, judging the service of Christ to be madness, began to persecute him and continuously tormented him with his curses. So the servant of God turned to a rather simple man of the people and had him act in his father's stead, so that each time his father cursed him, he asked that man to bless him instead. And so he carried out the meaning of the prophecy, *Let them curse, but do you bless*[25], illustrating it with deeds.

He gave his father back the money he would have liked to spend to construct the little church, persuaded by the pious bishop of the city that it would not be right to put money coming from illicit earnings to sacred use. In the presence of the many people who had gathered around, he exclaimed, "Now I can freely say, *Our Father who art in heaven*, and I will no longer have to call Peter Bernardone father. At this very instant, I am returning not only his money but also all my clothing and I shall go forth naked to meet the Lord!" O generous soul, to whom Christ alone is sufficient. It could then be seen that the man of God was wearing a hair shirt under his clothes and he did not delight in flaunting this but in possessing virtue.

Francis' blood brother[26], following his father's example, also persecuted him with venomous jeers. One winter morning,

---

[24] *Acts* 20, 28.

[25] *Ps* 109, 28.

[26] His name was Angelo.

seeing that Francis, clothed in poor garments and intent on his prayers, was shivering with the cold, he malevolently said to a fellow citizen, "Ask Francis to sell you a coin's worth of sweat." When he heard this, the man of God smiled happily and replied, "Oh, I will certainly sell it to my Lord at a high price." Nothing could be truer, since he earned not a hundred but even a thousand-fold on earth and he earned eternal beatitude for the future not only for himself but also for many others.

CHAPTER VIII
How he overcame his shame, and of his prophecy
about the poor Virgins

13. He strove to change his earlier habits of refinement into austerity and to adapt to nature a body that had once gone soft. One day as he was going through Assisi begging for oil for the lamps in the church of St. Damian, which he was restoring at that time, he was about to go into a house, but when he saw a little group playing in front of the door, he turned red and withdrew. However, lifting that generous spirit of his to heaven, he severely reproached himself for his cowardice[27] and immediately went back to that house. Confessing the reason for his shame before everyone in a steady voice, he zealously begged for the oil in French and obtained it.

He ardently urged everyone to repair that church and, speaking to everyone in French, he clearly foretold that it would become a monastery for the holy virgins of Christ. In fact, whenever he was filled with the fervor of the Holy Spirit, he would utter fiery words in French, foreseeing that he would be particularly revered in that country and would have special devotion there.

---

[27] *Jas* 3, 1.

CHAPTER IX

How he begged for food from door to door

14. Starting from the time he began to serve the Lord who is common to us all, he always liked to do common things, fleeing completely from singularity, which is stained with every vice.

As he toiled to restore that church as Christ had mandated, he had changed from the delicate young man he had once been to become as robust as a farmer, capable of withstanding the effort. The priest to whom the church was entrusted took pity on him when he saw how worn out he was from his constant work and he began to give Francis a bit of his food every day, although it was certainly no delicacy since he too was poor. While he thought highly of this kindness and appreciated the priest's piety, the young man said to himself, "You will not always find a priest everywhere who can give you food in this way. This is not the lifestyle of a man who has made a profession of poverty, nor is it fitting for you to get accustomed to this, because you will soon go back to being what you had despised and will once again abandon yourself to weakness. Therefore, get up without any further delay and go begging for your bread from door to door."

So saying, he went through Assisi begging for food from door to door. The first time he saw a bowl filled with all types of leftovers, he felt an initial wave of repulsion, but remembering God, he controlled himself and ate that mixture with spiritual delight. Love soothes everything and turns the bitter into sweetness.

CHAPTER X

Brother Bernard's renunciation of his property

15. A certain Bernard of Assisi, who would later be the son of perfection, wished to turn his back on the world following the example of the man of God and he begged him for some advice. Accordingly, he posed this question to him: "O my father, if after

one has long possessed the goods of a lord he should no longer want to keep them, how should he best get rid of them?" The man of God answered that he should give them back to the lord from whom he had received them, so Bernard declared, "I know that all my possessions were given to me by God and I am ready to give them all back to Him as you have advised me." The saint then concluded, "If you truly wish to implement what you have said, as soon as day breaks, let us go to church and, taking a book of the Gospel, let's ask Christ for counsel."

In the morning, they went into a church[28] and after saying a devout prayer, they opened the Gospel, willing to follow the first counsel that should appear before their eyes. They opened the book and Christ manifested His advice in it: *"If you seek perfection, go, sell your possessions, and give to the poor"*[29]. The second time they opened it there appeared the passage *"Take nothing for the journey"* and the third time they found *"If a man wishes to come after me, he must deny his very self"*.

Bernard carried everything out without delay and did not omit even one iota of this counsel[30].

Within a short time, many people freed themselves of the grip of worldly cares to return to infinite good and to their true homeland, under Francis' guidance. However, it would take too long to go on describing how each one achieved the prize of his heavenly vocation.

CHAPTER XI

Of the parable he narrated to the Supreme Pontiff

16. When he went with his followers to Pope Innocent to ask for the rule for his life[31], being the very prudent man that he

---

[28] The church of St. Nicholas in the main square of Assisi. This took place on April 16, 1209.

[29] *Mt* 19, 21; *Lk* 9, 3; *Mt* 16, 24.

[30] *Mt* 5, 18.

was, the pontiff, who considered that commitment beyond human strength, said, "My son, pray to Jesus Christ that He may show us His will through you. Then, once we know what it is, we can surely fulfill your pious desire more confidently."

The Saint obeyed the order of the supreme shepherd and turned faithfully to Christ. He prayed insistently and exhorted his companions to beseech God devoutly. Accordingly, while he was praying he got his answer and announced the salutary news to his sons. This was how Christ spoke to him simply through a parable. "Francis, this is what you must say to the pope. In the desert, there was a woman who was very poor but quite beautiful and because of her extraordinary beauty, a king fell in love with her. He joyfully married her and she bore him beautiful children. When they grew up and had been nobly educated, their mother said to them, 'Do not be ashamed of being poor, my dears, for all of you are children of that great king. Go to his court and ask him for what you need.' Happy and astonished at these words, they were comforted by the knowledge that they were of royal descent and were heirs of the sovereign, and they considered all their misery as wealth. They confidently went before the king and were not afraid of him, for their faces bore his own image. Upon seeing that they resembled him so closely, the king asked them in wonder whose children they were and as soon as they told him that they were the children of that poor woman in the desert, he embraced them, exclaiming, 'My children, you are my heirs. Have no fear[32]. Indeed, if strangers can be fed at my table, it is all the more fitting that I feed those who have a right to my entire inheritance.' Then he ordered the woman to send to his court all the children he had sired so that they would be fed."

The Saint rejoiced at this parable and promptly related it to the pope.

---

[31] It would be more precise to say, "to ask for approval of his rule of life", since the Saint had already formulated it using short evangelical passages.

[32] *Rm* 8, 17; *Mt* 14, 27 and 17, 7.

17. This woman symbolized Francis for the numerous children who were begotten in austerity and not in weakness. The desert was the world that, at that time, was a wasteland sterile of all virtue. The beautiful and numerous progeny represented the great number of brothers adorned with every virtue. The king is the Son of God, whom those fed at the king's table resemble through their holy poverty by shunning all cowardly shame: happy to imitate Christ, they live off alms, knowing that they will achieve eternal beatitude through the world's scorn.

The pope admired the parable and recognized beyond the shadow of a doubt that Christ had spoken through the mouth of that man. He recalled a vision he had had several days before and, illuminated by the Holy Spirit, he declared that it must be fulfilled by this man. In a dream, he had seen the Lateran basilica[33] that threatened to fall into ruin and a religious, a small and despicable-looking man[34] who was holding it up on his shoulders to keep it from falling. "Certainly," he thought, "he is the one who will sustain the Church of Christ through his works and his words."

This was why the pope so readily agreed to his request and why, full of devotion, he always loved the Servant of God in a special way ever afterwards. He granted what had been requested and promised to add other concessions.

So Francis, strengthened by the authority granted to him, began to spread the seed of virtue, preaching fervently throughout the towns and villages[35].

---

[33] The Basilica of St. John Lateran in Rome, which was the cathedral of the pope in his role as Bishop of Rome.

[34] This passage, as well as the analogous one in St. Bonaventure's *Major Life* (Chap. III, 9), was the inspiration for Dante's tercet in which he describes St. Francis as he goes before Pope Innocent to have his Rule approved:

> *No abjectness of heart abashed his brows*
> *That he was Peter Bernardone's son,*
> *Nor that he seemed such wondrous scorn to arouse.*

(Par. XI, 88-90)

[35] *Mt* 9, 35.

Of St. Mary's of the Porziuncola

CHAPTER XII

*Of the Saint's veneration for this place, of the brothers' life there
and of the Blessed Virgin's love for it*

18. Given that he was in the world, the Servant of God, Francis, small in stature, humble of mind, minor by profession, chose a portion of the world for himself and his own, for otherwise, if they did not use any worldly thing, they would not be able to serve Christ[36]. This was surely not without prophetic inspiration, because as far back as ancient times, the place that was destined for those who desired to own nothing of the world was known as the Porziuncola[37]. Built there was a church for the Virgin Mother who deserves, after her Son, to be head of all the saints because of her humility. And the Order of the Friars Minor began there and their noble edifice arose and developed there on that stable foundation. This was the place that the Saint loved above all the rest. He ordered his brothers to venerate it in a special way and he wanted it to be kept in humility and supreme poverty as the mirror of the Order, thus leaving its ownership to others[38] and keeping only its use for himself.

19. The strictest discipline was observed there, both in silence and in work as well as in all the other actions of normal life. No one could enter there except for brothers who had been chosen for this from many places and whom the saint wanted to be filled with true devotion to God and perfect all things. Access was likewise forbidden to all laymen, for he did not want the brothers who resided there, who were limited to a certain number, to interrupt their contemplation of heavenly things out of a craving to

---

[36] This entire paragraph is based on adaptations from *Is* 16, 14; *Mt* 11, 29; *Lk* 9, 48 and 22, 26; *Jn* 15, 19; 17, 9-11-14.

[37] From the Latin "portio", meaning "portion".

[38] It belonged to the Benedictines of Mount Subasio.

hear about mundane events and be enticed by chatterers to take up worldly things. No one was allowed to say idle words there, nor could they refer the words that others had said, and if anyone committed this offense, he was severely chastised so that he would learn never to do it again.

Day and night without pause[39], the brothers who lived there were intent on praising God and, emanating a marvelous fragrance of virtue, they led a truly angelic life, quite rightly so since, as its old inhabitants could testify, that place was also often referred to as Saint Mary's of the Angels. The blessed Father was accustomed to saying that God had revealed to him that, of all the other churches built throughout the world in her honor, the Blessed Virgin loved that one the most and so the Saint too loved it more than any of the others.

CHAPTER XIII
Of a vision

20. Before his conversion, a very devout brother had had a vision about that church that deserves to be told. He saw an infinite number of men, wretchedly struck with blindness, who were kneeling in a circle around the church with their faces turned towards heaven. In a wailing voice, all of them raised their arms and cried out to the Lord, asking for mercy and begging to be given back their eyesight. A great splendor then descended from heaven and flowed over them, giving each one his eyesight and longed-for salvation.

Of the life led by Saint Francis and his brothers

---

[39] *Jos* 1, 8 and *Acts* 12, 5.

CHAPTER XIV
Of their harsh discipline

21. Not once did that valiant soldier of Christ spare his body, exposing it to all harshness of words and deeds as if it were not his own[40]. Anyone who wants to enumerate the afflictions he suffered would have to go beyond the bounds of the Apostolic book that recounts the torments of the saints[41]. Like him, his entire first school submitted to every deprivation, so that it seemed to be a sin to seek any comfort other than spiritual consolation. In fact, they girded themselves with iron hoops and corselets and mortified themselves with continuous fasts and vigils, and many of them would have fainted if the constant admonishments of the pious Shepherd had not curbed such severe mortification.

CHAPTER XV
Of St. Francis' discretion

22. One night while the others were sleeping, one of those little lambs cries out, "I'm dying, brothers! I'm dying of hunger!". The good Shepherd got up at once and hastened to take care of that sick little lamb. He had the table set, covering it solely with delicacies from the field and, as usual, water made up for the lack of wine. He was the first one to start eating and invited the others to do this work of charity so that the brother would not feel ashamed.

---

[40] *Heb* 11, 9.

[41] Some have taken the term "Apostolic book" to mean the *Acts of the Apostles*, while others have understood it to be *Revelation*. Still others have interpreted this as a simple allusion to the verses of the letter of St. Paul to the *Hebrews*, 11, 13. None of these theories is totally convincing, but through no fault of these scholars: the text is extremely vague!

After they had finished their meal in the fear of God[42], in order to ensure that nothing would be lacking to complete their work of charity, the father told his sons a long parable about discretion. He urged them to offer God sacrifices that were seasoned with the salt of moderation[43], cautioning each of them to bear his own strength in mind in serving the Lord and declaring that depriving the body of its needs indiscriminately is a sin, just as giving it too much out of gluttony is also a sin. Then he added, "Dearest brothers, you should know that I made you eat out of indulgence and not on a whim, for brotherly love bid me to do so. Thus, let charity and not the act of eating be an example for you, because the latter serves gluttony while the former serves the spirit."

CHAPTER XVI
How he foretold the future; and how he entrusted
the Order to the Church of Rome, and of a certain vision

23. The holy Father continued to progress in merit and virtue, and seeing his progeny grow in number and grace, spreading its shoots to the ends of the earth and bearing marvelous fruits, he began to think assiduously and with concern about how to preserve this new plant and make it grow in the bond of unity. At that time, he saw many who were acting like ferocious wolves towards the little flock and, ingrained in evil[44], they were using the sheer novelty of the Institution against it.

Moreover, he predicted that even among his own sons there could arise conflicts contrary to peace and harmony and he feared that, as often occurs among the elect, there would be sev-

---

[42] *Acts* 2, 26 and 9, 31.
[43] *Lev* 2, 13.
[44] *Dn* 13, 52. See also Celano's' *First Life*, 74, concerning the difficulties faced by the new Order.

eral rebels puffed up with physical pride and contentious in spirit who would be prepared to create a scandal.

24. During the time in which the man of God worried about this and about other concerns, one night when he fell asleep he had the following vision. He saw a little black hen, similar to a tame dove, with its legs and feet covered with feathers. She had innumerable chicks that kept circling around her, but she was unable to gather them all under her wings. When he awoke and returned to the usual thoughts deep in his heart, he interpreted his vision in this way. "I am the hen, small in stature and dark by nature, and through the innocence of my life I must have dove-like simplicity which, the rarer it is on earth, the more quickly it will ascend to heaven. The chicks are the brothers, who have grown in number and grace and whom Francis' strength cannot succeed in defending from turmoil and from the opposition of slanderers[45]. Therefore, I will go to entrust them to the holy Church of Rome, so that the evil-minded will be punished by her powerful rod and the children of God everywhere can enjoy the full freedom to grow in eternal beatitude. The children will then recognize the sweet benefits of their mother and they will always follow in her venerable footsteps with special devotion. Under her protection, there will be no occasion for evil in the Order and the son of Belial[46] will not be able to pass through the Lord's vineyard with impunity. She will keep watch so that the glory of our poverty will remain holy and she will not allow the fog of pride to dim the splendor of our humility. She will keep the bonds of charity and peace steadfast in us, striking down dissidents with the harshest of punishment. Sacred observance of evangelical purity will flourish in her presence and she will not allow the good odor of our life to fail for even an hour."

It was this intention that drove the Saint of God to entrust the Order to the Church. This was the most holy counsel given to

---

[45] *Ps* 31, 31.
[46] *Deut* 13, 13.

him by his foresight concerning the need to take these precautions in the future.

CHAPTER XVII
How he asked for the Cardinal of Ostia as the pope's vicar

25. When he arrived in Rome, the man of God was received very devoutly by Pope Honorius and all the cardinals, and rightly so, since his saintliness, which was known through reputation, truly shone in his works and resounded in his words so that no one could help but venerate him.

He preached fervently before the pope and the cardinals without any preparation, speaking from his heart filled with love according to what the Spirit suggested to him.

Those high mountains[47] were moved by his words and sighing deeply, they cleansed their innermost spirit with tears. When the sermon as over and he had had a brief and informal conversation with the pope, he finally addressed the following petition to him: "As you well know, it is not easy for poor and base men to come to such a high majesty, since you, who sustain the whole world, have important affairs that prevent you from dealing with trifles. Therefore, I ask the mercy of your holiness to grant us this lord of Ostia as our pope so that, ever preserving the dignity of your preeminence, the brothers can turn to him in times of need and have the benefit of his protection and guidance."

Such a holy request was pleasing in the eyes of the pope and he soon put lord Hugolin at the head of the Order, just as the man of God had asked. That holy Cardinal took the flock entrusted to his care under his protection and until his blessed

---

[47] *Is* 54, 10; *Na* 1, 5 and other Gospel references.

death, he became its solicitous farmer, shepherd and student all at the same time[48].

The fondness and special care that the holy Church of Rome has always demonstrated towards the Order of the Friars Minor thus stems from this special respect.

End of part one

---

[48] Gregory IX died on August 22, 1241.

PART TWO

Preface to the second part

26. Handing down the excellent works of the fathers to the memory of their children is a sign of honor to the former and of love to the latter. Truly, those who have not had the fortune of knowing their forefathers in person will be led towards goodness at least through the account of their lives and will be induced to do their best, when the fathers, although far off in time, bear memorable witness to their children. Nevertheless, the foremost and not unimportant fruit we gain from this is an awareness of our insignificance when we see such an abundance of merit in them and an equivalent paucity in us.

I consider blessed Francis a most holy mirror of divine sanctity and the image of its perfection. Everything about him, I say, his words as well as his actions, have a heavenly fragrance about them, so that if they are studied diligently by the humble disciple and imbue him with their saving teachings, they will soon lead him to the love of that sublime knowledge.

Thus, now that I have recounted several events in his life, albeit briefly and poorly, I believe it would not be superfluous to report a few of the things, chosen from the numerous ones, that can do the Saint honor while reawakening our dulled affection at the same time.

CHAPTER I

Of Francis' spirit of prophesy [1]

27. The blessed Father, borne in spirit above worldly things, had subdued everything there is in the universe with a marvelous power, for with his mind's eye always set on the supreme Light, not only did he see through divine revelation what he must do, but with the spirit of a prophesy, he also foretold many events[2], laid hearts' secrets bare[3], knew of matters far away and foresaw and announced the future.

And the facts prove our statement.

CHAPTER II

How he knew that a brother reputed to be a saint
was an impostor

28. There was a brother who, judging by external appearances, led an extraordinarily holy and pious but quite singular life. He was always deep in prayer and observed silence so strictly that he would only make his confession with gestures and not with words. He would go into such rapture over the Scriptures that whenever he would hear them, he would gesticulate because of their extraordinary spiritual sweetness. Why mince words? Everyone considered him a saint three times over.

Now it happened that the blessed Father went to that convent, and he saw the brother and heard him being proclaimed a saint. So to all those who were praising and exalting him, he commented, "Let it be, my brothers, and don't go praise the devil's deception in him. Know that this is actually diabolical temptation and trickery. I am certain of this and the surest proof

---

[1] The original Latin text contains 24 chapters (rather than 25), the first of which is untitled.

[2] *Rev* 19, 10.

[3] *1 Cor* 14, 25.

is the fact that he does not want to make his confession." The brothers did not want to believe him, particularly the Saint's vicar[4], and they asked, "How could it be true that astute deception can be hidden under so many signs of perfection?" And the Father said to them, "Order him to make his confession at least once or twice a week. If he refuses, you'll realize that what I've told you is true." The vicar called the brother aside and began to joke with him at first, finally ordering him to make his confession. However, he refused and, placing a finger over his lips, shook his head to indicate that he did not want to make his confession. All the brothers fell silent, truly fearing the scandal of this false saint. In fact, a few days later he left the Order of his own will and returned to the world and to the vomit of sin until, multiplying his faults, he was deprived of both life and the possibility of repentance.

Singularity must always be avoided, for it is none other than an enormous precipice, a fact experienced by many of these lovers of singularity who climb up to heaven only to fall into the abyss.[5] At the same time, consider the virtue of devout confession, which not only produces saintliness but also demonstrates it.

CHAPTER III

A similar example against singularity

29. A similar case occurred with another friar, Thomas of Spoleto. Everyone had the most solid opinion about his saintliness. Instead, the holy Father considered him to be wicked and in the end, this judgment was confirmed by the man's apostasy. He did not persevere at length, for simulated virtue does not last long. He left the Order and, dying outside it, he realized his misdeed too late.

---

[4] Brother Peter Catanii if the event took place before March 10, 1221 (the date of his death), or Brother Elias if after that.

[5] *Ps* 107, 26.

CHAPTER IV

How he predicted the slaughter of the Christians at Damietta

30. When the Christian army besieged Damietta, the Saint of God was there with his companions, for he had crossed the sea out of his desire for martyrdom.[6] Thus, one day when our side was preparing to go into battle, the Saint was greatly saddened at the news and said to his companion, "If the battle should take place today, the Lord has shown me that victory will not smile upon the Christians.[7] Well, if I say this now, they'll think I'm mad, but if I remain silent, I will not have any peace of mind. Therefore, what do you think I should do?" His companion answered him, "Father, you must not worry about the judgment of men, especially since this is not the first time that you have been considered mad. Clear your conscience and fear God instead of man." The Saint then dashed outside and began to warn the Christians that they must not pitch battle, predicting their downfall, but they turned this truthful announcement to ridicule, hardened their hearts and did not want to believe the warning.

They advanced, gave battle and engaged in hand-to-hand combat with the enemy. During the battle, the Saint, trembling in spirit, had his companion get up to take a look, and after a first and then a second futile attempt to see, he ordered him to go look a third time. And lo, the entire Christian army had been put to flight, ending the war in shame instead of triumph. The slaughter of our soldiers was so terrible that the number of those slain and those taken prisoner rose to six thousand men.

---

[6] This was the third time that St. Francis tried to go among the infidels. After two futile attempts in 1212 and 1213, in the summer of 1219 he succeeded in reaching Egypt. It seems certain that after that he went as far as Palestine, accompanied by Brothers Illuminatus, Peter Catanii, Elias and Caesar of Speyer. The siege of Damietta had begun in May of 1218 and the Christians were defeated on August 29, 1219.

[7] *2 Kgs* 8, 10 and *Nm* 14, 41.

The Saint was filled with compassion and the Christians with remorse, and he mourned above all for the Spaniards, for he saw that because of their greater audacity, very few of them had been spared.

May these princes of the earth know and be convinced that it is not worthwhile to battle against God[8] or in other words, against His will. Pride usually leads to a ruinous end, since by trusting in its strength, celestial help is forfeited. In fact, if victory is to be expected from heaven, then battle must be joined following divine inspiration.

CHAPTER V

How he knew a brother's secret thoughts

31. At that time, having returned from the countries overseas[9] the Saint was with Brother Leonard of Assisi[10] and, exhausted and tired from his trip, he was forced to ride a donkey for a while. The companion who was following him and who was just as tired, allowed himself to be overcome by human weakness and began to say to himself, "His relatives and mine certainly never considered each other as equals, but there he is riding and I'm on foot, leading his donkey." While Brother Leonard was thinking these things, the Saint quickly dismounted from the donkey and said, "No, brother, it is not fitting for me to be riding while you are on foot, for in the world you were nobler and more honored than I." The brother was dumbfounded and, red-faced with shame, he realized that the Saint had read his heart. Thus he threw himself down and, shedding many tears, honestly confessed his thoughts and asked for forgiveness.

---

[8] *Sir* 46, 8.

[9] He returned in the fall of 1220.

[10] Not much else is known about him, but the name makes us think this was the nobleman Leonard of Gislerio, even though there is no proof that he entered the Order. Could the name Leonard be the full name of Brother Leo?

CHAPTER VI

Of the brother over whom he saw a devil and
against those who withdraw from the community

32. There was another brother who was distinguished before men by his fame and even more so before God through grace. His virtue stirred up the envy of the father of all envy, however, who schemed to cut down the roots of that tree, which was already touching heaven, and to tear the crown from his hands.

He tricked him, disturbed him and studied and assessed his tendencies and habits in order to find a way to thwart his saintliness. He instilled in his heart the desire for solitude, giving it the appearance of a search for greater perfection, so that by assaulting him when he was alone in this way, it would be easier to make him fall and so that, being alone, the man would have no one to pick him up from his fall.[11] Why mince words? He withdrew from the community of brothers and went wandering all over the world. From the robe of his habit, he made a small tunic without the hood stitched to it[12] and went about like this, mortifying himself in everything. But divine solace immediately disappeared, the waters seeped down into his very soul[13] and, desolate in body and spirit, he went around like a bird about to be trapped. Already on the edge of the abyss by this time, he was about to fall when the merciful eye of divine Providence benevolently looked upon the wretch[14] who, illuminated by suffering and finally returning to his senses, said to himself, "Miserable wretch, return to the Order for

---

[11] *Eccl* 4, 10.

[12] This is an interesting detail for anyone interested in the early Franciscan habit. Based on this passage, it would appear that the hood was supposed to be sewn to the cowl, whereas further ahead in N° 154, the opposite would seem to be the case.

[13] *Ps* 69, 2 and *Prv* 7, 23.

[14] *Sir* 11, 13.

there is your only salvation." And without further delay, he got up and hastened to find refuge in his mother's womb.

33. When he finally arrived at the brothers' abode in Siena, he found St. Francis there. Wonder! The Saint fled as soon as he laid his eyes on him, running off to retreat to his cell. The brothers, upset, asked him why he had fled and the Saint replied, "Why should it be any wonder to you that you don't understand the reason? I turned to the help of prayer to free him from his error. I saw something in my son that rightly distressed me, but through the grace of Christ, all illusion has now fallen away." And turning to the brother who, kneeling in shame, proclaimed his guilt, he said, "May the Lord forgive you, brother, but in the future beware of withdrawing from your community and from your brothers under the pretext of saintliness." That brother subsequently became a lover of the Order and of unity, devoted himself above all to those communities in which observance of the Rule is most strictly enforced.

O marvels worked by the Lord in the company and assemblies of the just![15] In company, those who are tempted can sustain themselves, the fallen can rise again and the tepid are inflamed, for iron sharpens iron[16] and one brother helped by another becomes as solid as rock, and even though amidst the crowds of the world you cannot see Jesus, the heavenly celestial throng is instead of no obstacle to you.[17] As long as you do not flee, by remaining faithful until death you will receive the crown of life.[18]

34. A short time later[19], a similar thing happened with someone else. A brother did not want to obey the Saint's vicar but followed another brother as his teacher instead. Admonished

---

[15] *Ps* 111, 1-2.

[16] *Prv* 27, 17 and 18, 19.

[17] *Lk* 19, 3.

[18] *Rev* 2, 10.

[19] St. Bonaventure would later specify that this event took place during a chapter (*Major Life* XI, 11), and that the Saint was off to one side in prayer.

through the intermediary of the Saint, who was present, he threw himself at the vicar's feet and, leaving his previous teacher behind, he turned to obey the one the Saint had given to him as his superior. St. Francis then drew a deep sigh and said to the companion who had been entrusted with giving this reprimand, "My brother, I saw a demon on the back of that disobedient brother and he was wringing his neck. By submitting to a knight of that kind and rejecting the bit of obedience, he allowed himself to be led by the reins of instinct. Then, as soon as I prayed to the Lord for that brother, the devil immediately disappeared in shame."

Such was the penetrating glance of our Saint, whose sight for material things was weak yet it was quite sharp for the spiritual ones.

Why should it be so amazing that he who did not wish to bear the Lord of majesty was burdened by such terrible weight? There is no middle ground: you will either carry a light burden that will instead bear you or, like a millstone around your neck, iniquity will weigh you down even more than a talent of lead.[20]

CHAPTER VII

*How he freed the people of Greccio from wolves
and from hailstorms*

35. The Saint willingly stayed the brothers' place in Greccio, not only because he saw it was rich in poverty but also because in a small and very solitary cell built there on a jutting rock[21], he could very freely abandon himself to contemplation. This is precisely the place where, some time before, he had celebrated birthday of the Child of Bethlehem, becoming a child with Him.

---

[20] *Mt* 18, 6 and *Zec* 5, 7-8. A talent was a large unit of weight used in ancient Greek and Rome.

[21] That cell was the first sanctuary dedicated to St. Francis.

Now it happened that those citizens were tormented by various calamities. Predatory packs of wolves devoured not only animals but also people and hail devastated the fields and vineyards each year. But one day as he was preaching to them, blessed Francis said, "For the honor and glory of God almighty, listen to the truth that I announce to you: if each one of you confesses his sins and does fruitful penance[22], I give you my word that this evil will go away and the Lord, looking benevolently upon you, will fill you with worldly goods. Listen to this too, however: I repeat to you that if you are not grateful for these benefits and return to sin, the wound will be opened again, punishment will be doubled and divine anger shall rage against you even more."

36. And it truly happened that through the merits and prayers of the holy Father, from that moment on their misfortune ceased and peril perished, and neither wolves nor hailstones gave them trouble any longer. Indeed -- an even greater miracle! -- if hail sometimes devastated the fields nearby, when it reached the boundaries of Greccio, it either stopped or turned off in a different direction. Having achieved tranquillity in this way, worldly goods grew and were enriched, but prosperity brought about its usual results: eyes were covered in fat and the fatness, or rather the dung, of worldly goods blinded them. In the end, falling into the gravest of sin, they forgot about the God who had saved them, but not with impunity, since divine justice does not punish the fall as much as the relapse. When divine rage was provoked against them, the previous scourges returned and added to them was a war among men, while an epidemic sent from heaven decimated many of them. Lastly, the entire town was burnt by the flames of punishment.[23] And it is quite fitting that those who turn their back on benefaction should fall into misfortune.

---

[22] *Lk* 4, 8.

[23] Perhaps in 1242, when Rieti, which was loyal to the Pope, was besieged by the troops of Frederick II.

CHAPTER VIII

*How, while preaching to the Perugines, he predicted
their sedition; and of his praise of unity*

37. Several days later, as he was leaving the cell that we mentioned[24], the blessed Father spoke to the brothers who were present and with sorrow in his voice, he said, "The Perugines have done much harm to their neighbors and their heart has become proud[25], but to their own shame. Now God's punishment is approaching and He has already placed His hand on the sword."

After a few days had gone by, he fervently set out for Perugia and the brothers safely deduced that he must have had some vision while he was in his cell.

When he reached Perugia, once the population had been assembled, he began to preach. Since the knights on horseback, racing and scheming as they are wont to do, kept the word of God from being heard, the Saint turned to them, exclaiming: "O the deplorable foolishness of you wretches, who do not consider or fear God's judgment! But listen to what the Lord is announcing to you through the mouth of this poor one. He has made you more powerful than all those around you. Therefore, you should be more benevolent with your neighbors and thankful to God but instead, ungrateful for divine grace, you assault your neighbors with your weapons, kill them and devastate their territories. Now I say to you that your sin will not go unpunished, but as the gravest of punishments, God will stir up an internal war among you, so that one will rise against the other, and heavenly indignation will teach those who have not learned their lesson from His favor."

---

[24] In paragraph 35 above.
[25] *2 Chr* 26, 16.

Just a few days later, conflict broke out[26] and arms were taken up. The citizens fought against the knights and the noblemen wielded their swords against the common people. The battle was waged with such deep hatred and such great slaughter that even the neighboring towns that had so often been offended by the Perugines felt sorry for them.

Rightful justice! Since they had drawn away from the one supreme God, there could remain no unity in them either. In public life, there can be no bond stronger than pious love towards God and sincere and unfeigned faith.

CHAPTER IX

How he predicted to a woman that her husband
would change from bad to good

38. At that time, while the man of God was going to Le Celle in Cortona, a noblewoman from Volusiano hastened to see him as soon as she heard the news. Since she was quite weak and delicate, by the time she reached him she was all out of breath from running. The most holy Father, seeing her so tired and short of breath, took pity on her and asked, "What do you want, Madonna?" And she replied, "Father, I want you to bless me." So when the Saint asked, "Are you married?" this is what she replied. "Father, I have a very strict husband who keeps me from serving Jesus Christ and this is my greatest sorrow. Because he is opposed to it, I cannot follow the Lord's good inspiration. Therefore, I ask you in grace, o saint, to pray for him so that his heart will be touched by divine mercy."

The Father admired the woman's manly strength and the mature wisdom in such a young woman and taking pity on her, he said, "Go, blessed child, and know that you will find comfort in

---

[26] The civil war, which started in 1214, broke out again in 1217 and then once again in 1223-1225. The nobility was exiled until 1228.

your husband." Then he added, "You must tell him on God's part and on my own, that now is the time for salvation and that the time of justice will come later." Having received this blessing, the young woman returned, found her husband and told him the words she had heard. The Holy Spirit immediately descended upon him and, transforming him into a new man, led him to respond very sweetly in this way: "Oh woman, let us serve God and we shall save the soul of our household." His wife replied, "It seems to me that we must make continence the spiritual foundation upon which we should then build the other virtues." He replied, "This is just as pleasing to me as it is to you."

After living in chastity for many years, they both died blessedly on the very same day, one of them as the morning holocaust and the other as the evening sacrifice.[27]

Blessed woman, who subdued her husband to the life of grace! The word of the Apostle was fulfilled in her: *the unbelieving husband is consecrated by his believing wife.*[28]   But to use a common proverb, today you can count these women on one hand.

CHAPTER X
How, in spirit, he knew about a brother who had given scandal to another and predicted that he would leave the Order

39. Two brothers once came from the Terra di Lavoro[29] and the elder one stirred up a great scandal in the younger one's regard. We could say that he was not a companion but a tyrant and the younger one bore everything in admirable silence out of the love of God. As soon as they arrived in Assisi, the younger

---

[27] *Ps* 141, 2.

[28] *1 Cor* 7, 14.

[29] No other information is available from other sources concerning the identity of the two friars. While the Saint was alive, the provincial Minister of Terra di Lavoro, an area in the Campania region north of Naples, was Brother Augustine of Assisi.

one went into the cell of St. Francis, to whom he was rather close, and the Saint asked him, among other things, "How did your companion act towards you during your trip?" "Oh, well enough, my dear father!" And the Saint said to him, "Beware, brother, not to lie under the pretext of humility. Because I know how he treated you, but just wait a bit and you'll see." The friar was quite amazed when he saw that, in spirit, St. Francis knew about things that had taken place far away. And not long afterwards, the one who had given scandal to his companion left the Order.

It is undoubtedly a sign of wickedness and proof of a lack of good spirit[30] to travel with a good companion without getting along.

CHAPTER XI
Of the young man he knew had not come into the Order through divine inspiration

40. At that same time, a young nobleman from Lucca came to Assisi out of the desire to enter the Order and when he was introduced to Saint Francis, he tearfully begged on his knees that he be accepted. Taking a closer look at him, however, the man of God immediately recognized in spirit that he had not been led by divine inspiration and said to him, "Miserable carnal man, what makes you think that you can deceive both the Holy Spirit and me? Your weeping is carnal and your heart is not with God. Go, for there is nothing spiritual about you."

As soon as he had uttered those words, it was announced that the young man's parents were at the door to ask if they could take their son away with them, so he left and returned with them quite willingly. The brothers, amazed, praised the Lord in his Saint.

---

[30] *Sir* 19, 21.

CHAPTER XII

*Of a cleric who was healed by him and to whom he predicted
worse punishment because of his relapse into sin*

41. During the time in which the holy Father lay ill at the bishop's palace in Rieti, a canon named Geodone, a lascivious and mundane man who was lying in bed struck by illness and wracked with pain throughout his body, had himself brought before St. Francis and tearfully beseeched him to bless him with the sign of the cross. So the Saint said to him, "How can I bless you with the sign of the cross if you have lived by the desires of the flesh, without any fear of God? As far as I am concerned, I can bless you in the name of Christ, but know that you will be struck even more severely if you fall back into sin after you've been cured."[31] Then he added, "The punishment that is given for the sin of ingratitude is always worse than the initial one."

He made the sign of the cross over him and the canon, whose muscles had been contracted, promptly got up healed and burst into praise of the Lord, exclaiming, "I'm cured!" His kidney stones creaked like dry wood being split and many people heard this. But after just a short time had gone by, forgetting God, he fell back into his indecent conduct. One evening when he had gone to have supper with another canon, one of his confreres, and was spending the night there, the roof of the house suddenly collapsed. While the others escaped death, that wretch alone was crushed and killed.[32]

It is no wonder that, as the Saint had prophesied, he was struck by a punishment that was even worse than the previous ones, since one must be grateful for the pardon he receives and repeated sin is doubly offensive.

---

[31] *Prv* 26, 11; *Mt* 12, 45; *Lk* 11, 26.
[32] The canon died sometime before August of 1246. He had been the treasurer of the cathedral of Rieti from 1213 to 1216.

CHAPTER XIII
Of a brother who was tempted

42. When the Saint was staying in this same place[33], a spiritual brother from the custody of Marsica[34] who was tormented by grave temptation, said deep within himself, "O! if I could just have even a small bit of St. Francis' fingernail, I believe that this whole storm of temptation would go away and through the Lord's favor, peace would return." Obtaining permission to go, he went to the place and explained the reasons for his trip to one of the holy Father's companions, who answered him, "I don't think I can give you any, because when we cut them, he orders us to throw them away and forbids us to keep them." But at that moment, the brother was summoned and ordered to go to the Saint, who wished to see him. "My son," he said, "look for a pair of scissors to cut my nails." The friar handed him the scissors, which he had already gotten out for that very purpose and collecting the bits that had been cut, he gave them to the other brother who had requested them. This brother, receiving them devoutly and guarding them even more devoutly, was immediately liberated from all the demon's assaults.

CHAPTER XIV
Of the man who donated the kind of cloth
that the Saint had previously requested

43. One time at this same place[35], the Father of the poor, dressed in a rather old tunic, said to one of the companions he

---

[33] At the bishop's palace in Rieti or at one of the nearby hermitages?

[34] Could Celano, who was born in Marsica, be referring to himself here?

[35] In this passage, the detail about the brother who goes into the city to get the cloth would appear to indicate that St. Francis was not staying at the bishop's palace, which was in the city. However, the palace of the Bishop of Rieti is expressly mentioned in the *Treatise of Miracles*, 35.

had chosen as a guardian, "Brother, if possible, I would like you to find me some cloth for a tunic." Having heard this, the brother began to think about how he could find the cloth that was so necessary and requested with such humility. The next day at dawn, he went towards the gate to go into the city to get the cloth and there, seated in front of the gate, was a man acting as if he wanted to speak to him and he said, "For the love of God, accept this cloth from me for six tunics. Keep one for yourself and give the other ones away as you think best, for the good of my soul." The happy friar returned to brother Francis and told him about this donation that had come from heaven. And the Father said to him, "Accept the tunics, for that man was sent precisely to help my needs, and let us give thanks to the One who has such great concern for us."

CHAPTER XV

How he invited his doctor to lunch although the brothers had nothing, and of what the Lord suddenly provided; and of divine Providence towards its own

44. While the blessed man was staying at a hermitage near Rieti[36], a doctor[37] visited him every day to treat his eyes. One day, the Saint said to his companions, "Invite the doctor and give him good food to eat." The guardian replied, "Father, we are embarrassed to tell you that we are ashamed to invite him, since we are poor right now!" But the Saint replied to him, "Why do you want to make me repeat it?" The doctor, who was present, added, "And I, dear brothers, will find your poverty delicious."

The brothers got busy, setting what was in the pantry out on the table and that is, a bit of bread and not much wine and then, to make the dinner more lavish, a few legumes were sent out

---

[36] Probably Fonte Colombo.
[37] This was probably Master Nicholas, a doctor who is also listed in local documents from 1203 to 1233.

from the kitchen. In the meantime, God's table was moved with compassion by the servants' table: someone knocked at the door and when they ran to open it, there was a woman carrying a basket full of lovely bread, fish and some shrimp pies, and it was also brimming with honey and grapes. The table of those poor men rejoiced at the sight and, putting the ordinary food aside for the next day, they ate the finer food. Sighing, the doctor exclaimed, "Neither you, brothers, nor we laymen realize this man's holiness!" And they would have satisfied their appetites further if the very miracle itself had not gratified them even more than the food.

Thus, the eye of the Father never abandons its own and indeed, Providence is even more liberal with those who are in greatest need. The poor man dines at a table that is much richer than the king's, for God is more generous than man.

CHAPTER XVa

How he freed Brother Riccerio from temptation

44a. A brother named Riccerio, who was noble in both morals and birth, placed so much faith in the merits of blessed Francis that he believed that anyone who obtained the Saint's indulgence would surely merit divine grace, but that if instead he were deprived of it, then he would deserve God's anger. Ardently aspiring to obtain this benefit, he greatly feared that the Saint would discover some fault in him and that for this reason, he would further withdraw his favor. Therefore, even though this brother was constantly and seriously tormented by this fear, he did not reveal this thought to anyone. Now it happened that one day, disturbed by his usual concern, he approached the cell in which St. Francis was praying.

Aware not only that the friar was approaching but also knowing his state of mind, the man of God beckoned him kindly and said to him, "In the future, fear no more. No temptation should upset you, son, since you are very dear to me and of all those who are dearest to me, I have a special love for you. You can safely come to me whenever you like and then leave again as you like."

That brother was quite amazed and he rejoiced over the words of the holy Father. Reassured of his love, he subsequently also grew in the Savior's grace, just as he had believed he would.

CHAPTER XVI
How, as he was leaving his cell, he blessed two brothers whose wish he knew in spirit

45. St. Francis used to spend the entire day in a solitary cell without returning among the brothers except when he felt he needed food. Thus, he did not go to eat at the established time, for he was often claimed by his even greater hunger for contemplation.

It happened one day that two brothers who led a life dear to God came to the hermitage in Greccio from far away, and the only reason for their visit was to see the Saint and receive the blessing they had long desired. However, when they arrived and could not see him because he had already retreated from the community to his cell, they were greatly saddened by this. Given that they did not know when he would come back out and that perhaps they would have had to linger there quite a while, they began to set out again disheartened, believing that they had not deserved that grace on account of their sins. Thus, accompanied by the blessed Francis' companions who tried to console them, they had already gone a stone's throw away from the hermitage when the Saint began to call after them in a loud voice, saying to one of his companions, "Tell my brothers who came here to look towards me." As soon as they turned their faces towards him, he made the sign of the cross over them and blessed them very affectionately. Then, made even happier since their desire had been fulfilled so miraculously, they went away praising and blessing the Lord.[38]

CHAPTER XVII

*How, by praying, he made water gush from a rock
to quench a farmer's thirst*

46. One time blessed Francis, who wanted to go to a hermitage[39] so that he could dedicate himself more freely to contemplation but was feeling rather weak, borrowed a donkey from a poor man. It was summertime and before they were halfway there, tired by the long steep walk, the farmer who was climbing the mountain with the man of God was worn out and felt as if he would faint from his burning thirst. So he cried out to the Saint with great urgency, begging him to take pity on him and declaring that he would die if he were not refreshed by something to drink. The Saint of God, who was always compassionate with those who suffer, dismounted at once, knelt down with his hands outstretched towards heaven and did not stop praying until he felt he had been answered. "Hurry," he then said to the farmer, "and over there you'll find running water that the Lord has just now mercifully made flow from the rock for you to drink." Marvelous kindness of God, who submits so readily to his servants! The man drank the water that was flowing from such hard rock[40] by virtue of Francis' prayer. There had never been any running water in that place before nor, despite all the diligent searching that was done, was any ever found there since.

What is there to marvel about if one who is filled with the Holy Spirit[41] should renew the miraculous gestures of all the just? It is nothing out of the ordinary that he who had the gift of being

---

[38] *Lk* 24, 53.
[39] The hermitage of Mount La Verna.
[40] *Is* 48, 21; *Ps* 78, 16 and *Dt* 32, 13.
[41] *Lk* 4, 1.

united with Christ through singular grace should do works similar to those of other saints.

CHAPTER XVIII

Of the birds he fed and how one of them died of greed

47. One day, blessed Francis was seated at the table with his brothers when along came two birds, a male and a female, that came at will every day to get crumbs from the table to feed their young. The Saint stroked them merrily as usual and gave them the provisions he had gathered. Another day, the two little animals brought their young to the brothers, almost as if to repay them for having fed them at their own expense, and then never returned. The little birds became accustomed to living with the brothers, perching on their hands, and they lived in the house, not as guests but as residents, avoiding laymen and considering themselves only the brothers' disciples.

The Saint observed all this and was amazed, and he invited the others to rejoice over this. "Can you see what our brothers, the robin redbreasts, have done, as if they could reason? They said, 'Here, brothers, we offer you our young, who were nourished with your crumbs. Do what you like with them and we will go somewhere else to make our nest'." And they were completely tame and ate with the brothers.

However, this harmony was ruined by greed, for the oldest one became proud and began to persecute the younger ones. He would sate his appetite at will and keep the others from eating. The Father said, "Look at what this miser is doing: even though he is full and satiated, he is nevertheless envious of his starving little brothers. He will surely die a bad death."

Punishment followed the Saint's words immediately. That unruly bird climbed up onto a jar of water to drink and suddenly drowned in the water, and neither cats nor any other beast dared to touch the little animal that had been cursed by the Saint.

What a dreadful evil greed must be in men if it is so harshly punished in birds! And the condemnation of saints must also be feared, for it is so quickly followed by punishment.

CHAPTER XIX
How all the prophesies about Brother Bernard
were fulfilled

48. On another occasion, this is what he foretold about Brother Bernard, the second one to enter the Order[42] : "I say to you that very astute demons who are worse than the other evil spirits[43] have been chosen to tempt Brother Bernard, but even if they are always alert in order to make him fall like a star from the heavens, everything will end quite differently. He will be tormented, tempted and afflicted, but in the end he will conquer all." Then he added, "When he is near death, once he has tamed every storm and overcome every temptation, he will enjoy marvelous peace and tranquillity and after he has completed his path, he will happily join Christ."

This is indeed what happened: his death was glorified by miracles and the prophecy of the man of God was fulfilled precisely. Thus, when he died, the brothers said, "Truly, we did not know the virtues of this brother while he was alive!"

But we will leave the praise of this Bernard for others to relate[44] .

---

[42] Either he is considered the second one because St. Francis was the first one, or this is a reference to the anonymous predecessor discussed in the *First Life*, 24. Nevertheless, further ahead (n° 109), he is referred to as "the first plant" of the Order.

[43] *Mt* 12, 45.

[44] *The Life of Brother Bernard* can be found in the *Chronica XXIV Generalium*, published in vol. III of *Analecta Franciscana*.

CHAPTER XX
Of the brother who was tempted and who wanted something
written in the Saint's own hand

49. While the Saint remained closed off in his cell on Mount La Verna, one of his companions yearned to have some comforting passage from the divine books written in St. Francis' own hand, for he believed that in this way, he could drive away a grave temptation -- not a carnal one but a spiritual one -- that was tormenting him, or if nothing else, endure it more easily. This desire gave him no peace, yet he did not dare manifest it to the most holy Father. Nevertheless, what was not said by man was revealed by the Spirit.

In fact, one day blessed Francis beckoned him and said, "Bring me paper and ink because I want to write the words of God and His praise, which I have meditated in my heart."[45] As soon as the things he had requested were brought to him, in his own hand he wrote the "Praise of God" and the words he had inside him and lastly, a blessing for the brother. Then he said to him, "Take this little piece of paper and safeguard it diligently until the day you die."

The temptation was immediately driven away and the writing he preserved later worked miracles.[46]

---

[45] *2 Jn* 12 and *Ps* 77, 7.
[46] This precious parchment is still preserved at the Sacred Convent in Assisi. The friar involved was Brother Leo, as indicated in the footnote that he himself wrote on the parchment to explain how he had received this dear and precious memento, the authenticity of which is unquestionable. Written on one side is *Laudes Dei Altissimi*, while on the other side is the austere and tender blessing of Brother Leo, which was taken from the Scriptures,

CHAPTER XXI

*Of the same brother, to whom he gave his tunic
as the brother had desired*

50. The holy Father had yet another miraculous intuition with regard to this same brother. During the time in which the Blessed One lay ill at the bishop's palace in Assisi[47], this brother thought to himself, "Here the Father is close to death and my soul would be greatly comforted if I could have my Father's tunic after he dies!" Just as if his heart's desire had been manifested aloud, shortly thereafter blessed Francis summoned him and said, "I want to give you my tunic. Take it and afterwards, it will be yours. I will wear it as long as I am alive, but it must remain with you after I die." Amazed by the Father's spiritual insight, the brother was finally comforted by receiving the tunic, which was later brought to France for sacred devotion.

CHAPTER XXII

*Of the parsley that, at his request, was found at night
among the wild herbs*

51. Towards the end of his illness, one night he had a craving for parsley and humbly requested some. The cook who had been called to bring it to him answered that he could not go out into the garden to pick it in the dark, saying, "I've picked so much of it every day that by now, I would hardly be able to find any even in broad daylight, much less can I manage to distinguish it from the other herbs now that it's pitch dark." And the Saint said, "Don't worry, brother. Go and bring me the first herbs you happen to find." The brother went into the garden, tore up the first wild herbs at hand and brought them inside. The brothers looked at the herbs carefully and when they picked them over,

---

[47] *First Life*, 108.

they found some tender leafy parsley in the middle. As soon as he had had a taste of it, the Saint was very comforted. Thus he told his brothers, "My dearest brothers, obey the very first word without having the order repeated to you and do not claim that it is impossible, because even if I were to order something beyond your capabilities, the strength of obedience will not fail you."

CHAPTER XXIII
Of the famine he predicted would come to pass after his death

52. At times, the saints are driven by the impulse of the Holy Spirit to say marvelous things about themselves, not only because the glory of God requires some truth to be revealed, but also because it is required by charity in order to edify one's neighbor. Therefore, it happened that the blessed Father recounted to a brother, whom he loved greatly, the words that had been said to him directly during an intimate and mysterious conversation with God. "Now," he said, "there is one of God's servants on earth and as long as he is alive, through his merit the Lord will not allow famine to decimate man."

He did not speak this way out of vanity, because indeed, this was a holy declaration that was manifested with modest words for our own good by that holy love that is not self-seeking[48], for the prerogative of Christ's marvelous love for his servant did not need to be hidden by useless silence.

In fact, all of us know -- because we saw it -- how quietly and peacefully time passed while Christ's servant was alive and how it was overabundantly rich in goods of all sorts. There was no dearth of the word of God, since the words of those who preached were particularly full of virtue and the hearts of all listeners were pleasing to the Lord. There were resplendent examples of saintliness in the religious habit and the hypocrisy of the

---

[48] *1 Cor* 13, 5.

whitewashed[49] had not yet contaminated such sacred souls, nor had the teachings of those in disguise[50] aroused any strange things. Thus, it was fitting that worldly goods should abound, since the eternal ones were loved so sincerely by all.

53. As soon as he was taken away from us, however, and the order of things was upset, a radical change took place.[51] War and sedition broke out everywhere and death, under a variety of forms, destroyed many countries. The scourge of famine also spread far and wide and, surpassing all other evil in its cruelty, it killed many people. Need turned all sorts of things into food and forced men to chew what even brutes were not accustomed to eating. Bread was made out of walnut shells and tree bark and as was learned through the confession of some, even parents, gripped by famine, felt no grief -- to use a less atrocious expression -- over the death of their children.

But in order to make it known with even greater certainty who this faithful servant was, for whose love divine justice had stayed the hand of vengeance, a few days after his death, blessed father Francis clearly manifested to the brother to whom he had foretold the imminent slaughter, that he was precisely that servant of God. In fact, one night as the brother was sleeping, he called to him aloud and said, "Brother, the famine the Lord kept from visiting the earth as long as I was alive is now at hand." The brother, awakened by the voice, then referred everything that had happened. Three nights later, the Saint appeared to him again and repeated similar words.

---

[49] See *Mt* 23, 27: "Woe to you scribes and Pharisees, you frauds! You are like whitewashed tombs...".

[50] *2 Cor* 11, 13-15.

[51] While this passage exaggerates to some extent, it is obvious that Celano considered the rebellion of Frederick II (who was excommunicated in 1227) and the war against Gregory IX to be extraordinarily serious offenses.

CHAPTER XXIV
Of the Saint's perception and of our ignorance

54. It should not seem strange to anyone that the prophet of our times shone because of such privileges for, released from the haze of earthly things and not subject to whims of the flesh, with his mind he soared freely to the heights of heaven and because of his purity, was able to enter into the realm of light. Thus illuminated by the splendor of the eternal Light, he learned from the Word what he then reiterated in his words.

O how different we are today, we who, cloaked in darkness, ignore even necessary things! And what do you think the reason for this is, unless it is the fact that, by living as friends of the flesh, we too sink into the dust of worldly thing? Instead, if we were to lift our hearts up to heaven together with our hands, if we were take make our home amidst eternal things, then perhaps we would come to learn what we do not know: God and ourselves. He who lives in mud necessarily sees only mud, but the eye that is set on heaven can't help but see heavenly goods

On poverty

CHAPTER XXV
Praise of poverty

55. Living in the vale of tears, this blessed Father spurned the poor riches of the children of man and out of the loftiest ambition, he aspired to poverty with all his heart. Considering her to be the constant companion of the Son of God who had been abandoned by the whole world by this time, he wanted to marry her in a bond of eternal love. In love with her beauty, in order to become as closely united to her as to a wife and to make two

spirits into one, not only did he abandon his father and mother[52], but he pushed everything else aside. He held her in chaste embraces and not even for one hour would he sustain that he was not her faithful groom. He would tell his sons that this was the path to perfection and that this was the pledge and promise of eternal wealth. No one was as covetous of gold as he was of poverty, no one more solicitous of guarding a treasure than he of this evangelical pearl. More than anything else, he loathed to see anything contrary to poverty in his friars, either within the house or without. In fact, from the time he became a religious until his death, he felt that his only wealth was his tunic, his cord and his underwear, and he had nothing else. The poverty of his habit showed where he placed his treasure. Thus happy, thus certain, thus unencumbered, he delighted in having exchanged the wealth that is destined to perish for a good that was a hundred times greater.

Of the poverty of their dwellings[53]

CHAPTER XXVI

56. He taught his brothers to make themselves poor dwellings and to build little huts out of wood and not out of stone, following a rough design. When speaking about poverty, he would often remind his brothers of that evangelical saying: *the foxes have lairs, the birds in the sky have nests, but the Son of Man has nowhere to lay his head.*[54]

---

[52] *Gn* 2, 24.
[53] In the Latin text, this title covers four chapters and chapter XXVI is untitled.
[54] *Mt* 8, 20.

CHAPTER XXVII
Of the house he began to tear down
near the Porziuncola

57. Since the time was approaching in which a chapter was to be held at Saint Mary's of the Porziuncola, the people of Assisi, seeing that there was no suitable building, hurried to build one for the chapter while the man of God was away and knew nothing about it. When the Father returned and saw the house, he was bitterly grieved by this, as if it were an insult. In order to tear it down, he was immediately the first to climb onto the roof and he energetically started to throw down bricks and tiles. He also ordered the brothers to climb up and completely destroy that horror contrary to poverty. In fact, he said that anything in that place that looked too ostentatious would immediately be heard about throughout the Order and taken as an example. And he would have destroyed the house from its very foundations if some soldiers who were present had not stopped him in his zeal by declaring that the house belonged to the city and not to the brothers.

CHAPTER XXVIII
Of the house in Bologna from which he drove out the sick

58. One time when he was returning from Verona with the intention of passing through Bologna, he heard that a brothers' house had just been built. Struck by the sound of the words "brothers' house", he took a different road and went elsewhere without even entering Bologna. Then he had the brothers notified that they were to leave that convent at once. They abandoned it and not even the ill dared to stay there and they were forced to leave with the others. They were not given permission to return

there until cardinal Hugolin, bishop of Ostia and legate in Lombardy[55], publicly proclaimed that the house belonged to him.

This is witnessed and written down by one who was forced to leave the house at that time even though he was ill.

CHAPTER XXIX

How he did not want to enter the cell
he had heard referred to as his

59. He did not want the brothers to live anyplace, even if it were small, unless he knew for certain that someone else owned it. He always wanted his sons to live as pilgrims and that is, to stay under someone else's roof and to pass by peacefully, yearning for the heavenly homeland.

Thus, it happened at the hermitage of Sarteano[56] that as soon he heard one brother reply to another one who had asked him whence he came, "I am coming from Brother Francis' cell", Francis exclaimed, "Since you have given the name of Francis to the cell, as if I were its owner, you can find someone else to live there, but I will never stay there again." And he added, "When the Lord stayed in the desert, where he prayed and fasted for forty days, he did not have a cell nor was any house built, but he took refuge in a cave. We can imitate Him according to the precepts of the Rule, since we possess nothing of our own, even though we cannot go without a dwelling place."

---

[55] He was legate in 1219 and again in 1223.
[56] In the province of Siena.

Of poverty of furnishings

CHAPTER XXX

60. Not only did that man despise the luxury of buildings, but he also abhorred having numerous or elegant furnishings. He did not want anything on the table, nor crockery, that had anything to do with the world, so that each thing would speak of pilgrimage and exile.

CHAPTER XXXI

Of the table that was prepared in Greccio on Easter;
and of how he appeared as a pilgrim, following Christ's example

61. It happened one time, on Easter[57], that the brothers at the hermitage in Greccio prepared the table with greater care than usual, using white table linens and glassware. Descending from his cell to go to the refectory, the Father found the table set on high[58] and prepared with vain refinement, but he did not smile at all at the delightful table. Slowly and secretly, he retraced his steps, donned the hat of a poor man who was present and, leaning on a cane, went outside. There, outside the main door, he waited for the brothers to start eating, for they did not usually wait for him if he did not come when the signal was given.

As soon as they started to eat, that true poor one cried from the doorway, "For the love of the Lord our God, give alms to this poor sick pilgrim." The brothers replied, "Come in, good man, for the love of Him whose name you have invoked." He entered at once and presented himself in this way to those who were dining. Imagine the amazement that the pilgrim caused in

---

[57] Instead, according to the *Legenda antiqua*, this event took place on Christmas day.

[58] Perhaps as opposed to the older custom of eating seated on the floor.

those leisurely citizens! At his request, they gave him a bowl and sitting down on the ground all alone, he placed the bowl amidst the ashes and said, "Now I'm truly sitting like one of the Friars Minor!" Then he said to the friars, "We, more than all the other religious, must feel ourselves bound by the example of poverty set by the Son of God. I saw the table all set and adorned and did not recognize it as the one of those poor ones who go begging from door to door".

This event proves how closely he resembled that Pilgrim who was alone in Jerusalem on that same day of Easter. Like Him, he too made his disciples' heart burn inside when he spoke.[59]

CHAPTER XXXII
Against the excessive desire for books

62. He cautioned that in books, the word of the Lord[60] and not material value, edification and not beauty of form, should be sought. He wanted them to have only a few, and those few should always be ready for the brothers who needed them. One minister, who had asked him for permission to keep luxurious books of great value, was given this reply: "I do not wish to lose the book of Gospel, which I have promised to observe, over your books. You can do what you want, but I cannot approve of something that conceals a trap."

---

[59] *Lk* 24, 32.
[60] *Ps* 19, 8.

On the poverty of their beds

CHAPTER XXXIII
An episode about the Bishop of Ostia and his praise

63. With their pallets and beds, poverty was honored so greatly that anyone who had worn-out fabric to lay out over straw thought he had a sumptuous bed. Now it happened that during the time in which a chapter was being held in St. Mary's of the Porziuncola, the Bishop of Ostia[61] went there with a crowd of knights and clerics to visit the brothers. When he saw them sleeping on the ground and examined those beds, which you would have thought were straw beds for animals, he said to everyone, weeping, "Here's how the brothers sleep!" adding, "What then will become of us wretches, who live overindulgently with so many superfluous things?" All those present, moved to tears, went away greatly edified.

This was the famous bishop of Ostia who, later becoming the highest gateway of the Church, always held out against enemies until he gave his blessed soul up to heaven like a sacred victim.[62]

O merciful heart, womb of charity! Placed so highly, he grieved that he did not have any high merits, whereas truly he was more sublime in virtue than in office.

---

[61] Cardinal Hugolin.

[62] This passage is play on three Latin words that resemble the word *Hostiensis*, name of Hugolin's episcopal see: *ostium* (gateway), *hostibus* (enemies), *hostiam* (victim).

CHAPTER XXXIV

What happened to him one night because of a feather pillow

64. Given that we have already mentioned beds, there is also another episode that perhaps it would be useful to recount.

Starting from the time that the Saint, converting to Christ, had forgotten about all the things of the world[63], he no longer wanted to rest on a mattress or keep a feather pillow beneath his head, and this strictness was not curbed either by his illness or by his staying at other people's houses. Instead, it happened at the hermitage in Greccio that, bothered more than usual by his eye disease, he was forced to use a small cushion against his will. Accordingly, after the first night, he called to a brother companion at dawn and said, "Brother, I couldn't sleep last night nor could I stay awake in prayer. My head is shaking, my knees are trembling and my whole body is unsteady, as if I had eaten bread made of chaff. I believe that the devil is right in this cushion I have under my head. Take it away, because I don't want to keep the devil under my head any longer." At that complaint, the brother, feeling compassion for the Father, took the cushion that was tossed to him in order to take it away. As he was leaving, however, he suddenly lost the power of speech and was so greatly oppressed and blocked by fright that he could not even lift his feet off the ground or move his arms in the least. A short time later, realizing what had happened, the Saint called to him and, thus liberated, the brother returned and recounted his plight.

The Saint said to him, "Last night while I was saying complines[64], I clearly sensed that a devil was entering the cell." Then he went on, "Our enemy is very astute and has a subtle mind: since he cannot do any harm within the soul, he tries at least to give the body reason to complain."

---

[63] *Acts* 11, 21; *2 Cor* 7, 33-34.
[64] The last evening prayers.

Those who place cushions around on all sides[65] so that they will find softness wherever they turn should think about this! The demon willingly follows the abundance of comfort and enjoys staying near sumptuous beds, especially when there is no need for them or they are forbidden by the religious profession. And the ancient serpent[66] is equally ready to flee from the man who is stripped of everything, because he despises the simplicity of the poor man and fears the nobility of poverty. If a brother considers that under the feathers lies the devil, he will be happy to lay his head on straw.

Examples of his aversion for money

CHAPTER XXXV
The harsh correction of the friar who had
touched money with his hands

45. Although that great lover of God disdained all of the world's vanities, he execrated money above all. He held it in contempt from the very beginning of his conversion and he instilled in his followers that they should flee from it as if it were the devil in person. This is the trick he suggested to his own: they should consider money as dung.

Now it happened that a layman who had come into the church of St. Mary's of the Porziuncola to pray placed an offering of money at the foot of the cross. As soon as he had left, a brother simply picked it up and flung it onto the windowsill. The Saint heard about the action of this brother who, finding himself to be at fault, ran to beg forgiveness and, throwing himself down on the ground, he prepared himself to receive his punishment. The Saint scolded him harshly for having dared to touch money

---

[65] Adaptation of *Ez* 13, 18.
[66] *Rev* 12, 9.

and then ordered him to pick it up from the window with his mouth, take it outside the fence of the convent and place it, with his mouth, onto donkey dung. As the brother willingly obeyed this order, all the others were filled with fear.

For the future, all of them learned to disdain even more what had been compared to dung in this way and each day, they were stimulated by new examples of such scorn.

CHAPTER XXXVI
The punishment of a brother who once picked up money

66. Walking together one time, two friars arrived at a leper hospital. Along the way, they found some money and stopped to discuss the best thing to do with this sort of dung. One of them, laughing over the other's scruples, tried to pick it up to offer it to the lepers' servants. His companions stopped him, telling him that he had been deceived by false piety and repeating to this dare-devil the words of the Rule, which instilled in them that found money must be trod upon like dust.[67] But the other one, who was proud by nature, turned a deaf ear to these warnings and, violating the Rule, bent over and touched the coins. He did not escape divine punishment, however, for he immediately lost the power of speech, his teeth chattered and he was unable to speak. The unhealthy was thus visibly afflicted and through punishment, that proud man learned to obey the laws of the Father.

After throwing that filth away, at last his contaminated lips, washed with the waters of penance, burst into praise according to the ancient proverb: Correct a fool and he will become your friend.[68]

---

[67] *Rule of 1221,* chap. 8.
[68] *Prv* 28, 23.

CHAPTER XXXVII
*His reproach of the brother who wanted
to set money aside under the pretext of need*

67. One time the Saint's vicar, Brother Peter Catanii[69], seeing that St. Mary's of the Porziuncola was often visited by a crowds of foreign brothers and that the alms were not sufficient to provide for their needs, said to St. Francis, "Father, I don't know what to do, because I do not have enough to be able to provide for the numerous brothers who flock here from all over. I ask that you please arrange for part of the property of the novices entering the Order to be set aside, so that we can resort to it to spending it when necessary." The Saint replied, "My dear brother, far be it that such piety, which arises out of love towards man, should lead us to become impious in our observance of the Rule."[70] So the other man asked, "Then what should I do?" He said, "Strip the altar of the Virgin and take the decorations away if there is no other way to assist the needy. Believe me, she will be much happier to see her Son's Gospel observed and her own altar bare than to see the altar fully adorned but her Son scorned. The Lord will then take care of sending someone who will give the Mother what she has lent to us."

CHAPTER XXXVIII
Of the money that turned into a snake

68. The man of God, who was traveling through Apulia with a companion, found a large bag filled with money -- the kind of bag that shopkeepers call a "saddle-bag" -- on the road near Bari. His companion urged him insistently to pick up the bag and donate the money to the poor, praising piety towards the needy

---

[69] Peter Catanii died at the Porziuncola on March 10, 1221 and was buried there, as indicated in the thirteenth-century epigraph on the outside wall of the chapel.
[70] *Rule of 1221* and *1223*, chap. 2.

and lauding the distribution of that money as a work of mercy. But the Saint soundly refused, stating that it was a trick of the devil. "It is not right, son, to take others' things, and donating the property of others is a sin that will be punished rather than being considered merit and glory." Off they went, hurrying to complete the journey they had begun.

That brother, however, deceived by false charity, was not satisfied and continued to suggest this breach. The Saint agreed to return to that spot, not to satisfy his companion's wish but to demonstrate God's secret to that fool. He called over to a young man seated near a well along the way, so that the secret of the Trinity would be manifested in the presence of two or three witnesses[71].

The three of them went back to the bag and saw that it was stuffed with money. The Saint ordered that no one go near it so that the demon's deception would be revealed by virtue of prayer. Then he stepped back by about a stone's throw[72] and began to pray. When he returned from his prayers, he ordered the brother to pick up the bag which, through his prayers, now held a snake instead of money. The astonished brother trembled and through an ashamed premonition, was of quite a different mind than before. Nevertheless, out of fear that he would fail to fulfill holy obedience, he set all uncertainty aside and picked the bag up and a large snake jumped out, thus showing the brother this diabolical trap.

And the Saint admonished him, "Brother, for the servants of God, money is none other than a devil and a poisonous snake."

---

[71] *Mt* 18, 16; *2 Cor* 13, 1.
[72] *Lk* 22, 41.

Of the poverty of their clothing

CHAPTER XXXIX

How through his words and examples, the Saint rebuked, those who dress luxuriously and elegantly[73]

69. Clothed in virtue from on high[74], this man warmed himself more from the divine fire within than with bodily garments on the outside. He detested the brothers of the Order who wore triple layers of clothing and those who needlessly used luxurious habits. He asserted moreover that this need, which was not dictated by any reason but was put forward by pleasure as an excuse, was the sign of a dead spirit. He would say, "When the spirit is lukewarm and is gradually losing the heat of grace, it necessarily ensues that flesh and blood will follow their instinct. When the soul no longer finds its delight, what else is left but for the flesh to turn to its own delights? At that point, animal appetite is disguised with the word 'need' and the senses shape the conscience." He also added, "Even if our brother should find that he is truly in need and is oppressed by some want, if he hurries to satisfy and eliminate this need, what reward can come of this? An opportunity for merit was offered to him, but he clearly felt that it was a burden to him."

With these and other arguments, he needled those who were insufferable of need, since failure to bear it patiently is none other than a return to Egypt.[75]

Lastly, on no occasion did he want the brothers to have more than two tunics, but he would allow them patch them. He ordered them to abhor fine clothing and in front of everyone, he would sharply rebuke anyone who did the opposite. To shame

---

[73] See *Rule of 1221* and *1223I*, chap. 2.

[74] *Lk* 24, 49.

[75] In other words, to the land of pleasure and slavery instead of the Holy Land. This is an allusion to the Hebrews who, in the desert, looked back with regret on their slavery in Egypt. See also *Nm 14, 2-4.*

them through his example, he had a rough sackcloth stitched onto his tunic and even as he was dying, he requested that his burial robe be covered with sackcloth.[76] However, he allowed the brothers who were ill or who were forced by other needs to wear a softer tunic underneath against their skin so that the roughness and poverty of their habits would be preserved on the outside nevertheless. In fact, he would say, "Rigor will yet be relaxed greatly and warmth will dominate, so that the sons of such a poor father will not even be ashamed to wear scarlet clothing[77], changing it only in color."

We degenerate sons, and not you, Father, have belied this and it is rather our iniquity that bears false witness in its own interest[78] and so it is that laxity becomes as clear as daylight and grows more and more by the day.

CHAPTER XL

He declared that those who withdraw from poverty will be punished with indigence

70. At times he would also repeat, "When our brothers withdraw from poverty, the world will likewise draw away from them and they shall seek but will not find.[79] Instead, if they have remained in the embrace of my lady poverty, the world will maintain them because they will have given themselves to the world for its salvation." He also said, "There is a sort of contract between the world and the brothers: they must give the world a good example and the world must provide for their needs. If they go back on this agreement by failing to provide a good example, the world will withdraw its hand in just punishment."

---

[76] The cloth used for his last tunic was brought from Rome by Jacomina de' Settesoli.

[77] The finest cloth was dyed scarlet, so what is meant here is precious fabric.

[78] *Ps* 27, 12.

[79] A play on *Mt* 7, 8.

Attentive towards poverty, the man of God feared that his brothers would grow too much in number, because this look like wealth even though this was not the case. Therefore, he would say, "O! If it could come to pass[80], I say, let it come to pass that the world, rarely seeing the Brothers Minor, should esteem them because of their small number!"

Tied to Lady Poverty by an unbreakable bond, he expected her dowry, not in this life but in the next. The psalms that talk about poverty, such as *The needy shall not always be forgotten*[81] or *See, you lowly ones, and rejoice*[82], were sung aloud by him with more fervent love and greater joy.

On begging for alms

CHAPTER XLI
In its praise

71. The holy Father would use those alms begged from door to door with much greater pleasure than the ones offered spontaneously. He said that being ashamed of begging was an obstacle to salvation, whereas the shame that one felt in begging without withdrawing on account of it, was holy. He praised the blush that rises to one's face out of frailty, but not the shame of embarrassment. At times, in order to exhort his own to go begging, he would say, "Go, because the Friars Minor have recently been given to the world so that the elect might do works for them through which they will be praised by the Judge: *As often as you did it for one of my least brothers, you did it for me.'*[83] Because of this, he said that his order was beloved by the great Prophet[84] who had so

---

[80] *Mk* 14, 35.

[81] *Ps* 9, 19.

[82] *Ps* 69, 33.

[83] *Mt* 25, 40-45.

[84] Jesus Christ.

indicated it through its very name, and therefore he wanted the brothers to stay not only in the towns, but also in the hermitages, so that there would be grounds for merit for all and the reprobate would lack any semblance of excuse.

CHAPTER XLII
The example the Saint gave of seeking alms

72. In order not to offend his holy bride even once, this is what the servant of the Most High would usually do. At times, if he was to be honored with sumptuous tables when invited by gentlemen, first he would beg for pieces of bread from the houses nearby and thus enriched by misery, he would sit down at the table. When asked sometimes why he did this, he would reply that he did not want to lose a permanent inheritance over a fief granted for an hour. He would explain, "It is poverty that makes us heirs and kings in the kingdom of heaven, and not your false riches."[85]

CHAPTER XLIII
The example given to the Curia of the bishop of Ostia;
and of his reply to the bishop

73. One time when St. Francis was a guest of pope Gregory of venerable fame but who was still of lesser rank[86] at that time, he went off to beg when it was time for dinner and, upon his return, he placed bits of black bread on the table of the bishop, who was somewhat embarrassed at the sight of this, especially since new guests were also there. But with a happy face, the Father distributed the alms he had received to the knights and chaplains

---

[85] *Jas* 2, 5 and *Rm* 8, 17.
[86] When he was still a cardinal.

who were dinner guests. All of them picked them up with great devotion, some of them eating them while others set them aside out of devotion.

When dinner was over, the bishop got up and, calling the man of God to his chamber, he opened his arms and embraced him. "My brother," he said, "why did you insult me this way in the house that is yours and your brothers' by going around for alms?" And the Saint said to him, "Instead, I honored you by giving honor to a greater Lord, for God is pleased by poverty and above all by willing mendicancy. Furthermore, I consider it to be royal dignity and illustrious nobility to follow that Father who, though He was rich, made himself poor out of love for us."[87] And he added, "I feel greater delight in a poor table set with small alms than in a large one at which you can hardly even count the number of courses." And the bishop, who was quite edified, concluded, "Son, do what is best in your eyes, for the Lord is with you."

CHAPTER XLIV
Of his exhortation to beg for alms, through his example and his words

74. Sometimes for his own mortification and other times out of regard for his brothers' embarrassment, in the beginning he alone would go begging. Then, seeing that many did not respond to their vocation out of duty, he once said, "Dearest brothers, the Son of God was nobler than we are, yet He made Himself poor in this world of us.[88] Out of love for Him, we have chosen the path of poverty and therefore, we must not feel embarrassed about going begging. It is not fitting for the heirs to the kingdom to blush over the pledge of heavenly inheritance. I say to you that many nobles and learned men will join our congregation and they

---

[87] *2 Cor* 8, 9.
[88] *2 Cor* 8, 9, also included in the *Rule of 1223*, chap. 6.

shall consider it an honor to go begging. And you, who are the first fruits, rejoice and be glad and do not refuse to do what you will be handing down for those saints to do!"

CHAPTER XLV

How he reprimanded a friar who did not want to beg

75. Blessed Francis often said that the true Friar Minor should never hesitate to go begging. "And the nobler one of my sons is," he would say, "then the more prepared he is to go, since his merits will grow in this way."

There was a brother in a convent who didn't do enough begging even for one, but who ate enough for many. Seeing that he was a person who loved his belly and shared in the results but not in the effort, this is how the Saint once reprimanded him: "Go your own way, brother fly, since you want to eat of the sweat of your brothers and lie lazily in God's field. You are like the drone who, shirking the bees' efforts, wants to be the first one to eat the honey."

When he saw that his gluttony had been revealed, that carnal man returned to the world that he had not yet fully abandoned. He left the Order and he who had not done enough begging even for one was no longer counted as a brother. He who had done the work of many at the dinner table became a very capable demon.

CHAPTER XLVI

*How he went out to meet a brother who was bringing alms
and kissed him on the shoulder*

76. Another time at the Porziuncola, as soon as a brother who was on his way back from Assisi with alms drew near the convent, he began to chant songs, praising the Lord aloud. When

he heard him, the Saint jumped up, bounded outside and, kissing the brother on the shoulder, he took the bag upon his own shoulder, saying, "My blessed brother, who goes forth readily to beg humbly and then returns exultant!"

CHAPTER XLVII
How he persuaded some lay soldiers to ask for alms

77. It happened that while blessed Francis, quite ill and already close to death, was staying in the convent in Nocera[89], he was requested by people of Assisi, who sent a solemn embassy to get him so that the glory of possessing the body of the man of God would not be left to anyone else.[90] When the knights who were reverently accompanying him on horseback reached a very poor little town by the name of Satriano, they felt that they needed some food, both out of hunger and because of the time of day. However, unable to find anything to buy no matter how hard they looked, they went back to St. Francis and said to him, "You'll need to give us some of your alms, because we can't find anything to buy here." The Saint replied, "You can't find anything because you put more trust in your flies (he referred to coins as flies) than in God. But," he added, "go back to the houses you have just visited and, offering the love of God instead of money, beg humbly for alms. Do not be ashamed, for all good has been granted as alms after sin and that great Almsgiver donates with clement generosity to the worthy as well as the unworthy."

Setting aside their embarrassment, the knights went to ask for alms and obtained much more through the love of God than they would have with money, since everyone hastened to donate willingly. Hunger no longer prevailed where rich poverty had prevailed.

---

[89] The town of Nocera Umbra is east of Assisi along the Flaminian Way.
[90] *Is* 42, 8 and 48, 11.

CHAPTER XLVIII

Of the piece of capon that was turned into a fish
in Alexandria

78. As far as alms are concerned, he sought them more to gain souls than for the sustenance they gave to the flesh and he was an example to others in both giving as well as receiving.

In Alexandria of Lombardy[91], where he had gone to preach the divine word, he was the guest of a God-fearing man who enjoyed a good reputation. When the man asked him to eat every good thing that would be set in front of him, in order to observe the holy Gospel[92] he nodded kindly, won over by his host's attentions. Having obtained this promise, the man hastened to have a seven-month capon prepared for dinner. While the Patriarch of the poor was seated at the table with that festive family, there came to the door a child of Belial, devoid of all grace, and feigning that he was without the essentials of life, he astutely begged for alms out of the love of God and asked mournfully to be helped in God's name. The Saint, hearing the blessed name that, above all else, was sweeter to him than honey[93], solicitously took a piece of the chicken that was in front of him, put it on some bread and had it given to the beggar. Well, this wretch saved the gift as an affront to the Saint.

79. The next day, the Saint was preaching the word of God to the people who had assembled, as was his custom, when that scoundrel suddenly shouted and tried to show everyone the piece of capon. "Here," he prattled, "who is this Francis who is preaching and who is honored by you as a saint? Look at the meat he gave me last night while he was eating." But everyone reproached him and accused him of being possessed by the devil. In fact, what he declared to be the thigh of capon appeared to every-

---

[91] The city founded by the Lombard League against Frederick Barbarossa. The city is now in the Piedmont region.

[92] The passage from *Lk* 10, 8 is included in *Rule of 1223*, chap. 3.

[93] *Ps* 72, 17 and 19.

one to be a fish. Even that rogue, amazed by the miracle, was forced to acknowledge what the others were saying. In the end, he felt ashamed and through penance, he was cleansed of the sin for which he was guilty. He begged the Saint for forgiveness in front of everyone, revealing his poor intentions.

The meat then regained its original appearance after that corrupt man had returned to his senses.

Of those who renounce the world

CHAPTER XLIX

The example of one man who distributed his property to his relatives rather than to the poor, and of how the Saint reproached him

80. The Saint taught those who entered the Order to renounce the world first of all and to offer God their exterior goods before donating the interior gift of the soul.[94] He would only admit those who had stripped themselves of everything without keeping anything, not only in deference to the words of the Holy Gospel[95] but also so that there would be no scandal on account of any goods that were kept aside.

81. It so happened in the March of Ancona that, after one of the Saint's sermons, a man went up to him and humbly asked if he could enter the Order. And Francis said, "If you want to join the poor ones of God, first distribute your possessions to the poor of the world." When the man heard this, he went away and, led by bodily love, he gave his things to his family and gave nothing to the poor. But when he returned and told the saint of his munificent generosity, the Father reproached him, saying, "Go your own way, brother fly, for you have not left your house or

---

94 *Mt* 5, 30. *Rule of 1221*, chap. 2 and *Rule of 1223*, chap. 2.
95 *Mt* 19, 21, which is also included in the first chapter of *Rule of 1221*.

your kinsfolk yet.[96] You have given your things to your relatives and have cheated the poor. Therefore, you are not worthy of the saintly poor ones. By starting from the flesh, as you have done, you have laid a ruinous foundation for the edifice of your spirit."

That natural man[97] went back to his family and wanted all his things back, soon losing his virtuous intentions because he had not wanted to leave his property to the poor.

Many people today allow themselves to be deceived by a similar pitiable semblance of detachment and they seek sainthood by starting out as worldly people. Yet no one consecrates himself to God in order to make his relatives rich, but does so to redeem himself from his sins at the price of mercy and thus to gain eternal life through the fruits of good works.[98]

He also often taught that "whenever the friars are in need", they must rely on others rather than on their novices, first of all as an example, and then to avoid any appearance of base profit.

CHAPTER L

Of a vision about poverty

82. Here I would like to report one of the Saint's visions that deserves being recalled. One night, at the end of a long prayer, he got drowsy and slowly fell asleep. In a dream, that saintly soul who had entered the sanctuary of God[99] saw among other things a strange-looking woman: her head seemed to be made of gold, her chest and arms of silver, her belly of crystal and her lower limbs of iron. She was tall, slender and shapely, yet the woman, so lovely in appearance, was clothed in a filthy cloak.

---

[96] *Gn* 2, 1.
[97] *1 Cor*, 14.
[98] *Rm* 2, 7 and *Phil*, 22.
[99] *Ps* 73, 17.

When he got up in the morning, the Father recounted his vision to a holy man, Brother Pacificus[100], but without explaining its meaning.

Even though many have interpreted it in their own way, I believe that we can unerringly accept the interpretation of the aforesaid Brother Pacificus, which was suggested by the Holy Spirit even as he heard the vision being recounted. That is, the woman of extraordinary beauty was St. Francis' beautiful soul, the golden head was the contemplation and knowledge of eternal possessions, the silver chest and arms were God's words as they were contemplated in the heart and put into practice through deeds; the crystal stood for moderation in its rigidity and chastity in its splendor; iron was steadfast perseverance. Lastly, the filthy cloak was the wretched body that covers the precious soul.

Instead, many people filled with the divine inspiration saw the woman as the Father's bride, Poverty, saying, "She is made to resemble gold for the prize of glory, silver to illustrate fame, crystal for the total renunciation that is the same both inside and out and iron for final perseverance, while the opinion of bodily men has woven a wretched cloak over this noble woman."

The majority trace this as a symbol of the Order, following Daniel in his division of the eras.[101] Nevertheless, it seems obvious that it represents the Father, above all because of the fact that he was unwilling to give his interpretation of it in order to avoid pride. Instead, if it had alluded to the Order, he would not have remained silent.

---

[100] Whose conversion is the subject of n° 106 below.

[101] *Dn* 2, 31-45. This image, varied somewhat, is reminiscent of Dante's allegory of the Guardian of Crete (*Inferno* XIV, 94-120).

Of St. Francis' compassion towards the poor

CHAPTER LI
*Of his compassion towards the poor and
how he envied those who were poorer than he*

83. Who can repeat how compassionate this man was towards the poor? Certainly, he was already compassionate by nature, but his goodness was doubled by the charity instilled in him
by heaven. He felt his spirit moved to pity for the poor and if he
could not offer someone material help, he would offer his love.
Any need, any deprivation he saw in anyone, he would relate to
Christ with rapid and thankful consideration. Thus, in all the poor
he would see the Son of the poor Madonna, carrying Him naked
in his heart just as she had carried him naked in her arms. Indeed,
he who had driven out all feelings of envy could not help but envy
poverty. Whenever he saw anyone who was poorer than he, he
would immediately envy him and would be afraid that the other
one would surpass him in the contest of poverty.

84. One day while the man of God was going about
preaching, he happened to meet a poor man and, seeing that he
was half naked, filled with compunction he turned to his companion to tell him, "That man's misery puts us to great shame and
greatly reproaches our poverty." His companion asked him,
"Why, brother?" And in a mournful voice, the Saint answered, "I
have chosen poverty as my wealth and my wife and here it is, even
more resplendent in this man. Perhaps you don't know that we
are renowned throughout the world as being the poorest of all out
of love for Christ, but that man persuades us that this isn't so."

O unprecedented envy! Emulation that the sons, in turn,
should emulate. This is not the envy that is saddened by someone
else's good, nor is it the one that is darkened by the rays of the
sun, nor the one that opposes mercy or is tormented by spite. Do
you believe that evangelical poverty possesses nothing that is

worth envying? It has Christ and because of Him, it possesses everything in all things.[102]

Clergy of our times, why do you covet gain? Tomorrow you will realize how rich Francis was, once you find the gains of affliction on your hands.

CHAPTER LII

How he corrected a friar who was speaking badly
about a poor man

85. Another time during his apostolic preaching, a poor man, who also happened to be ill, went to his refuge. Commiserating with the man's double misfortune, meaning his misery and illness, he began to speak to his companion about poverty. Given that his compassion for the afflicted man had already become heartfelt affection, his companion said to him, "Brother, it's true that he is poor, but perhaps there is no one in the whole province who loves wealth more than he." The Saint immediately upbraided him and, as the latter was acknowledging his fault, he ordered him, "Quickly, take off your tunic, throw it at that poor man's feet and confess your offense. And it is not enough for you just to beg his forgiveness: you must also ask him to pray for you." The brother obeyed him, went to do his penance and returned. The Saint said to him, "O brother, when you see a poor man, remember that the mirror of the Lord and of his poor mother has been placed before you. Likewise with the sick, think about the illness that He bore out of love for us!"

Thus, that little sachet of myrrh was always deep in Francis' heart and he always had the Man of suffering who knows all infirmities in his mind![103]

---

[102] *1 Cor* 12, 6.
[103] *Sg* 1, 12; *Ps* 84, 10 and *Is* 53, 3.

CHAPTER LIII

Of the cloak he gave an old woman in Celano

86. It happened near Celano that during the winter, St. Francis was wearing as a cloak a piece of cloth given to him by a man from Tivoli who was a friend of the brothers. In the palace of the bishop of Marsi, an old woman went up to him to ask him for alms. He immediately loosened the cloth from around his neck and even though it was not his, he gave it to her saying, "Go, make yourself a dress because you really need one!"

The old woman smiled and, dumbfounded -- I don't know whether out of fear or pleasure -- she took the cloth from his hands and quickly ran off. Then, in order to avoid the risk of being asked to return it, she cut it with some scissors without waiting another second. However, realizing that the cloth that had been cut by this time would not be enough for a dress and feeling encouraged by the goodness she had already experienced, she went back to the Saint and showed him that there was not enough cloth. He glanced over at his companion, who was wearing a cloth of the same size around his shoulders, and said, "Brother, do you hear what this poor woman is saying? Out of the love of God, let us bear the cold and give her your cloth so she can finish her dress." Just as Francis had given, so did his companion and they unclothed themselves so that the old woman could be clothed.

CHAPTER LIV

Of another cloak given to another poor person

87. Another time, on his way back from Siena, he encountered a poor man and the Saint said to his companion, "We must give this poor man the cloak that belongs to him! We received it as a loan until we could find someone poorer than we are." The companion, knowing how much the merciful Father needed it,

was firmly opposed to the idea that he should neglect himself to provide for others. But the Saint said, "I don't want to be a thief. We would be accused of robbery if we failed to give the cloak to the person who needs it the most." The other brother was forced to give in and he gave the cloak away.

CHAPTER LV

Of another similar event

88. The same thing happened to him at Le Celle in Cortona. Blessed Francis was wearing a new cloak that the brothers had taken the trouble to find for him. A poor man came up, weeping over his dead wife and his poor abandoned family. The Saint said, "I will give you this cloak out of the love of God, as long as you do not give it to anyone unless they buy it from you for a good price."

The brothers immediately ran to take the cloak away and prevent such generosity. But the poor man, who had become bolder at the sight of the holy Father's kind face, defended it tooth and nail as if it were his own. In the end, the brothers bought the cloak back from him and the poor man went off with the money he had gotten in exchange.

CHAPTER LVI

How he gave a cloak to someone
so he would not hate his master

89. One time at Colle, in the countryside around Perugia[104], St. Francis saw a poor man whom he had already met while he was still in the world and he asked him "Brother, how are you?"

---

[104] At Collestrada, a town that marked the boundary between the Communes of Assisi and Perugia. St. Francis' family owned a piece of land here.

However, the man began to curse his master with great animosity for he had taken away all his possessions. He said, "Thanks to my master -- Almighty God curse him! -- I can only be badly off."

Moved to pity more for his soul than for his body, since the man persisted in mortal hatred, blessed Francis said to him, "Brother, pardon your master for the love of God, in order to free your soul from sin, and perhaps he will give you back what he has taken. Otherwise, just as you have lost your possessions, you'll also lose your soul." But the man replied, "There is no way that I can forgive him unless first he gives me back what he has taken from me." Blessed Francis, who was wearing a cloak, said to him, "Here, I'll give you this cloak and I beg you to forgive your master out of love for the Lord our God."

The other man, who became meeker and was moved by this benefaction, took the gift and forgave the wrongs he had received.

CHAPTER LVII
How he gave a poor man a strip of his tunic

90. One time, when he heard a poor man asking him for alms but had nothing on hand, he unstitched a piece of his tunic and gave it to him. Sometimes he would also take off his trousers for the same reason.

He was compelled by such deep piety towards the poor and through these feelings, he followed in the footsteps of poor Christ.

CHAPTER LVIII
*How he had the Order's first New Testament
given to the poor mother of two brothers*

91. The mother of two friars went to the Saint one day to ask him confidently for alms. The holy Father felt compassion towards her and asked his vicar, Brother Peter Catanii, "Can we give our mother some kind of charity?" In fact, he referred to each friar's mother as his own mother and as the mother of all the friars. Brother Peter replied, "There is nothing left in the house for us to give her!" Then he added, "All we have is a New Testament which we use to read lessons at matins since we don't have a breviary." So blessed Francis said, "Then give our mother the New Testament so that she can sell it to take care of her needs, since it is precisely this New Testament that instructs us to help the poor. Therefore, I believe that the Lord would be more pleased by this gift than by the readings."

The book was given to the woman and thus the Order's first New Testament was given away out of holy charity.

CHAPTER LIX
*How he gave a cloak to a poor woman
with an eye disease*

92. At the time in which St. Francis was staying at the bishop's palace in Rieti to have his eyes treated, a poor woman from Machilone, who had the same disease as the Saint, went to see his doctor. Turning to address the guardian, Francis began to hint to him, "Brother guardian, we must return what belongs to others." And the latter replied, "Let's give it back, Father, if we've got it!" He replicated, "This cloak that was lent to us by that poor woman -- let's give it back to her because she doesn't have any money for her expenses." The guardian then replied, "But brother, this cloak is mine and it wasn't lent to me by anyone.

You can use it as long as you like, but when you don't need it anymore, give it back to me." In fact, the guardian had bought it just a short time before because St. Francis needed it. The Saint answered, "Brother guardian, you have always been courteous to me. Now please demonstrate your courtesy!" The guardian replied, "Father, do freely what the Spirit has suggested to you."

The Saint then called a very devout layman and said to him, "Take this cloak and twelve loaves of bread, and go say to that woman, 'That poor man to whom you lent your cloak thanks you for the favor, but now you should take what belongs to you'."[105] The man went and related what he had heard, but the woman, thinking she was being made fun of, turned red and replied, "Leave me alone with that cloak of yours. I don't know what you mean." The other one insisted and, indeed, put everything right into her hands. Thus, seeing that she was not being tricked and afraid that this unhoped-for gain would be taken away from her, she got up during the night and no longer caring about her treatment, went home with the cloak.

CHAPTER LX

How three women appeared to him on the road
and then disappeared after they had greeted him in a singular way

93. I will briefly recount a miraculous event whose interpretation is uncertain but whose occurrence is really most certain. On his way from Rieti to Siena for his eye treatment, the Poor One of Christ was crossing the plains near Rocca Campiglia with a physician devoted to the Order as his travel companion, when three poor women appeared on St. Francis' path. They were so similar in height, age and appearance that you would have thought that all three of them had come from the same mold. When St. Francis arrived, they reverently bowed their heads and extolled him with

---

[105] *Mt* 20, 14.

this unusual greeting: "Welcome, Lady Poverty!" The Saint was immediately filled with unspeakable joy, for there was no title with which men could address him that pleased him more than the one the three women had just bestowed upon him. At first, he thought that they were truly three poor women and turning to the doctor who was accompanying him, he said, "I beg you, for the love of God, let me give something to those poor women." The doctor immediately took out his purse and dismounted from his horse to give each of them some coins. They had proceeded a little further when, looking around suddenly, the brothers and the doctor could no longer see a single woman across the entire plain. They were greatly surprised and counted this event as one of the Lord's miracles, realizing that they who had flown away faster than birds could not have been women.

Of St. Francis' love of prayer

CHAPTER LXI
Of the time, place and fervor of his prayers

94. Exiled from the Lord in body[106], Francis, the man of God, sought to bring his spirit to heaven and he had already become a fellow citizen of the angels, from whom only the shield of the flesh separated him. His entire soul thirsted for his Christ and he dedicated not only all his heart, but also his whole body to Him.

Of the marvels of his prayers, we will relate just a few parts of what we have seen with our own eyes, insofar as they can be conveyed to human ears, for those who come after him to imitate.

---

[106]   *2 Cor* 5, 6.

He turned all his time into sacred repose, during which he wrote the teachings of Wisdom in his heart, out of fear that if he did not always keep moving forward he would fall back.

At times, if there were visits from laymen or there was some business to handle, he would interrupt them rather than waiting until they were over and would withdraw in meditation. In fact, since he had eaten heavenly sweetness, the world held no flavor for him and with his palate refined by divine delights, he could not stand the coarse food of mankind.

He always looked for secluded places where he could be united with God not only in spirit but practically with all his limbs as well. And if he suddenly felt that the Lord was visiting him while he was with others, he would make a cell out of his cloak in order not be without one. Then, if he even lacked this at times, in order to keep the secret of hidden manna from being seen, he would cover his face with his sleeve. He always placed something between himself and those present so that they would not be able to perceive his contact with the Groom. Thus, in narrow places he would pray unseen even though he was among many people. Lastly, if none of these things were possible, he would make his chest into a temple: when he was in ecstasy, he would even forget about weeping and wailing[107] and, fully absorbed in God, would not sigh or give any external signs.

95. This was among men. But when he would pray in the forest and in solitude, he would fill the woods with sighs, bathe the ground with tears, beat his chest with his hands and there, as if he had found a more recondite sanctuary, he would often converse aloud with his Lord. There, he would respond to Him as to a judge, beseech Him as a father, converse with Him as with a friend and he would delight in his Groom. In fact, in order to make every fiber of his heart a holocaust in different ways, he would gaze upon Him who is One in essence under many appear-

---

[107] Intended as external manifestations of his feelings.

ances.[108] Often he would talk to himself without moving his lips and by concentrating all external senses internally, he would make his spirit ascend to heaven. In this way, he would turn his whole mind and heart only to what the Lord asked. No longer was he a man praying, but he himself became a true prayer.

How much sweetness do you think must have inundated him if he was accustomed to praying this way? He knows[109] and I cannot help but admire him. Anyone who has experienced this will be given to know it, but it will not be granted to whomever has not experienced it. And when his keen spirit burned this way, his whole glance and his entire ecstatic soul too were already set in the highest spheres of the heavenly kingdom.[110]

It was the blessed Father's custom not to miss any visit of the divine Spirit out of his own carelessness and instead, he was ready to welcome it each time it was offered to him and would enjoy the sweetness given to him for as long as the Lord would allow. Thus, if while he was occupied with some task or was traveling he felt the touch of grace, he would savor that sweetest manna often but at intervals. Truly, even on the road, he would let his companions go ahead, stopping in order to enjoy the new inspiration and thus he did not receive grace in vain.[111]

CHAPTER LXII
Of his devout recitation of the canonical Hours

96. He would recite the canonical hours with no less reverence than devotion. In fact, although his eyes, stomach, spleen and liver were diseased, during their chanting he did not want to lean against the wall of the wooden partition of the choir but al-

---

[108] Adaptations from *Ps* 66, 15 and 101, 3 and from *Wis* 7, 22.
[109] *Jb* 28, 23.
[110] *Jb* 41, 22; *Wis* 7, 22; *Sg* 5, 6.
[111] *2 Cor* 6, 1.

ways fulfilled the duty of the hours upright and without his hood on, without looking around and without interruption.

If he was traveling on foot, he would always stop to recite the hours and if he was on horseback, he would dismount. Thus, one day as he was coming back from Rome under driving rain, he dismounted from his horse to recite the Office and since he had stayed on his feet for a long time, he was soaked through and through.

And sometimes he would explain the reason: "If a body tranquilly eats the food that will become a meal for worms along with it, how much more peace and tranquillity will the soul need to takes its food, which is God Himself?"

CHAPTER LXIII
How he would drive away distraction during prayer

97. He considered it a grave sin if he was distracted at times by vain reverie during prayer. If this were the case, he would not hesitate to make his confession in order to atone for his error, and he took such diligent care to pay attention that he was very rarely disturbed by flies[112] of this sort.

Once during Lent, he had been working on a vase during his spare time so that he would not pass this time lazily. So one day, as he was devoutly reciting Terce[113], since his eyes happened to fall on it, he felt the inner man hindered in his fervor and regretting that the voice of his heart had ceased to rise to the ears of God, as soon as Terce was over, the brothers heard him exclaim, "Ah, frivolous work that had the great power to distract my soul to it! I will thus sacrifice it to the Lord, since it hindered my sacrifice to Him." So saying, he took the vase and threw it on the fire to burn, adding, "We should be ashamed of letting ourselves be

---

[112] Note Francis' custom of calling all worldly things "flies" (see also n° 77 above).

[113] The third prayer of the Divine Offices, recited at mid-morning.

distracted by foolish daydreams when in prayer we can speak to the great King."

CHAPTER LXIV
Of an ecstasy

98. Many times, he would be so taken up with the great sweetness of contemplation that, rapt in ecstasy, he then would not want to tell anyone about the superhuman things he had experienced. Nevertheless, through a single event that took place in public, we can deduce how frequently he was engrossed in heavenly sweetness.

One day, while he was riding on the back of a donkey, he had to pass through Borgo San Sepolcro[114] and since he had planned to rest in a leper hospice, many learned that he would be passing through there. Men and women hastened there from all over to see him and out of their usual devout desire to touch him. So what happened? They touched him, shook him and cut pieces of his cowl in order to put them aside, but he seemed to be insensitive to everything and like dead man, he did not notice anything. They finally drew near the hospice long after they had left Borgo and, as if he were returning from some other place, that contemplator of heavenly things pensively asked when they would reach Borgo.

CHAPTER LXV
How he acted after prayer

99. Whenever he returned from his solitary prayers, during which he was virtually transformed into a different man, he would

---

[114] In Tuscany, near Arezzo. The Saint was returning from Mount La Verna after he had received the Stigmata.

strive to make himself like the others again so that he would not lose what he had gained on account of the admiration that his inflamed appearance would have caused.

In this regard, he would often say to those close to him, "When God's servant, in praying, is visited the Lord with some new consolation, before leaving his prayers, he must raise his eyes towards heaven and, putting his hands together, say to the Lord: 'You have sent this sweet solace, Lord, from heaven to me, an unworthy sinner, and I am entrusting it to you again so that you can keep it for me, for I am a thief who has stolen your treasure.' And then 'Lord, take your good away from me in this world to give it back to me in another life'." He went on, "This is how one must act so that when he leaves his prayers, he shows himself to the others as a wretch and a sinner, as if he had never achieved any grace at all." He would also say, "It can happen that for a small reward, one can lose an inestimable benefit and easily provoke Him who granted it never to give it again."

Lastly, he was in the habit of getting up to pray so secretly and quietly that none of his companions would be aware of when he got up or when he prayed. Instead, in the evening when he was going to bed, he would make noise, loudly even, so that everyone would hear that he was going to rest.

CHAPTER LXVI

*How a bishop who surprised him as he was praying
lost the power of speech*

100. When St. Francis was praying at the Porziuncola, it happened that the bishop of Assisi came to him for a friendly visit, as usual. As soon as he reached the convent, he went to the Saint's cell somewhat irreverently without being summoned and, having knocked on the door, he was about to go in. Accordingly, as soon as he poked his head in and saw the Saint praying, he immediately began to shiver and while his limbs turned stiff, he also

lost the power of speech. Then through divine will, he was violently driven back and dragged far away.

I think that this occurred either because he was not worthy of observing that mystery or because the other man was worthy of keeping the grace he was already enjoying for a longer time.

Amazed, the bishop returned to the brothers and he first of all attempted to confess his fault, thus regaining the power of speech.

CHAPTER LXVII
How an abbot felt the efficacy of St. Francis' prayer

101. Another time, the abbot of the monastery of San Giustino[115], which is in the diocese of Perugia, ran into St. Francis and quickly dismounting from his horse, he stopped to dwell a bit with him about the state of his soul. Finally, as he was leaving, he humbly asked Francis to pray for him. The Saint replied, "I will pray willingly, lord." The abbot had gone off a little way when the Saint said to his companion, "Wait a minute, brother, because I want to keep my promise." In fact, it was his custom never to neglect requests for prayers but rather, to fulfill this kind of promise as soon as possible. And as the Saint was interceding with God, that abbot immediately felt an unusual warmth and sweetness of spirit that he had never felt before so that, rapt in ecstasy, he thought he would faint. He stopped for a while and when he returned to his senses, he understood the efficacy of St. Francis' prayer. Because of this, he felt even greater love towards the Order and told many people that this event was a miracle.

It is fitting that the servants of God should give each other such gifts and that there should be this exchange of favors between them. That holy love, which at times is called spiritual love, is content with the goodness of prayer and charity considers

---

[115] The Benedictine monastery of San Giustino at Massa d'Arno.

worldly gifts base. I believe it is part of sacred love to help and to receive help in spiritual battles, to defend and be defended before the tribunal of Christ.[116]

But if, through his merits, he could raise up another man, what great heights do you suppose he himself must have reached in prayer?

CHAPTER LXVIII
Of the Saint's knowledge of the Holy Scriptures, and of the efficacy of his words

102. Although this blessed man was not nourished by the study of human knowledge[117], he was nevertheless learned in the wisdom that comes from God and, shining with the splendor of eternal light, he understood the core of the scriptures well. In fact, his mind, which was not darkened by any stain, penetrated the difficult mysteries and through his love, he could enter where the learning of doctors was left outside. Every so often, he would read sacred books and what he had allowed to enter his spirit even once would be written indelibly in his heart. "His memory took the place of books," for if a truth came to his ears even once, it was the constant subject of his devout and loving meditation. He would say that, as opposed to leafing through thousands and thousands of treatises, this way of learning and reading yielded many good results. He considered anyone who placed nothing before the desire for eternal life to be a true philosopher. He also asserted that anyone who was a humble and unpresumptuous seeker in applying himself the Scriptures would move easily from knowing himself to knowing God. He often resolved dubious matters accurately and, without refined words, he revealed a treasure of intelligence and virtue.

---

[116] *2 Cor* 5, 10.

[117] This is an exaggeration meant to counter scholarly fanaticism. Nevertheless, the Saint certainly was not as ignorant as he claimed to be.

CHAPTER LXIX

Of a prophetic saying that a preaching friar asked him to explain

103. While he was staying in Siena, a friar from the Order of Preachers, a spiritual man who was a doctor in sacred theology, stopped there. When this man went to visit St. Francis, the scholar and the Saint held a long and very sweet conversation about the words of the Lord. Now, this teacher also questioned him about this passage from Ezechiel: *If you do not warn the wicked man of his wicked conduct ... I will hold you responsible for his death*[118], adding, "O good Father, I know that many people with whom I am acquainted are in mortal sin, but I don't rebuke them for their fault. Could this mean that I will have to answer for their souls?" And since the Blessed said that he was a simpleton who needed to be taught by him rather than be the one to give an answer about a sentence from the Scriptures, that humble teacher went on, "Brother although I have heard the explanation of this passage from several wise men, I would nevertheless like to hear your opinion." Blessed Francis answered him, "If this saying is to be understood in general terms, I believe it means that the servant of God must be so burning in holiness within himself that he will reprimand all the wicked with the light of his example and the eloquence of his actions.[119] So I say that the splendor of your life and the odor of its fame will show everyone their own iniquity." The other man was greatly edified and, as he was leaving, he said to the Saint's companions, "My brothers, the theology of this man, which is based on purity and contemplation, soars like an eagle[120]. Instead, our learning slithers with its belly on the ground."

---

[118] *Ez* 3, 18.

[119] Here the Saint states the importance of bearing witness through one's way of life.

[120] *Jb* 9, 26.

CHAPTER LXX

Of how he answered a cardinal's questions

104. While he was in Rome at a cardinal's house on another occasion, when he was questioned about some obscure passages, he elucidated such profound ideas that you would have thought he had always lived among the Scriptures. And the lord cardinal said to him, "I am not questioning you as if you were a scholar, but as one who has the spirit of God within him, and I joyfully welcome your explanations because I know that they proceed solely from God."

CHAPTER LXXI

*How he explained his idea of learning to a brother who exhorted him
to the zeal of reading*

105. While he was ill and completely wracked with pain, one of the brothers who was close to him said, "Father, you have always turned to the Scriptures and there you have always found a remedy for your pain. Therefore, I beg you, now too, have one of the passages of the prophets read to you and perhaps your spirit will rejoice in the Lord." And the Saint said to him, "Reading the testimonials of the Scriptures is a good thing and seeking the Lord our God there is a good thing too, but I have already taken in so much of them that all I have to do to think about them again is meditate. I don't need anything else, son: I know the poor and crucified Christ!"[121]

---

[121] *1 Cor* 2,2.

CHAPTER LXXII

*Of the resplendent swords that Brother Pacificus saw on the
Saint's face*

106. In the March of Ancona, there was a worldly man,
unmindful of himself and unaware of God, who had given himself over completely to the vanities. He had been nicknamed "the
king of verse" for he was the prince of vain singers and the writer
of secular songs. To be brief, I will just say that this man had risen
to such great glory that he was crowned by the emperor in great
pomp.[122]

Now, as he was walking this way in darkness, dragging a
sinful life along by the cords of vanity[123], divine mercy was moved
to compassion for that wretch and decided to summon him so
that he who was lying on the ground would not perish[124].

By divine arrangement, he met blessed Francis at one of
the cloisters of Poor Sisters[125], where the blessed Father had gone
with his companions to greet his daughters, while the other man
had gone with his cohorts to visit a relative of his.

But as the hand of the Lord came upon him[126], with his
bodily eyes he saw St. Francis pierced by two very dazzling swords
set like a cross, one of which went from his head to his feet while
the other sword went across his chest from one hand to the other.
He did not know blessed Francis yet, but he quickly recognized
him through that miraculous indication. Amazed by that visit, he
resolved to live a better life, even though he thought he would put
off carrying this out. However, as soon as the blessed Father began to preach before everyone, he struck him by the sword of the
word of God. Then he warned him secretly and sweetly, especially

---

[122] Frederick II.

[123] *Is* 5, 18.

[124] *2 Kgs* 14, 14.

[125] The monastery of the Poor Women of the Holy Savior in Colpersito, near
San Severino.

[126] *Ez* 1, 3.

about vanity and contempt for the world, and lastly, he pierced his heart with threats of divine judgment. Hesitating no longer, the other man replied, "What's the use of going any further? Let's move into action: take me away from man and give me to the great Emperor!"

The next day, the Saint gave him a habit and he named the man he had brought back to the peace of God Brother Pacificus. His conversion edified at least as many people as there had been in his multitude of companions in vanity.

Happy over his intimacy with the blessed Father, Brother Pacificus began to experience a sweetness that he had never felt before. Truly, once again he was able to see what was concealed from the others. In fact, a short time later, on blessed Francis' forehead he saw a large "Tau" sign[127] that, eyed with little multi-colored circles, was as beautiful as peacock feathers.

CHAPTER LXXIII
Of the efficacy of his words;
and of the testimony given by a physician

107. Even though Francis, proclaimer of the Gospel, preached slowly and simply to ignorant men, knowing full well that there is greater need for virtue than for beautiful words, he nevertheless uttered life-giving and profound words among spiritual and more learned men.

He would concisely explain what was almost impossible to say and, accompanying his words with fiery gestures and energy, he would bear his listeners up to heaven. He did not make use of the device of distinction, since he did not need to organize discourses that did not require him to exert his imagination.[128] His

---

[127] *Ez* 9, 4. St. Francis loved to sign his writings using the Greek letter "tau", which is shaped like a cross.

[128] Since he spoke through divine inspiration.

voice was given the force of virtue by true virtue and wisdom, Christ.[129]

A physician, a learned and eloquent man, once said, "I remember other men's sermons word for word, but St. Francis' are the only ones I can't remember this way, and even if I can commit part of them to memory, they no longer seem to be the ones that originally came from his lips!"

CHAPTER LXXIV

How through the power of his words, he drove the demons from Arezzo through Brother Sylvester

108. His words were not only very effective when spoken directly, but at times they achieved the required goal even if they were uttered through an intermediary. It thus happened that one time, he arrived in the city of Arezzo while the city, devastated by civil war, was on the brink of disaster. The man of God, who had received hospitality in a quarter outside the city, saw exultant demons over it who were urging the citizens to slaughter their fellow countrymen. He thus called a friar by the name of Sylvester, a suitably simple man of God, and he enjoined him, "Go before the gates of the city and, on God's behalf, order those demons to leave immediately." The pious and simple man hastened to carry out this obedience and offering praise before the Lord[130], he vigorously shouted in front of the gate, "On God's behalf and by order of our father Francis, go far from here, all you demons!"

A short time later, peace returned to the city and civil rights were maintained in great peace. Thus, when blessed Francis subsequently preached to the people of Arezzo, his preamble would start like this: "I am speaking to you, who were once subjugated

---

129 *Ps* 68, 34.
130 *Ps* 95, 2.

and enthralled by the devil, but whom I know were liberated through the prayers of a poor man."

CHAPTER LXXV
The conversion of this same brother Sylvester;
and of one of his visions

109. I believe it would not be out of place here to add the account of the conversion of the aforesaid Sylvester, of how he was moved by the Spirit to enter the Order.

Sylvester was a secular priest in the city of Assisi and the man of God had bought some stones from him to repair a church.[131] Now, having seen at that time that Brother Bernard, who was the first little plant in the Order after the Saint of God, had given up everything he possessed and had given it to the poor, Sylvester, burning with greed, complained to the man of God about the stones he had sold him, as if he had not been paid in full. Francis smiled compassionately, realizing that the priest's spirit had been poisoned by avarice. Nevertheless, since he wanted to quench that cursed thirst, he filled the man's hands with coins without even bothering to count them. The priest Sylvester was pleased by the gift, but was even more amazed by the generosity of its donor and when he was home again, he began to reflect on what happened. He continued to rebuke himself, wondering why, as he was getting older, he still loved the world and in the meantime, he also wondered how that young man could spurn everything in that way. When he had been filled with these good inclinations at last, Christ opened up the bosom of His mercy towards him.

In a vision, He showed him the great worth of Francis's works, how they shone before His eyes and how magnificently

---

[131] It seems that he was canon at the Cathedral of San Rufino. The church referred to was St. Damian's, the first one of the three restored by St. Francis.

they filled the whole world. In fact, in a dream he saw that coming out of Francis' mouth was a golden cross "with its top reaching to the heavens, whose outstretched arms"[132] encircled the world in their embrace.

Filled with compunction at this sight, the priest avoided any further harmful delay, abandoned the world and became a perfect imitator of the man of God. He began to live a perfect life in the Order, completing it most perfectly through the grace of Christ.

Yet why should it be any wonder that Francis appeared to him crucified, since the cross was all he had? What prodigy is it that the miracle-working cross, which had become so deeply rooted in him, should bring flowers and branches forth from such good earth and produce such wonderful fruit? Nothing else could have sprung from that ground but the marvelous cross that had claimed him as its own from the very start.

But now let us return to our subject.

CHAPTER LXXVI
Of a brother who was liberated from a demon's assaults

110. A brother had long been afflicted by spiritual temptation, which is far more subtle and worse than the urgings of the flesh. At last, turning to St. Francis, he humbly threw himself at his feet and bathing them with the bitterest of tears, he was unable to utter a single word because he was sobbing so heavily. The merciful Father was moved to compassion by him and, realizing that he was being disturbed by the influence of evil, he said, "O demons, in the name of God I order you to stop assaulting my brother the way you have dared to do until now." The veil of darkness was lifted at once, the brother got up liberated and, as if nothing had ever happened, he was never troubled again.

---

[132] *Gn* 28, 12.

CHAPTER LXXVII
Of the cursed sow who ate a lamb

111. The miraculous power that his words also had over beasts has been revealed elsewhere.[133] However, here too I will recount an anecdote that I have on hand.

One night while the servant of the Most High was a guest at the monastery of San Verecondo in the diocese of Gubbio, a ewe gave birth to a little lamb. A cruel sow was also there and without any consideration for the life of that innocent, it killed it in one voracious bite. When the men got up in the morning, they found the dead lamb and realized that the sow was guilty of the misdeed. Upon hearing this news, the pious Father was moved to great compassion and remembering another Lamb, he grieved over the death of the little animal and exclaimed in front of everyone, "Ah, little brother lamb, innocent little animal who offers mankind such a useful image! Cursed be the piteous one who killed you: let no one, either man or beast, eat of its flesh!" Miracle! The evil-doer immediately fell ill and after three days of agonizing pain, was punished by death. It was tossed into the ditch near the monastery, where it remained for a long time, drying out like a piece of wood without being eaten by anyone, no matter how hungry they were.

Against familiarity with women

CHAPTER LXXVIII
About avoiding familiarity with women;
and of how he spoke with them

---

[133] N° 167-171 and *First Life*, n° 58-71.

112. The sweet poison of familiarity with women, which can lead even saints astray, taught him to avoid it completely.[134] In fact, he feared that the weak in spirit would quickly be broken by this and that at the very least, even the strong would often be weakened. He said that unless a man of proven virtue is involved, keeping their company while escaping their seduction, as it says in the Scriptures, is as easy as walking on fire without scorching the soles of one's feet![135]

In order to reinforce this teaching with deeds, he offered an example of such virtue within himself.[136] Women were so troublesome to him that you would have thought it wasn't because of prudence and example, but out of true fear or horror. When he had to face their importunate loquacity, he would impose silence through the brevity and humility of his words, lowering his eyes. Instead, at times he would remain with his eyes looking up to heaven, as if he would find the answer there to that worldly babbling.

Instead, with his marvelously brief discourses, he instructed those women whose spirits had become a temple of wisdom through assiduous devotion. Whenever he spoke with any woman, he would utter each word in a loud voice so that it could be heard by all.

One time, he said to a companion, "Dear one, I honestly confess that if I were to look them in the face, I would only recognize two of them. I know both of their faces very well, but I don't know anyone else's."[137]

Quite so, O Father, for no one is sanctified by looking at them. Quite so, I must add, because they do not bring any profit but great harm and even temporal ruin. They are an obstacle to

---

[134] *Rule of 1221*, chap. *12* and *Rule of 1223*, chapter *11*.

[135] *Prv 6, 27-28.*

[136] *Ru 4, 11* and *Ti 2, 7.*

[137] Most scholars feel that St. Clare and Jacomina dei Settesoli are being referred to here, although a few retain that the reference is to Francis' mother and to St. Clare.

anyone who wishes to undertake the arduous path of sanctity and see the divine face shining with grace.

CHAPTER LXXIX
A parable against looking at women

113. With the following parable, he also wanted to condemn immodest eyes.

A very powerful king sent two messengers to the queen, one after the other. The first one returned and related only the words of the sovereign, for his eyes had been prudent[138] and had not rested on her. The other one came back and, after referring the brief embassy, sang the praises about the lady's beauty. "Truly, o sire, I saw a most beautiful woman. Happy the man who can delight in her!" And the king said, "Disgraceful servant,[139] you laid your indecent eyes upon my bride? Of course you would want to make yours the creature that you have gazed upon with such attention!" He had the first one called and asked him, "What do you think of the queen?" The messenger replied, "Excellent impression, since she listened in silence and replied sagely." And he insisted, "And isn't she beautiful?" "Lord, she is for you to look at. My only duty was to bring the message." So the king pronounced, "You whose eyes are chaste and whose body is even more chaste can remain in my chambers, but he must leave my palace so that he will not violate my nuptial bed."

The blessed father also said, "Being overly self-confident makes us less cautious of the enemy. If the devil can have even a man's single hair at his mercy, he will immediately enlarge it to the size of a beam. And even though he has not succeeded in bringing down the man he has been tempting for many years, this does not mean he will give up, just as long as he can get him to surrender in

---

138 *Eccl* 2, 14.
139 *Mt* 18, 32.

the end. This is, in fact, his task and day and night, he is interested in nothing else."

CHAPTER LXXX
The Saint's example against excessive intimacy

114. It once happened that St. Francis, who had planned to go to Bevagna, was unable to get as far as the town on account of the weakness that fasting had caused him. Therefore, his companion sent a messenger to ask a devout woman humbly for a bit of bread and wine for the Saint. As soon as she heard this, she hastened bring him what he needed, going together with one of her daughters, a virgin consecrated to God. The Saint, quite refreshed and invigorated, rewarded the woman and her daughter by speaking to them about God, but during his discussion he never looked them in the face.[140] After they left, his companion asked him, "Brother, why didn't you look at that virgin, who came to you with such devotion?" And the Father replied, "Well, why shouldn't one be afraid of looking at the bride of Christ? Because if one's eyes and face made preaching more effective, she could look at me, but there was certainly no need for me to see her!"

When he spoke on this subject, he often declared that, with the exception of confession or some brief spiritual advice, any other dialogue with women was useless. In fact, he explained, "What does the Friar Minor have to do with women, except when holy penance or counsel on a better life have devoutly been requested of him?"

---

[140] *Ps* 83, 10.

Of the temptations he had to suffer

CHAPTER LXXXI
Of the Saint's temptations and how he overcame one of them

115. As St. Francis' merits grew, so did his clashes with the ancient serpent, because the more grace the former received, then the more subtle the cunning and the stronger the violence the latter would use to fight him. Although he had found him to be a courageous and valiant warrior, who had not ceded in battle for even an hour, he nevertheless kept striving to attack the invincible.

During one period in his life, the holy Father underwent enormous spiritual temptation that is certain to have increased his reward. Thus, he was tormented and, filled with anguish, he afflicted his body with mortification and prayed and wept bitterly. After many years of this struggle, one day while he was praying at St. Mary's of the Porziuncola, he heard a voice within him saying, "Francis, if you have faith the size of a mustard seed, you will tell this mountain to move on, and it will move."[141] He replied, "Lord, what is the mountain that I should wish to move?" And again he heard, "That mountain is your temptation".

Weeping, he concluded, "Lord, let it be done as You have said!" The temptation was immediately gone, and he was freed and completely at peace within himself.

CHAPTER LXXXII
*How the devil, calling him by name, tempted him
with lust and how the Saint overcame this*

---

[141] *Mt* 17, 19.

116. At the friars' hermitage in Satreano, the evil one, who always envies the progress made by the children of God, dared to tempt him in this way.

Seeing that the Saint was becoming more and more sanctified[142] and that he never renounced the gain of the current day like those who are content with what they gained the previous day, one night while Francis was praying in his cell, he called him three times by name: "Francis! Francis! Francis!" And when he replied, "What do you want?", he answered, "There is no sinner in this world that the Lord will not forgive if he converts, but anyone who kills himself through harsh penance will not find eternal mercy." Through divine revelation, the Saint immediately recognized his enemy's trickery, understanding that he was trying to turn him to a life of tepidness.

What happened then? The enemy did not refrain from mounting a new assault against him. Realizing that he had not succeeded in disguising that trap, he prepared another one: the urge of the flesh. This was another vain attempt, for this carnal intent could not deceive one who had already unmasked that spirit's cunning. Thus the devil sent him a terrible temptation of lust, but as soon as the blessed Father felt it, he took off his habit and flogged himself violently with his cord, saying, "Come on, brother donkey, it is fitting for you to stay there like this and submit to these blows: the cowl belongs to the Order and cannot be stolen. If you want to go somewhere else, then go ahead."

117. However, seeing that he could not drive temptation away through discipline, even though all his limbs were already blotched with bruises, he left the cell to go into the garden and threw himself stark naked into the deep snow. Then he picked it up by the handful, made seven tall piles, sat down in front of them and began to tell his body, "Here, the tallest one is your wife, these other four are your two sons and two daughters and the last two are the servant and the maid that you need at your

---

[142] *Rev* 22, 11.

service. Now hurry up and dress all of them because they are dying of cold. Instead, if it's a burden for you to take better care of them, then quickly give yourself over to serving only the Lord."

At this point, the devil left disconcerted and the Saint returned to his cell, glorifying the Lord.

A spiritual brother, who had been praying as he kept watch, was able to see all this by the light of the moon. Shortly afterwards, since the Saint realized that he had been seen during the night and deeply regretted this, he ordered the other brother not to tell anyone what had happened for as long as lived.

CHAPTER LXXXIII
How he freed a brother from temptation, and of the benefits of temptation

118. One time, a brother who had fallen prey to temptation said to the Saint as he was sitting alone with him, "Pray for me, good Father. Indeed, I believe that I will be delivered of my temptations at once if you would deign to pray for me. I am truly tormented beyond my strength and I know that you yourself have perceived this." St. Francis answered him, "Believe me, son, it is precisely because of this that I think you are a servant of God. Know that the more you are tempted, the dearer you are to me." He went on, "In truth, I say to you that no one must consider himself a servant of God until he has gone through temptation and hardship. In a certain way, temptation that has been vanquished is the ring with which the Lord takes the soul of his servant as his bride. Many congratulate themselves on the merits they have gained over the years and rejoice that they have never experienced temptation of any kind, but they should also know that this is a sign that the Lord has taken their spiritual weakness into consideration, since terror alone would have sufficed to conquer them even before the battle. In fact, hard battles are only stirred up in those whose strength of spirit has been tested."

How the demons beat him

CHAPTER LXXXIV

*How the demons beat him
and how courts must be avoided*

119. Not only was this man assaulted by Satan through temptation, but he even engaged in hand-to-hand combat with him. Once when he was invited by lord Leo, Cardinal of the Holy Cross[143], to stay with him in Rome for a while, he chose a secluded tower that was divided into nine vaulted corridors that looked somewhat like small hermit-like cells. The first night as he was getting ready to rest after prayer, the demons arrived to pitch battle against the Saint of God and they beat him so long and so violently that they nearly killed him. After they had left and the Saint had gotten his breath back, he called to his companion who was sleeping under another vault and said to him, "Brother, I want you to stay near me because I am afraid of being on my own. Just a while ago, the demons beat me." In the meantime, his limbs had started to tremble as if he had a high fever.

120. After having spent that entire night wide awake, St. Francis said to his companion, "The devils are our Lord's stewards, whom He has destined to punish our sins. Indeed, it is a sign of even higher grace if they leave nothing unpunished in His servant as long as he lives in the world. I truly don't know if I have committed any offense[144] that the mercy of God[145] has not washed away through atonement. In fact, through his paternal goodness, the Lord has always been accustomed to showing me in prayer and meditation what pleases Him and what offends Him, but perhaps he has allowed his stewards to assault me precisely

---

[143] Leo Brancaleone was cardinal of the order of deacons, with the title of St. Lucille in Settizonio, and was subsequently cardinal of the order of priests, with the title of the Holy Cross in Jerusalem. He died around 1240.

[144] *Phil* 1, 10.

[145] *Rm* 12, 1.

because I set a poor example for others by staying at the court of great men. When my brothers who live in poor places hear that I am staying with cardinals, perhaps they'll suspect that I'm abounding in delight. Therefore, brother, I think it would be best for the one who has been set up as an example for others to imitate to flee the courts in order to encourage those who must bear hardship[146] by suffering the same way himself." When morning came, they told the cardinal what happened and took their leave of him.

Let the palatine friars[147] learn of this and know that they should consider themselves the unnaturally-born sons of such a mother.[148] I am not condemning their obedience here, but their ambition, their laziness and their laxity. Lastly, I propose Francis as a model for all obedience. Abandon everything that is displeasing to God, since it is pleasing to men![149]

CHAPTER LXXXV
An example in this regard

121. An example that I do not want to overlook comes to mind.

Upon seeing several religious who were living at a curia, a brother, enticed by I don't know what ambition, wanted to become a courtier together with them. During the time in which he longed greatly for a courtly life, one night in a dream[150] he saw that the aforesaid brothers were being kept out of the brothers' residence and segregated from the community. Moreover, he saw

---

[146] *Prv* 28, 27.

[147] The "palatines" were the friars who lived with noblemen and prelates as chaplains, under obedience to their superiors. In several of his letters, Innocent III also stated his case against the custom of certain religious to reside at court.

[148] *1 Cor* 15, 8 and *Lk* 1, 15.

[149] *Eccl* 5, 3 and *Ps* 52, 6.

[150] *Gn* 31, 24.

that they were eating chickpeas mixed with human feces from a filthy trough. The brother was very surprised at this sight and when he awoke at dawn, he no longer cared about the curia.

CHAPTER LXXXVI
Of the temptations he suffered in a solitary place,
and of a brother's vision

122. One time, together with a companion the Saint arrived at a church located outside of town. Wishing to pray in solitude, he informed his companion, "Brother, tonight I would like to stay here alone. You go to the hospice and come back to me early tomorrow morning."

Left on his own to address long and devout prayers to God, at last he looked around for a place to lay his head down to go to sleep. All of a sudden, his spirit was troubled and he began to feel afraid and distressed[151] and his whole body started to tremble. He could clearly feel that he was being assailed by the demon and heard the clamor of hordes of devils running along the roof of the church. He immediately got up and went outside, and making the sign of the cross on his forehead, he exclaimed, "In the name of Almighty God, I say to you, o demons, that you can do what you want against my body and I will bear it willingly. Indeed, since my own body is my worst enemy, you will be taking out my revenge on my adversary, punishing him in my stead." When those who had gathered together to terrify him saw that within the weak flesh the spirit was quite prepared, they quickly fled in shame.

123. When his companion returned in the morning, finding the Saint prostrate before the altar, he waited outside the choir and began to pray fervently before the cross. And there, as he was rapt in ecstasy, in the heavens he saw many chairs and in the middle was one that was more beautiful than the rest, adorned

---

[151] *Mk* 14, 33.

with precious stones and completely resplendent. He looked at it in admiration and began to wonder whose it was. Then, in the meantime, he heard a voice saying to him, "This chair belonged to one of the fallen angels and now it has been awarded to humble Francis."

When he finally came to his senses, the brother saw blessed Francis coming from his prayers and he quickly prostrated himself with his arms outstretched into a cross, as if he were before a spirit that is already triumphant in heaven rather than a man living in the world, and he said to him, "Pray for me, o Father, that the Son of God will not impute my sins to me!" The Saint stretched his hand out to him and picked him up, realizing that he had had a revelation. As they are leaving, the brother finally asked blessed Francis, "Father, what is your opinion of yourself?" and he replied, "I think I'm the greatest of sinners, because if such great divine mercy had been given to a scoundrel, he would certainly be ten times more spiritual than I am."

At this reply, the Spirit spoke within the friar's heart to say, "Acknowledge the truth of the vision you had, for humility will raise this most humble man to the throne that was lost through pride!"

CHAPTER LXXXVII
Of a brother who was freed of temptation

124. A brother of great spirituality who was one of the oldest ones in the Order, was tormented by a strong temptation of the flesh, so that he almost seemed to be swallowed up by the depths of desperation. His suffering doubled by the day and in the meantime, his conscience, which was even more scrupulous than it was judicious, compelled him to confess for no reason, since one does not feel bound to confess with great diligence to avoid suffering from temptation, but only if one has given in to it, even if just a little. He thus felt so very ashamed that, since he did not

dare to reveal everything that appeared to him to be a sin -- and was not -- to just one priest, he divided his disturbing thoughts and confided some things to one and some to another.

One day as he was walking with blessed Francis, however, the Saint said to him, "Brother, I say to you that you must no longer confess your tribulations to anyone. And fear not[152], for everything that takes place around you and that does not have your consent, will be attributed to you as merit and not as sin. The next time you are tempted, you should say seven *Our Fathers* on my instructions."

The other man was amazed that the Saint knew of his suffering and experiencing great joy, shortly thereafter he was freed of all temptation.

Of true spiritual joy

CHAPTER LXXXVIII
*Of his praise of joy
and of the negative effect of despondency*

125. The surest remedy against the thousands of traps and cunning of the enemy, our Saint declared, was spiritual joy. In fact, he would say, "The devil rejoices greatly when he can take a joyful spirit away from a servant of God. He brings dust that, just as soon as he can toss it through a small crack in the conscience, will sully candor of the mind and purity of life. But when hearts are filled instead with spiritual joy, the serpent spurts his deadly poison in vain. The demons cannot offend the servant of Christ when they see he is full of sacred joy, but they can when the spirit is bent on weeping, is desolate and afflicted, allows itself to be won over easily by sadness or lets itself be transported in vain pleasure."

---

[152] *Gn* 15, 1.

Therefore, he himself always tried to be happy and to maintain the anointment of the spirit and the oil of gladness.[153] He took great pains to avoid the terrible illness of despondency, so that when he could feel it seeping into his spirit even slightly, he would start to pray at once. He would also say, "As soon as the servant of God feels somewhat troubled, as can happen, he must immediately get up to pray and remain in the presence of the heavenly Father until salutary joy has been given back to him.[154] In fact, if he lingers in melancholy, that Babylonian evil[155] will grow and unless it is finally let out through tears, it will rust the heart indelibly."

CHAPTER LXXXIX

Of the lute he heard being played by an angel

126. During the time in which he was staying in Rieti for his eye treatment, he summoned one of his companions who had played the lute when he was in the world[156], and he said to him, "Brother, the children of the world do not understand the divine mysteries. Even musical instruments, which were once set aside to praise God, are used instead by men, greedy for pleasure, for the delight of their ears. Now brother, I would like you to have a lute given to you in secret. Then bring it here to me and so that with some honest music, you can give some relief to my brother body that is so full of pain." The friar answered, "Father, I am more than a bit embarrassed, because I'm afraid that men will think I've been tempted by levity of spirit!" And the Saint said to him, "Well then, brother, let's think no more about it. It's a good idea to give

---

[153] *Ps* 45, 8.

[154] *Ps* 51, 14.

[155] Francis would often use the term "Babylon" to mean mundane lifestyles. See also *Ez* 24, 6 and subsequent verses.

[156] This would probably have been Brother Pacificus, although it could also have been Brother Angelo of Rieti.

up a number of things in order to avoid offending others' feelings."

The next night as the Saint was sleeplessly meditating about God, there was suddenly the marvelous harmony and sweetest melody of a lute: there was no one to be seen, but the movement of the lute-player going to and fro could clearly be understood, because the sound would first come from over here and then from over there. With his spirit turned towards God, the holy Father felt himself overcome with such great sweetness at that sweet melody that he thought he had gone on to another world.

When he awoke the next morning, he called the aforesaid friar and told him everything that had happened, commenting, "The Lord, who comforts the afflicted, has never left me without solace and so, since I couldn't hear lutes played by men, I heard an even more delightful lute."

CHAPTER XC

How the Saint would sing in French when he was happiest

127. This is what he would do at times: the sweet spiritual melody running inside him would be expressed on the outside with songs in French, and the stream of divine whispers, furtively picked up by his ears, would spring forth in a jubilant hymn in the language of France. At times, as I myself have seen, he would pick a piece of wood up from the ground and would lay it in his left arm, while with his right arm he would take a small bow bent with string and scrape it along the wood like a viola, accompanying this with fitting gestures and singing the Lord's praise in French.

This jubilation would often end in tears and his jubilee would turn into compassionate weeping over the passion of Christ. Then he would breath deep sighs and, sobbing continuously and heedless of what was in his hands, he would remain engrossed with heaven.

CHAPTER XCI

*How he reproached a despondent brother
and taught him how he should behave*

128. One day he saw a companion of his with a sad and gloomy face and since he was not pleased by this at all, he said to him "It is not fitting for the servant of God to show himself to men as being sad and irate, but he must always be affable. Think about your sins in your cell and weep and wail there before your God, but when you come back among the brothers, set sadness aside and adapt yourself to the others." After a while, he also added, "The adversaries of human salvation envy me greatly and always try to give my companions the disturbance that they are unable to give me."

Indeed, so greatly did he love the man who was full of spiritual grace that one time during a chapter[157] , he had the following words written down as general advice: "Let the brothers beware of appearing gloomy and hypocritically sad on the outside. Instead, they should always show themselves to be happy in the Lord, smiling and cheerful and fittingly gracious."

CHAPTER XCII

How the body should be treated so it won't grumble

129. The Saint also said once, "Brother body must be provided for with moderation, so that it will not arouse the tempest of despondency. In order to keep it from feeling burdened by the vigils it keeps and the devout prayer it endures, it is a good idea to eliminate any opportunity for it to complain. In fact, it would have good reason to say, 'I'm fainting from hunger, I cannot bear the burden of your exercises in piety.' Instead, if it grumbles after it has had enough food, then you know that this lazy beast of

---

[157] Probably the one held in 1221.

burden needs to be spurred and that this reluctant donkey is waiting to be prodded."

This was the only teaching in which the actions of the most holy father went against his words. In fact, he kept his body in bondage with whips and fasting even though it was innocent, multiplying its punishments without cause[158], for the warmth of the spirit had shaped his body so much that just as his soul thirsted for God, his most holy flesh likewise thirsted just as much.[159]

Of foolish gaiety

CHAPTER XCIII
Against vainglory and hypocrisy

130. While spiritual happiness was dear to him, he took the greatest of care to avoid foolish joy, knowing that what is beneficial must be loved ardently and that what is harmful must be shunned just as promptly.

He thus tried to suffocate the seed of vainglory, not tolerating in himself even for an instant anything that could offend the eyes of his Lord. Many times, in fact, hearing that he was exalted with much praise, he grieved and moaned over this, immediately becoming sad.

One winter, since his poor body was clothed with a single tunic that had been reinforced with rather crude patches, his guardian, who was also his companion[160], bought a fox skin and gave it to him saying, "Father, your spleen and stomach are diseased. Out of the love you have for God, please let this skin be stitched inside your tunic. If you don't want to use all of it, at least

---

158 *Prv* 23, 29.
159 *Ps* 63, 2.
160 Probably Brother Angelo.

have a piece put over your chest." And the Saint replied, "If you want me to have this put under my tunic, then have a patch of the same size put on the outside so that the stitching on the outside will make people realize that I have a skin hidden inside!" The brother was reluctant to agree to this proposal and insisted again, but got no further. Finally, the guardian gave in and a patch was sewn on top of the other one, since Francis did not want his external appearance to be any different than what he truly was.

O consistency of words and of life, the same inside and out, subject as much as prelate! You did not want external glory, nor did you want any of your own, for you wanted to take pride only in the Lord! Yet I do not want to offend anyone who wears furs -- heaven forbid! -- when I say that they are wearing skin for skin[161], since we know that they needed fur when they were stripped of their innocence![162]

CHAPTER XCIV

One of his confessions against hypocrisy

131. Near the hermitage of Poggio[163] at around Christmas time, he once had large crowd assembled for his sermon and began by saying, "You believe that I am a holy man, and thus you have come here with devotion, but I must confess to you that throughout the entire Lenten season of Advent, I ate food seasoned with lard."[164] In fact, he often accused himself of gluttony over things that he had had to concede above all because of illness.

---

[161] *Jb* 2, 4.

[162] *Gn* 3, 21.

[163] Poggio Bustone, in the Rieti valley.

[164] During this forty-day period, which started on All Saints' Day, it was customary to eat food that was seasoned only with oil.

CHAPTER XCV
One of his confessions of vainglory

132. If his spirit was tempted by vainglory, he would immediately reveal this with a frank confession before everyone with just as much fervor. As he was walking through Assisi one day, he was approached by a little old woman who asked him for something.[165] Since he had nothing except his cloak, he generously gave it to her right away, but when he felt the workings of vain satisfaction creeping into his soul, he immediately confessed to everyone that he had felt conceited about it.

CHAPTER XCVI
His words in response to those who praised him

133. He tried to hide the Lord's gifts deep in his heart, for he did not want them to be his downfall by gaining him human glory. Therefore, when many people called him blessed, he would often reply by saying, "I can still have sons and daughters, so don't praise me as if I were safe! Never praise anyone whose end you don't know yet. If He who has given all good should want to take back what He has lent me, only body and soul would be left, things that infidels also possess."

This was his reply to those who praised him. Then he would say to himself, "If the Most High had given such great gifts to a thief, he would certainly be more grateful than you, Francis!"

---

[165] *Mt* 20, 20.

CHAPTER XCVII
His words against those who praised themselves

134. Then he would often say to the brothers, "No one should take undue pride in anything that a sinner can do as well. Indeed, the sinner can easily fast, pray, weep and mortify his own flesh. There is only one thing he cannot do: remain faithful to his Lord. Therefore, what we should be proud of is that we have rendered to God the glory that is due Him and that by serving Him faithfully, we have attributed to Him everything that He gives us. Man's greatest enemy is the flesh: it can remember nothing to grieve over and can foresee nothing to fear. Its aim is to abuse the present time and what is worse," he added, "is that it claims as its own and glories over things that have not been given to it but to the soul. It goes about seizing external praise for virtue and admiration for vigil and prayer. Leaving nothing to the soul, it even seeks to profit from tears."

Of the care he took to conceal the Stigmata

CHAPTER XCVIII
*What he replied to those who questioned him,
and of the care with which he hid it*

135. No silence must be kept about how many veils he used, about the great pains he took to hide those marks of the Crucified that were worthy of being venerated even by the highest spirits.

Right from the time in which the true love of Christ had virtually transfigured the lover into the image of his Beloved[166] , he very carefully began to hide and conceal that treasure, which not even those close to him perceived for a long time. Yet divine

---

[166] *2 Cor* 3, 18.

Providence would not allow it to remain hidden or be kept from the eyes of those dear to him. Indeed, since they were imprinted on the uncovered parts of his limbs, it was impossible for them to remain hidden.

One time, when one of his companions saw the Stigmata on his feet, he asked him, "What on earth is that, good brother?"

And he replied, "Mind your own business."

136. On another occasion, this same brother, who had gotten Francis' tunic to shake it out, saw that it was bloody and when he returned it to the Saint, he asked him, "What's that blood that seems to have stained your tunic?" So putting his finger over one eye, the Saint replied, "Why don't you ask me what this is as well, if you don't know that it's an eye!"

Thus, he would rarely wash his hands entirely but would just get his fingers wet so that nothing would be discovered by those present and he would wash his feet even more rarely and circumspectly. If anyone asked to kiss his hand, he would give half of it, extending his fingers just far enough for them to be kissed and sometimes, instead of giving his hand, he would even offer his sleeve. He covered his feet with woolen socks so that they couldn't be seen, putting a small patch of leather over the wounds to avoid any contact with the rough wool. Even though he was unable to hide the Stigmata on his hands and feet from his companions completely, he nevertheless suffered greatly when someone would look at them. Therefore, whenever he was forced to uncover his hands or feet, even his companions would very prudently look elsewhere.

CHAPTER XCIX
How a brother used a pious trick in order to see them

137. While the man of God was staying in Siena[167] , there arrived a brother from Brescia who ardently wished to see the holy Father's Stigmata and thus begged Brother Pacificus to let him do so. The latter said to him, "When you are getting ready to leave, I'll ask for his hands to kiss them and when he stretches them out to me, I'll wink at you and that way, you'll be able to see them." When he was preparing to leave, they both went to the Saint and, kneeling down, Brother Pacificus said to St. Francis, "Bless us, dearest mother[168] , and give me your hand so I can kiss it." The Saint reluctantly give it to him, Brother Pacificus kissed it and signaled for the other brother to look. Then he also asked for the other hand, kissed it and showed it to the brother as well. As soon as they had gone off, however, the Father suspected that there had been a pious stratagem and deeming that holy curiosity to be irreverent, he immediately had Brother Pacificus summoned again and reproached him, "May the Lord forgive you, brother, for at times you cause me great suffering!" Pacificus threw himself at his feet and humbly asked, "What suffering have I given you, dearest mother?" Blessed Francis did not reply and everything ended in silence.

CHAPTER C
Of the wound in his side that was seen by one of the brothers

138. Even though the very need to keep his hands and feet uncovered revealed the Stigmata to some, no one was worthy of seeing the wound in his side during his lifetime, with the exception of a single friar and even then just one time. In fact, every

---

[167] Winter/spring of 1226.
[168] A term of endearment to show their great affection for the Saint.

time he had his frock shaken out, he would cover the wound in his side with his right arm and sometimes, he would also cover the blessed wound by placing his left hand over his pierced chest.

Nevertheless, while one of the companions[169] was giving him a rub, he let his hand slip over the wound, causing Francis great pain.

Another one of the brothers[170], curious to see what had been concealed from the others, said to the holy Father one day, "Father, would you like me to shake your cowl out a bit?" and the Saint replied, "May the Lord reward you, for I need it." Thus, observing him closely as he was getting undressed, the brother saw the wound in his side uncovered. He was the only one to see it while the Saint was still alive and no one else saw it until after his death.

CHAPTER CI

How one's virtues are to be concealed

139. This man had thus renounced all glory that did not taste of Christ[171] and in this way he had placed an eternal anathema on human favor. He was well aware that the price of fame diminishes inner worth, and that it is much more harmful to abuse virtues than not to have any at all. He also knew that it is no less of a virtue to preserve them than it is to acquire them[172].

Alas! We instead are driven more by vanity than by charity and the world's favor prevails over the love of Christ. We do not examine our love, we do not ensure ourselves of the spirit that moves us[173] and when conceit spurs us into action, we believe we

---

[169] Rufino, as indicated in Celano's *First Life,* 95, as well as in the *Treatise of Miracles*, 4 .

[170] Indicated by some scholars as John "de Laudibus".

[171] *Phil* 3, 19.

[172] Ovid, *Art of Love*, II, 213.

[173] *1 Jn* 4, 1.

have been led by charity. Moreover, if we do even a bit of good, we are unable to bear its weight[174] and rid ourselves of it in this life, no matter what it may be, so that we no longer have it when we are about to set foot on the other shore. We patiently bear not being good, but we find it unbearable not to appear and not to be considered good. Thus, we live completely through the praise of men, for we are nothing more than men.

On humility

CHAPTER CII

*St. Francis' humble demeanor, feelings and habits;
and against self-esteem*

140. Humility is the guardian and the pride of all virtues. If the spiritual edifice lacks this foundation, when the structure appears to be rising[175] it is instead even closer to ruin. Not only could such a virtue not be lacking in a man so rich in gifts, but indeed it was most abundant in him. In his own eyes, he was no more than a sinner -- him, embellished and dazzling with every form of sanctity! It was on this basis that he endeavored to construct his spiritual edifice, laying the foundation that he had learned from Christ. Heedless of his assets, he only kept his faults before his eyes, convinced that he lacked far more good than what he possessed. He was avid only to better himself and, not content with the initial virtues, he always wanted to gain new ones.

Humble in demeanor, even more so in spirit, humblest in self-esteem. There was no sign to indicate that this great man of God was a prelate, with the exception of this most dazzling gem, the least of the Minors.[176] This was the virtue, this the title, this

---

[174] *Jb* 31, 23.

[175] *Eph* 2, 21.

[176] This play on words is unfortunately lost in English. A very literal translation would be "the minimum among the minors".

the insignia that marked him as minister general. All arrogance was far from his words, all pose far from his gestures, all pomp far from his actions.

He had understood the meaning of many things through revelation, yet in expounding them, he preferred other men's interpretation. He deemed his companions' judgment as surer and others' views as better than his own. In fact, he would say that anyone who attaches importance to his own way of thinking has not left everything for the Lord. As for himself, he preferred reproof to praise, since the former spurred him to correct his faults while the latter drove him to fall.

CHAPTER CIII

His humility toward the bishop of Terni and toward a farmer

141. When he preached to the people of Terni, in order to commend him publicly when the sermon was finished the bishop of the city[177] said, "In this final hour[178], God has illustrated his Church through this contemptible, simple and unlettered poor man. Therefore, we must always praise God, knowing that He has not done this for every nation."[179] When he heard these words, the Saint was most pleased that the bishop had so explicitly declared that he was contemptible and as they were entering the church, he threw himself at his feet, exclaiming, "Truly, lord bishop, you have done me great honor, since only you have fully given me what is mine, whereas the others take it away from me. What I mean is that as a perspicacious man, you have separated what is precious from what is vile, giving God the praise and me my wretchedness."

---

[177] This was Rayncrius (1218-1253).
[178] *1 Jn* 2, 18.
[179] *Ps* 147, 20.

142. But the man of God was not only humble with magnates, since also with his peers and with those beneath him he was more willing to be admonished and corrected himself that to correct. Thus, one day as he was riding on the back of a donkey -- since, being as weak and ill as he was, he could not go on foot -- and he crossed through the field of a peasant who was working there, the man ran over in curiosity to ask him if he was Brother Francis. When the man of God humbly replied that he was the very person the man was asking about, the peasant warned him, "Take care to be as good as everyone says, because a lot of people have faith in you. Therefore, I exhort you never to do anything that is contrary to our hopes." At those words, Francis, the man of God, dismounted from the donkey and, prostrating himself before the farmer, he humbly kissed his feet[180], thanking him for deigning to caution him.

Even though he was so famous that many believed him to be a saint, he considered himself base before God and man, without taking pride in his fame nor in the image of sainthood that he enjoyed, nor also in the innumerable and holy brothers and sons that he had been given as the initial rewards for his merits.

CHAPTER CIV
How he renounced the office of General during a Chapter and of his prayer

143. In order to preserve the virtue of sacred humility, a few years after his conversion, during a Chapter he resigned the office of General before all the brothers, saying, "Now I am dead for you, but here is Brother Peter Catanii, whom you and I must obey."

Promptly bowing before him, he promised him obedience and reverence.

---

[180] *Lk* 7, 38.

The brothers wept and wailed sorrowfully, almost considering themselves as having been orphaned of such a father. When blessed Francis got up, he joined his hands together and raised his eyes towards heaven, saying, "Lord, I commit to You the family that You have entrusted to me until now. Since I can no longer take care of it because of the illnesses that You know about, sweetest Lord, I am entrusting it to the ministers. May they be held to account for it before you on Judgment Day, Lord, if any brother should perish either out of neglect or through their poor example or even because of the harshness of one of their reprimands."

He remained a subject until death and lived more humbly than anyone else.

CHAPTER CV
How he gave up his companions

144. Another time, he gave his companions up to the vicar, saying, "I do not wish to appear different from the others because of this privilege of freedom, but my companions should accompany me from place to place[181] as the Lord inspires them to do." And he added, "I've also seen a blind man who has a little dog to guide his way."

This, in fact, was his glory: he stayed away from any appearance of singularity and pride so that Christ's virtue would live within him

CHAPTER CVI
His words against those who aspired to office, and his description of the Friar Minor

---

[181] "Place" should be taken to mean "convent."

145. Seeing that some aspired to high office but that, aside from anything else, they were made unworthy of it by their very ambition of being at the head, he would say that those men were not Friars Minor but that they had forgotten their vocation and had fallen because of their pride. With numerous reprimands, he upbraided several wretches who had taken it very badly when they were exonerated from their office, in which they sought only honor and not duty.[182]

On this subject, he once said to his companion, "If I did not have the demeanor that I will describe to you, I would not consider myself a Friar Minor." He went on, "Now since I am the brothers' superior, I go to the chapter, preach, admonish the brothers and at the end, they go against me, saying, 'An unlettered and contemptible man is not fitting for us. Therefore, we do not want you to rule over us[183] since you don't speak well and you are simple and ignorant.' In the end, I am driven out ignominiously and am scorned by everyone. Now I say that if I have failed to listen to these words with my customary demeanor, with the usual heart-felt happiness and with the same intention of holiness, then I am not a Friar Minor at all."

He further added, "The prelacy is occasion for the downfall of the soul and praise for ruin, while a subject's humility is occasion for gain. Why then should we seek danger over sure gain, when we have only enough time to gain merit?"

CHAPTER CVII

How he wanted the brothers to be subject to the clergy and why

146. While he wanted his sons to live peaceably with all men[184] and to belittle themselves before everyone, he taught

---

[182] Here again, the word play is lost in English: *onus* (duty) is set against *honoris* (honor).

[183] *Lk* 19, 14.

[184] *Rm* 12, 18.

through his words and demonstrated through his examples that they must especially be humble with the clergy. Indeed, he would say, "We have been sent to assist the clerics in saving souls, in order to compensate for their shortcomings. Each one will receive his reward according to his toil and not according to the authority he enjoyed.[185] Know, brothers, that the good of the soul is most pleasing to God and that this is best carried out by being at peace with the clergy rather than by going against them. If then they are an obstacle to the salvation of the people, revenge is up to God and He will punish them in due course.[186] Therefore, be subject to the prelates so that no envy will be aroused insofar as you are concerned. If you are children of peace, you will gain both clergy and the people for God, which is what is dearest to God, rather than gaining only the people but outraging the clergy. Cover their falls, compensate for their many faults and be even more humble in accomplishing all this."

CHAPTER CVIII
Of his reverence toward the bishop of Imola

147. One time when St. Francis arrived in Imola, a city in Romagna, he presented himself before the bishop[187] and asked for permission to preach. The bishop said, "Brother, I am more than enough to preach to my people." St. Francis humbly bowed his head and left, but after a short time, he went back in and the bishop said to him again, "But what do you want, brother? What else are you asking for?" So blessed Francis replied, "Lord, if a father kicks his son out one door, he must go back in through the other one." Won over by this humility, the bishop embraced him with a smile and said to him, "From now on, you and all your

---

[185] *1 Cor* 3, 8.
[186] *Deut* 32, 35.
[187] Mainardino Aldighieri was bishop of Imola from 1207 to 1229.

brothers have my general permission to preach in my diocese, since your saintly humility fully deserves it."

CHAPTER CIX

Of his humility with Saint Dominic and of Saint Dominic's toward him, and of their mutual affection

148. Together with the bishop of Ostia, who later became Supreme Pontiff[188], those resplendent luminaries of the world, St. Francis and St. Dominic, happened to meet in the Eternal city.[189] After both of them had spoken most sweetly about God, that bishop said at last, "In the early Church, the shepherds of the Church were poor and burned with charity rather than cupidity. Why then don't we elect bishops and prelates from among your friars, who would teach the others and set an example for the others."

The two saints raced to answer, not to try to surpass each other, but in order to urge and, indeed, to force the other one to be the first to answer. Truly each one was greater than the other, for each one admired the other. In the end, humility prevailed in Francis because he did not want to be the first to reply, and in Dominic because he obeyed by being the first to respond, and his answer to the bishop was, "Lord, if they have understood this, my friars have been elevated to a good position and insofar as I am able, I will not allow them to obtain any other sort of rank." After these very brief words, blessed Francis bowed down before the bishop and said, "Lord, my friars are called minor so that they will not presume to become greater. This very name teaches them to remain lowly and to follow in the footsteps of Christ's humility so that in the end, they will be exalted to the presence of the saints even more than the others. If you want them to yield good results

---

[188] Gregory IX.

[189] This meeting probably took place in 1220 or at the very beginning of 1221. In fact, Dominic died on August 6, 1221 and was canonized on July 3, 1234.

in the Church of God, maintain and preserve the state of their vocation, and even if they should want to elevate themselves, bring them down. Therefore, father, to keep them from becoming prouder than they are poor and to keep them from becoming arrogant with others, I beg you not to allow them to ascend to the prelacy in any way."

These were the answers that the two blessed ones gave.

149. What do you say, children of saints? Jealousy and envy are proof of your degeneracy, just as the ambition for honor demonstrates your illegitimacy. You bite and devour each other and war and quarrels arise solely out of cupidity. You should struggle against the hordes of darkness, battle strongly against diabolical armies, yet instead you twist the sword around against yourselves. With their faces looking toward the propitiatory[190] the fathers very wisely gazed upon each other amicably, while their children, full of envy, cannot bear the sight of each other. What then will the body do if its heart is divided?

The teaching of piety would certainly yield greater fruits the world over if the ministers of the word of God were united by a stronger bond of charity.

Indeed, what we are saying or teaching is rendered suspect by the fact that obvious signs have shown that a certain spark of hatred exists between us. I am well aware that on both sides it is not the good who are involved, but the bad, whom I believe should be eradicated so that they will not ruin the saints as well.

What shall I say then about those who are ambitious? It is through the way of humility and not the path of loftiness that our fathers have reached the kingdom. If their sons walk in the labyrinth of ambition, they will not seek the way to the heavenly city that is their home.[191] What else can remain but that we who fail to follow their same path will also fail to achieve their glory? O Lord, far be such evil from us![192] Make the disciples humble under the

---

[190] *Ex* 25, 20.

[191] *Ps* 107, 4.

[192] *Jos* 24, 16.

wings of such humble teachers, keep the brothers in spirit united by the bond of affection, and may you see your children's children as pledges of peace in Israel.[193]

CHAPTER CX

How they commended themselves to each other

150. When God's servants had finished answering as we said, the cardinal of Ostia, supremely edified by the words of both of them, gave great thanks to God. As he was about to leave, blessed Dominic asked St. Francis if he would kindly give him the cord he wore around his waist. Francis showed great reluctance, refusing with a humility that was equal to the charity of the other man's request, but in the end, the pious devotion of the petitioner prevailed and Dominic very devoutly tied the cord that had been given to him under his tunic. They shook hands and sweetly commended themselves to each other's prayers, and then the one Saint said to the other, "Brother Francis, I would like my order and yours to be made into a single Order and to live in the Church under the same Rule!"

When at last they took leave of each other, St. Dominic said to many of those present, "In truth I say to you that all the other

---

[193] *Ps* 128, 6. Over the course of the centuries to follow, history has extensively documented the unity and, in essence, the brotherhood that existed between these two orders through their spirit and their leaders, as well as the conflicts and contrasts that could be observed in their followers and that were envisioned by Celano from the very moment the Orders were founded. Even today, it is worthwhile repeating the causes, exceptions, blame, prayers and hope set forth by our author who, both here and elsewhere, has shown himself to be an impartial, strict and happy reporter of the genuine spirit of humility and charity that represented the sole competition between the two founders, Francis and Dominic.
Also worth mentioning is the saintly praise that was sung by the Dominican, St. Thomas, in Francis' regard and then by the Franciscan, St. Bonaventure, in Dominic's regard, in Dante's *Divine Comedy* (*Paradise* XI and XII).

religious should follow this holy man, Francis, so perfect is his saintliness!"

About obedience

CHAPTER CXI
How he always wanted a guardian in order to practice true obedience

151. To achieve further gain in various ways and to convert his whole lifetime into merit, that very shrewd merchant wanted to be guided by the reins of obedience and place himself under someone else's direction. Therefore, not only did he resign from the office of general, but in even greater merit of obedience, he asked to have a personal guardian who was to be considered his special superior. Thus, he said to Brother Peter Catanii, to whom he had already pledged obedience, "I beg you in God's name to make one of my companions responsible for acting in your stead in my regard and whom I must obey as devoutly as I obey you. I know what an asset obedience is and how anyone who has submitted to the yoke of another does not let one second go by without reaping profit."[194]

Since his request was accepted, he was subordinate everywhere until he died and always obeyed his guardian reverently.

One time he said to his companions, "In addition to the other gifts that divine clemency has bestowed upon me, I have also been given the grace that I would obey a novice of one hour, if he were given to me as my guardian, just as diligently as I would one of the oldest and most experienced brothers." Then he went on, "In his superior, the subject must not see the man, but the One for whose love he subjugated himself. Moreover, the more contemptible the person in command is and the more God is pleased by the humility of the one who obeys."

---

[194] *Sir* 51, 26.

CHAPTER CXII

*How he described the truly obedient man,
and of the three kinds of obedience*

152. Another time while he was sitting among his companions, blessed Francis sighed, "In the whole world, it would be hard to find some religious who obeys his prelate perfectly!" Intrigued by this, his companions asked him, "Then tell us, Father, what perfect and sovereign obedience is." Using the image of a corpse to portray the truly obedient man, he replied, "Take a lifeless body and put it wherever you want. You'll find that it will not resist if it is moved, it won't grumble about where it has been put and it won't protest if you move it again. If it is placed on a bishop's throne, it will not look up but will face the ground and if it is surrounded by purple[195], it will look twice as pale." He commented, "This is the truly obedient man: he does not judge why he has been moved, doesn't care about where he is put and doesn't insist on being taken away from there. When elevated to office, he maintains his usual humility and the more he is honored, the more he considers himself unworthy."

On another occasion, when he was discussing the same subject, he referred to what was granted undoubtedly upon request as permission and called holy obedience those provisions that had been granted but not requested. He said that both of them were good, but that the second one was more certain. Then, he considered supreme obedience to be obedience in which flesh and blood take no part, the obedience with which "by divine inspiration one goes among the infidels"[196] both for the salvation of one's neighbor as well as through the desire for martyrdom. And he thought that asking for this sort of obedience must be very pleasing to God.

---

[195] Meaning purple robes, or the rank of cardinal.
[196] *Rule of 1221*, chap. 16 and *Rule of 1223*, chap. 12.

CHAPTER CXIII
That obedience must not be ordered lightly

153. Consequently, he established that a command must rarely be given out of holy obedience and said not to hurl first what should be the last weapon. He said, "The hand should not go immediately to the sword!" Anyone who does not hasten to carry out the order of obedience, he said, has no fear of God or respect for man.

Nothing could be truer. In fact, in an imprudent superior, what else could the authority to command be but a sword in the hands of an angry man? And what could be more wretched than a religious who disdains to obey?

CHAPTER CXIV
Of the brother whose hood he had thrown on the fire
because he had come without obedience,
even though he had been compelled by devotion

154. One time, he had a brother take off his hood and toss it onto a roaring fire because he had come alone without obedience.[197] No one dared to pull it out because they were afraid of the Father's glowering expression, but when the Saint then ordered them to pull it out of the flames, it was intact. Perhaps this happened through the Saint's merits, but perhaps the brother's own merit also had some weight. In fact, he had been overcome by the pious desire to see the most holy Father, but had lacked discretion, which is virtue's only guide.

---

[197] Even today, the written authorization issued to brothers in order to leave their residence is referred to as an "obedience".

Of those who set a good or bad example

CHAPTER CXV
Of the example set by a good brother;
and of the behavior of the older brothers

155. He stated that during those recent times, the Friars Minor had been sent by God precisely as an example of light for men, who were enveloped by the darkness of sin. He said that he felt himself inundated by the sweetest of fragrance and felt as if he had been anointed with a precious ointment when he heard of the beautiful gestures of the holy friars far away throughout the world.

It happened one time that a brother by the name of Barbaro insulted another brother in front of a nobleman from the isle of Scipio[198], but then, seeing that the brother had been hurt by the harshness of his words, angry with himself, he picked up donkey dung and he put it in his mouth in punishment, saying, "Let this tongue that spewed the poison of rage onto my brother eat dung!" The knight was amazed and edified at this sight and from that moment on, he placed himself and his possessions at the friars' service.

It was an ongoing custom with the brothers that if anyone said a word that upset someone else, he would immediately throw himself down on the ground and cover the other brother's feet with holy kisses, even though the one who had been offended would try to dodge this. The Saint would rejoice when he heard

---

[198] Barbaro was one of Francis' original twelve disciples. Since one codex of the *Legend of the Three Companions* specifies that the event took place in Limiso, this was thought to refer to Limissol on the island of Cyprus. However, the scholar A. Fortini points out that "de insula cipii", as indicated in a different edition of Celano's work, must have been in Limisano (now called Limigiano), located on the outskirts of Assisi on the island at the fork of three streams. This island, which was also known as "insula Albrici", probably belonged to Scipio, father of Brother Rufinus, who was one of the three companions.

that, through their examples of holiness, his sons were edifying each other in turn and he would heap his sought-after blessings on those brothers who, through their words and their deeds, had persuaded sinners to love Christ. He wanted his sons to resemble him in the zeal for the salvation of souls that filled him to perfection.

CHAPTER CXVI

How the Saint cursed some of the brothers who were
setting a bad example, and of how unbearable this fault was to him

156. Likewise, those who violated the sacred Order with sinful works or examples also drew upon themselves the terrible oath he uttered.

One day, he received a report that the bishop of Fondi[199] had said to two brothers who had gone before him and who had let their beards grow under the appearance of greater self-contempt, "Beware of marring the beauty of your order through the presumptuousness of such novelties!" Bathed in tears, the Saint sprang up and with his arms stretched towards heaven, he burst into the following words of prayer or, rather, of malediction: "Lord Jesus Christ, you elected twelve Apostles and even if one of them fell, instead all the others remained faithful to you and preached the holy Gospel animated by that same Spirit. O Lord, mindful of ancient mercy[200], in this final hour you have planted this Order of brothers to uphold your faith and accomplish the mystery of your Gospel through them. Then which of them will give you any satisfaction if, by neglecting their mission, not only do they fail to give everyone an example of light, but they even go so far as to demonstrate deeds of darkness?[201] Let those who,

---

[199] Near the Gulf of Gaeta in southern Italy. Roberto, a Cistercian, was bishop from 1210 to 1227.

[200] *Ps* 88, 50; *Sir* 51, 11.

[201] *Rm* 13, 12.

through their poor example, bring shame and ruin upon what you first built through the work of the saintly brothers of this Order -- and that you have never ceased to build -- be damned by you, most holy Lord, by the entire Heavenly Court and by me, your poor one!"

Where are those who go about glorying in his blessing and boasting that they have won his friendship through their own talent? If -- God forbid! -- they should be found unrepentant for having demonstrated deeds of darkness within themselves to the peril of others, woe betide them -- woes of eternal damnation![202]

157. "The finest brothers," he would say, "are covered in shame by the deeds of the bad brothers and, without having sinned themselves, they are condemned by the example of the wicked. Unfortunately, I am pierced by a sword of sorrow and, all day long, they run it through my bowels over and over again."

He thus isolated himself from the company of the brothers, particularly in order to prevent the news of some evil committed by one of them from renewing his sorrow.[203]

And he said, "The time will come when God's chosen Order will be defamed by these bad examples, so that its members will be ashamed to go among the people. Then, those who will come to embrace the Order will be led only by the grace of the Holy Spirit and flesh and blood will not blemish them, and they will truly be blessed by the Lord[204]. Even if they do not accomplish acts of great merit because the charitable fervor that animates the saints will have cooled, since they will be assailed by terrible temptation nevertheless, those who remain strong at that time will be better than their predecessors. But woe to those who, content with keeping up only the semblance of religious life, become numb in idleness and fail to offer constant resistance to the

---

[202] *Jude* 11.

[203] It is worth examining this further reason for the Founder's voluntary isolation since it indicates that it was not motivated solely by his desire to lead a life of silence and contemplation.

[204] *Mt* 16, 17 and *Ps* 115, 15.

temptations that have been allowed in order to test the chosen ones, for only those who have been tested will receive the crown of life[205], once they have struggled against the malice of the reprobate."

CHAPTER CXVII
Of the revelation God gave him about the state of the Order and that the Order will never perish

158. He was nevertheless quite comforted by God's visits, through which he was assured that the foundations of his Order would always remain solid. He was also promised that those who were lost would undoubtedly be replaced by other chosen ones.

Once when he was troubled by some bad examples and had begun to pray with that anxiety in his heart, the Lord reproached him as follows: "Poor little man, why are you troubled? Did I perhaps make you the shepherd of my Order so that you can ignore the fact that I am its head and protector? Indeed, I chose you, simple man, so that those who wish to do so can follow what I will have accomplished in you as a guide. I called you, I myself will preserve you and I will nourish you[206] and, to fill the void left by the friars who fall, I will make other ones rise and if none of them have been born yet, then I will ensure that they are born if necessary. Therefore, please don't be troubled, but work towards your own salvation, for even if the Order were to go down to just three people, it will always remain standing through my patronage."[207]

From that day on, it would be his custom to say that the virtue of a single saint exceeds the demerits of an enormous number of imperfect people, just as a single ray of light will dissipate profound darkness.

---

[205] *Jas* 1, 12.
[206] *Is* 48, 15.
[207] *Gn* 18, 24-32.

Against idleness and the idle

CHAPTER CXVIII

Of the revelation made to him about when
he was a servant of God and when he wasn't

159. From the time that this man abandoned fleeting things and began to be united with the Lord, he did not want to waste even the least amount of time. Although he had accumulated a great abundance of God's treasured merits, it always seemed as if he were at the beginning, ever more prepared for spiritual exercises. He considered it a serious fault not to do some good[208] and deemed any lack of progress to be a setback.

When he was staying in a cell near Siena once, he roused his sleeping companions one night to tell them, "Brothers, I have prayed to the Lord so that He might deign to indicate to me when I am His servant and when I am not, since all I want is to be His servant. Out of His goodness, the Lord has answered me most mercifully, 'Know that you are truly my servant when you think, speak and act in holiness.' Therefore, I have called you, o brothers, because I want to be shamed into turning red in front of you if at times I should I fail to do any of these three things."

CHAPTER CXIX

Of the penance he gave to the brothers of the Porziuncola
for their idle words

160. At Saint Mary's of the Porziuncola another time, considering that what had been gained by praying was lost through the idle words pronounced after the prayers, as a remedy against the flood of useless words, the man of God ordered: "Any brother who utters an idle or vain word must immediately confess

---

[208] *Rm* 9, 11.

his fault and recite an *Our Father* for each word. I also want the brother to say an *Our Father* for his soul if he is the first to admit his fault spontaneously. Instead, if he is initially admonished by someone else, then he should say it for the soul of the brother who reprimanded him."

CHAPTER CXX

How, being so hardworking, he detested the idle

161. He said that those lukewarm men who, as a habit, do not apply themselves to any work, had been spit from the mouth of God.[209] No idle person could appear before him without receiving a biting reproach. The model of all perfection, he himself worked with his hands so that no part of that excellent gift of time would be wasted. He also said once, "I want all my brothers to train themselves to work and those who do not have a profession should learn one."[210]

He also explained the reason for this. "This is so that we will be less of a burden to men and so that the tongue or the heart will not turn to evil out of idleness." Moreover, he would not leave the earnings or the pay for a job to whomever was doing the work, but he wanted it to be entrusted to the guardian or to the community.

CHAPTER CXXI

Lament to the Father against idlers and gluttons

162. O holy Father, let a complaint be lifted to heaven today against those who claim to be yours. There are many who detest the practices of virtue and by wanting to rest before they

---

[209] *Rev* 3, 16.
[210] *Rule of 1221*, chap. 7 and *Rule of 1223*, chap. 5.

toil, they thereby prove that they are not children of Francis but of Lucifer.

We abound more in those who are falsely ill than in fighters, whereas although they are born to labor, they should consider their own lives a battle![211] They do not like having to progress through deeds, and they are unable to do so through contemplation. After having troubled everyone with their singularity, working more with their jaws than with their hands, they detest those who blame them openly[212] and do not tolerate being touched even with the tips of one's fingers. And, in accordance with the words of blessed Francis, I am even more amazed by their impudence, for they would not have lived at home except by their own sweat, yet they want to live off the sweat of the poor now without any effort. Wondrous shrewdness! They do nothing and yet you would think they're always busy! They know when it's mealtime and if they feel pangs of hunger, they accuse the sun of having overslept! And should I judge the ugly actions of these men as being worthy of your glory, o good Father? Why, not even of your very cowl! You always taught that the wealth of merit must be sought in this indecent and fleeting life in order to avoid the danger of having to beg for it in the next. Instead, they do not even know how to take advantage of their homeland, moving on then to exile.

This disease prevails among the subjects because the superiors pretend not to notice, as if it were possible to bear another man's vice without also sharing the penalty.

---

[211] *Jb* 5, 7 and 7, 1.
[212] *Am* 5, 10.

Of the ministers of the divine word

CHAPTER CXXII
What the preacher must be

163. He wanted the ministers of the divine word to be occupied with spiritual study so that they would not be hindered by other offices. In fact, he said that a great King has entrusted them to proclaim his orders to the people after having received them straight from his own mouth. Accordingly, he also said, "First of all, the preacher must draw from the secret of prayer what he will then need to propagate with holy preaching, so that he must be inflamed from within before giving out cold words." He thought that such an office must be revered and that those who practice it should be venerated by everyone. He said, "They are the life of the body, the conquerors of the demons, the light of the world."[213]

He judged doctors of theology to be even more worthy of honor and in fact, he had it written as a general precept, "We must honor and venerate all theologians and those who dispense the divine word as the ones who administer to us the spirit and the life."[214]

Once when he was writing to blessed Anthony[215], he had "To Brother Anthony, my bishop" put at the top of the letter.

---

[213] *Mt* 5, 14.

[214] *Second Testament.*

[215] At the time Celano was writing this work, Anthony, who died in 1231, had already been beatified by Gregory IX (May 30, 1232).

CHAPTER CXXIII

Of those who are avid for vain praise;
and his explanation of a prophetic saying

164. He said that those preachers who often sell their ministry for the reward of vain praise should be pitied instead. Sometimes, he tried to cure their pomposity with this remedy: "Why do you glory in the conversion of men who instead were converted by the prayers of my simple little friars?"

Then he gave the following explanation of that prophecy that says: *In the end, the sterile woman bore many sons into the world.* "The sterile woman is my poor brother, who does not have the power to generate sons in the Church. On Judgment Day, however, he will have many sons for at that time, the Judge will attribute to his glory those he is now converting through his hidden prayers. Instead, *the woman who already has many will be disappointed,* for the preacher who exults as if he had generated so many of them through his own virtue will see then that there is nothing of his own in them."

He had little love for those who yearn to be praised more as rhetoricians than as preachers and who speak elegantly but without love. He said that they divide things badly, giving everything to the exterior form of preaching and nothing to devotion. He did praise the preacher, as long as he was able to seek wisdom for himself from time to time and also be nourished by it himself.

Of his contemplation of the Creator in His creatures

CHAPTER CXXIV

The Saint's love for creatures, animate and inanimate

165. Although he was in a hurry to leave the world soon, land of exile, this blessed pilgrim also knew how to take more

than a little advantage of the things of the world.[216] Certainly, he used them against the princes of darkness[217] as a battle ground, and for the glory of God as a clear mirror of His goodness. In all the things that had been created he praised their Creator and all that he could find in things that had been made he referred to the Maker.

He rejoiced in all the works of the Lord's hands[218] and through those joyful visions he perceived the life-giving reason and the cause. He recognized supreme Beauty in beautiful things, just as in all good things he could hear the song, "He who made us is Goodness!" He followed the Beloved everywhere through the marks He left in things and used everything as a step to rise to His Throne.[219]

He embraced all things with unprecedented devout love, speaking to them of the Lord and exhorting them to praise him. He would leave lights, lamps and candles burning, not wanting to put out with his own hand the glimmer that is the symbol of Eternal Light.[220] He tread over stones with veneration out of respect for Him who is called "the Rock"[221] and when he had to recite that little verse *"You will set me high upon a rock"*[222], he would say, "You have set me high beneath the feet of the Rock" in order to speak with greater respect.

The brothers in charge of cutting wood were forbidden to chop down the whole tree, so that it would have a chance to sprout new shoots. He ordered the gardener to leave a strip of untilled land around the garden so that in due time, green grass and beautiful flowers could praise the most beautiful Father of all

---

[216] *Jn* 17, 11. One of the aspects distinguishing Francis of Assisi was his reconsideration of earthly reality within the cosmic framework of creation, as seen by a mystic.

[217] *Eph* 6, 12 and *Wis* 7,26 and 8, 6.

[218] *Ps* 92, 5.

[219] *Ps* 100 and *Jb* 23, 3.

[220] *Wis* 7, 26.

[221] *1 Cor* 10, 4.

[222] *Ps* 61, 3; *Ps* 18, 39.

things and he wanted a little plot set aside within the garden for fragrant herbs and flowers, so that they would remind everyone who looked at them of the eternal fragrance.

He would pick little worms up from the ground so that they wouldn't be stepped on and would set out honey and fine wine for the bees so that they wouldn't die of starvation in the winter cold. He called all animals "brother", although he preferred meek little animals above all.

But who could possibly recount everything? Indeed, for this saint that original Goodness that will be all in all things[223] already shone clearly in everything.

CHAPTER CXXV

How the creatures themselves returned his love;
and of the fire that did not burn him

166. On their part, all the creatures tried to return the Saint's affection and to reward him with their gratitude: they smiled when he stroked them, answered his questions and obeyed his orders. Perhaps the reader would be pleased by a description of a few examples.

During the time in which he was suffering from his eye disease, since he was obliged to allow treatment to be done on him, he had a surgeon called to the convent. The man arrived with a cauterizing iron and had it put into the fire to get it red-hot. To console his body, which was trembling in horror, the blessed Father said to the fire, "My brother fire, marvelous among all the other creatures, the Most High has made you very strong and beautiful and useful.[224] Be benevolent to me now and be kind to me, for I have loved you in the Lord. I beseech the wonderful God who created you to temper your heat a bit so that you will

---

[223] *1 Cor* 12, 6 and 15, 28.
[224] The part is highly reminiscent of Francis' *Canticle of Brother Sun*.

burn gently and I will be able to withstand you." At the end of this prayer, he made the sign of the cross over the fire and waited bravely. The doctor took the glowing and scorching-hot iron in his hand while the brothers fled, overcome with compassion, and the Saint offered himself up with a smile, ready to be burnt. The iron was plunged into his tender flesh with a crackle and the cauterization stretched from his ear to his eyebrow.

We can find out how much pain was inflicted by that fire through the words of the one who knew best, the Saint himself. In fact, when the brothers who had run away returned, the Father said to them with a smile, "Cowards and men of little courage, why did you run away?[225] In truth I say to you that I felt neither the heat of the fire nor any pain in my flesh." Then, turning to the doctor, he said, "If the meat isn't done enough yet, burn it again!" The doctor, who was accustomed to seeing such an operation borne quite differently, declared that it was a miracle. "I say to you, brothers, that I have seen wonderful things today!"[226]

As for me, I believe that he must surely have returned to that early innocence, since through his will, cruel elements became meek.

CHAPTER CXXVI
Of the little bird that perched on his hands

167. On his way to the hermitage in Greccio, blessed Francis was crossing the lake of Rieti in a little boat and a fisherman offered him a tiny aquatic bird so that he would be amused by it in the Lord. The blessed Father took it very gladly and then, opening his hands out, he kindly set it free. Since the bird did not want to leave and, instead, crouched in his hands as if they were a nest, raising his eyes towards heaven, the Saint gave himself up to

---

[225] *1 Thes* 5, 14, *Mt* 14, 31; *Lk* 4,25.
[226] *Lk 5, 26.*

prayer. After a long time, he returned to his senses as if he had been elsewhere and he sweetly ordered the bird to return fearlessly to freedom. Thus, having received this blessing, it flew off in a burst of joy.

CHAPTER CXXVII
Of the hawk

168. While blessed Francis was staying at a hermitage[227], avoiding the sight and conversation of men as was his custom, a hawk that was nesting there became friends with him. Every night at the hour in which the Saint was used to getting up for the Divine Office, the little animal would awaken him by singing and making noise, giving him great pleasure by taking such care to rouse him from the drowsiness of his sleep.

Nevertheless, when the Saint was weaker than usual because of some illness, the hawk would feel compassion for him and would not rouse him as early. As if it had been instructed by God, it was only towards dawn that the hawk would ring the bell of its voice in soft knells.

It is no wonder that the other creatures should venerate one who, more than anyone else, loved the Creator.

CHAPTER CXXVIII
Of the bees

169. One time, a little hut was built on a mountainside where the Servant of God did very harsh penance for forty days.[228] When he left again at the end of the established time, since it was so isolated, the cell was left uninhabited and a clay jar

---

[227] St. Bonaventure indicates that the event took place on Mount La Verna during the Lent of St. Michael and thus in 1224 (*Major Life*, VIII, 10).

[228] Again, this is thought to be Mount La Verna.

that the Saint used to drink from was left behind. Several people who went there afterwards out of devotion for the Saint discovered the jar full of bees that, with wonderful artistry, were making the little cells there for their honeycombs, symbolizing the sweet contemplation that the Saint of God had tasted in that place.

CHAPTER CXXIX
Of the pheasant

170. A nobleman from the land of Siena sent a pheasant to blessed Francis during his illness. He gladly accepted it, not because he wanted to eat it, but because he was accustomed to delighting in these little creatures out of his love for the Creator, and he said to it, "Blessed be our Creator, brother pheasant!" Turning to the brothers, he went on, "Now let's see if brother pheasant wants to stay with us or if he would prefer to return to his usual home, which is more suitable for him." The Saint had a brother bring the pheasant and place it in a vineyard far from there, but the little animal quickly returned to the Father's cell. Again, he had it brought even further away, but with great speed, it returned to the doorway of the cell and practically pushed its way past the cowls of the brothers who were at the door. The Saint thus ordered that it be fed conscientiously and then embraced and stroked it, whispering sweet words to it.

One of the people observing this scene was a doctor who was very devoted to the Saint of God and he asked the brothers if he could have the pheasant, not to eat it but to keep it out of devotion and in memory of the Blessed One. In short, he brought it to his house, but the pheasant, almost as if it were indignant over the affront he had received by being separated from its friend the saint, refused to eat anything as along as it was kept apart from him. The doctor was amazed by this and brought the pheasant back to the Saint, telling him what had happened. As soon as the little animal had been set down on the ground and saw the Father, it set all sadness aside and began to eat gladly.

CHAPTER CXXX
Of the cricket

171. Near the cell of the Saint of God at the Porziuncola, a cricket sitting on a fig tree sang incessantly. One day, the blessed Father stretched out his hand out and called to it sweetly, "My sister cricket, come to me!" And as if it had the faculty of reason, it sprang onto his hand and then he said to it, "Sing, my sister cricket, and praise the Lord, your Creator, with your merry hymn!"

Obeying without further delay, it began to sing and did not stop until the man of God, who had interwoven his own praise with the cricket's songs, ordered it to hop back to its usual place, where it stayed for eight days in a row as if it had been tied there.

As he was leaving his cell, the Saint would take it in his hands and order it to sing and it was always ready to obey. At last, he said to his companions, "Now let's give our sister cricket permission to leave so that our bodies will not have any reason for conceit, for until now she has delighted us with her songs." After it had bidden him farewell, it went off and was never seen there again.

The friars who witnessed all this were filled with admiration.

Of charity

CHAPTER CXXXI
*Of his charity and how, for the good of souls,
he showed himself to be a model of perfection*

172. There is nothing to wonder about that he who had become the brother of other creatures out of love, should also have been united, through the love of Christ, in an even closer bond of fraternity to all the creatures marked with the image of the Creator.

In fact, he said that nothing is more important than the salvation of souls and often showed this through the fact that God's Only Son had allowed himself to be nailed to the cross out of His love for our souls. This is what guided his efforts in prayer, his continuous travels to preach, his incessant care in setting a good example. He could not consider himself a friend of Christ unless he too loved the souls that He had loved, and this was the most important reason behind his reverence toward doctors[229], because as Christ's assistants, they practiced Christ's same office. However, above all, he loved the friars with the fullness of deep affection, because, like him, they were the servants of a special faith and were united through their participation in the eternal inheritance.

173. Each time he was admonished for the harsh severity of his life, he would reply that he had been given to the Order to be their model so that, like an eagle, he could teach his young to fly.[230] Therefore, although his innocent flesh, which submitted spontaneously to his spirit, had no need to be scourged for sins it had committed, he continued nevertheless to torture it in order to set an example, walking along harsh paths solely as an encouragement to others.

And with good reason, for one looks at the actions of one's superiors more than at their words. Through your example, Father, more sweetly did you plead, more easily did you convince and with greater evidence did you give proof. If superiors were to speak the language of men and of angels, but did not give examples of charity[231], this would do me little good and would do

---

[229] "Doctors" in its original sense, meaning "teacher" or "learned man".

[230] *Deut* 32, 11.

[231] *1 Cor* 13, 1.

themselves none. But in places where the censor is not feared and will takes the place of reason, can seals[232] possible be enough for salvation?

One must nevertheless follow their orders so that running water can reach the flower beds even through channels that have dried up. Let the rose sometimes be picked from the thorns, so that the elder will always benefit the younger.

CHAPTER CXXXII
Of concern towards the subjects

174. Who will take over Francis' attention towards his subjects now? He always lifted his hands up to heaven[233] on behalf of the true Israelites and, often heedless of himself, he would prefer to think about the health of his brothers. Prostrate before the divine Majesty, he would offer a spiritual sacrifice on behalf of his sons and would force God to help them. With trembling love, he would take pity on the little flock[234] that he had following behind him to ensure that, after having renounced the world, they wouldn't lose heaven as well. He thought that he would be deprived of heavenly glory if he did not lead the souls entrusted to him, and in spirit he gave birth with pains even greater than the ones felt by a mother's womb.

---

[232] In other words, what moral value can their authority have? The seal was one of the emblems of their jurisdiction.
[233] *Ex* 17, 11.
[234] *Lk* 12, 32.

CHAPTER CXXXIII
Of his compassion for the sick

175. Great was his compassion for the sick and great was his concern for their needs.[235] When he sometimes received some choice food through the mercy of laymen that he would have needed more than anyone else, he would give it to other sick people.

Inside, he experienced all the suffering of the sick and would offer them words of compassion when he was unable to help them in any other way. He would even eat on days of fasting so that the sick would not be ashamed of eating and would not hesitate to go begging publicly in the city for meat for a sick friar.

He nevertheless cautioned the weak that they should bear deprivation patiently and not be outraged if they could not be satisfied with everything. Thus in a Rule[236], he had the following words written: "I beg all my sick friars not to get angry over their illnesses, and not to feel troubled towards God and towards the friars. They should not ask for medicine with excess concern, driven by the desire to heal the flesh that soon must die and that is the enemy of the soul. They should thank God for everything, and should desire only to be the way God wants them to be. In fact, by inciting them through scourges and disease, He trains those He has destined for eternal life[237], just as He Himself has said: *Whoever is dear to me I reprove and chastise.*[238]

176. When he learned once that a sick friar wanted to eat some grapes, he led him to the vineyard, sat under the trellis and in order to encourage him, was the first to start eating.

---

[235] *Rule of 1221*, chap. 10, *Rule of 1223,* chap. 6. See also *Writings.*
[236] *Rule of 1221*, chap. 10.
[237] *Acts* 13, 48.
[238] *Rev* 3, 19.

CHAPTER CXXXIV
*Of his compassion towards the sick in spirit
and of those who do the contrary*

177. It was with even greater indulgence, however, that he loved and patiently bore the sick whom he knew were anguished by temptation and had no moral strength, just like weak children. Therefore, he avoided harsh punishment when he saw that mildness would do no harm and he spared the rod to spare the soul.[239]

He said that the prelate, who is a father and not a tyrant, must eliminate the occasion of sin and keep from falling those who would find it difficult to get back up again after a fall. Ah wretched insanity of our times! Not only do we fail to pick up or sustain the weak but often, we even push them to make them fall! We have no scruples over taking away from the Shepherd a little lamb for whom He gave His powerful cry from the cross as He wept![240] You acted very differently, holy Father, for you preferred to correct the erring rather than lose them.

Nevertheless, we are well aware that there are some who are so profoundly diseased in will that they need a caustic and not an ointment. It is clear that for many, it is sounder to be thrashed with an iron rod than to be treated with a gentle hand. But oil and wine, the rod and the staff, severity and indulgence, cauterization and unction, imprisonment and embracing, must all be used in their own due time.[241] All this is what the God of vengeance and the Father of mercies desires, and yet He desires mercy more than sacrifice.[242]

---

[239] *Ps* 77, 4 and *1 Mc* 13, 5.
[240] *Heb* 5, 7.
[241] *Lk* 10, 34; *Ps* 23, 4; *Eccl* 3, 1.
[242] *Ps* 94, 1; *2 Cor* 1, 3; *Mt* 9, 13.

CHAPTER CXXXV
Of the Spanish brothers

178. This most holy man would go into marvelous rapture with God and his soul would be elated whenever the good fragrance of his sons reached him.

A very devout Spanish cleric was once lucky enough to have the pleasure of seeing and conversing with St. Francis. And among his other news, he also gave him this happy report about the brothers in Spain: "Your brothers in our land, who are living in a poor hermitage, have established a way of life for themselves according to which half of them are busy with material affairs and the other ones attend to contemplation. And thus each week they go from active life to contemplation and from contemplative repose back to manual practice. Now one day, when the table had been set and those who were absent had been signaled to come, everyone came except for one of the contemplatives. After waiting a bit, they went to his cell to call him to the table, but he was comforted by the Lord with much more lavish food! He was found lying on the ground with face down, his arms outstretched in the shape of a cross, and he was breathless and still. Two candelabra were burning near his head and his feet, giving off a blazing light in the cell. They left him alone in order not to disturb his ecstasy and the beloved did not awaken until she pleased[243]. The brothers peered through the openings in the cell, staying behind the wall and peeking through the cracks. In short, as his friends gazed at the garden-dweller[244], the radiance suddenly disappeared and the brother returned to his senses. He got up quickly, went to the refectory and excused himself for being late. This", concluded the Spaniard, "is what happens in our country!"

Saint Francis was beside himself with joy, intoxicated by such great perfume in his sons. As if his sole pride were to hear

---

[243] *Sg* 2, 7 and 2, 9.
[244] *Sg* 8, 13.

his brothers spoken highly of, he arose to praise the Lord and from the bottom of his heart, he burst out, "I thank you, Lord, sanctifier and guide of the poor, for you have delighted me with this beautiful news about my little brothers. I beg you to bless them with your greatest blessing and to sanctify with special grace all those who, through their good example, are making the world redolent with the perfume of their religious profession!"

CHAPTER CXXXVI

Against those who live poorly in the hermitages;
and how he wanted everything to be held in common

179. Here we have learned of the charity that made him happy over the progress of his beloved sons, but we think that he scolded those who lived quite differently in the hermitages with equal severity. In fact, many had converted the place of contemplation into a place of idleness and turned hermitic life, established to lead souls to perfection, into a den of pleasure!

This is the constitution of Anachorites in our day: each one lives as he pleases. This does not apply to everyone. In fact, we know that there are still some saints who live according to excellent laws. We also know that the fathers who preceded them have been true solitary flowers. May God keep the hermits of our time from degenerating that early beauty whose sanctity will rightly be praised for eternity!

180. Lastly, counseling everyone to be charitable, St. Francis exhorted them to set a special example of courtesy and domestic harmony. He said, "I want my brothers to act like the children of a sole mother and if anyone should ask for a tunic or a cord or anything else, then the other one should give it to him generously. Books and anything else that may be appreciated should be held in common and indeed, they should oblige each other to accept them."

Here too, he was the first to carry all this out so that he would not command something that had not been accomplished by Christ through him.[245]

CHAPTER CXXXVII

Of the two French friars to whom he donated his tunic

181. Two French friars of great holiness met St. Francis. This gave them immense joy twice over since they had wanted to see him for a long time. After kind greetings and sweet conversation, in fervent devotion they asked him for his tunic. He took it off at once, remaining without a habit, and gave it to them and he then got dressed again in the very poor tunic that one of them had given in pious exchange.

He was always prepared to donate not only his clothing, but his very self and with sublime joy he would give up anything that was asked of him.

Against detraction

CHAPTER CXXXVIII

How he wanted slanderers chastised

182. Lastly, since the charitable soul detests those who are hateful to God, this was also St. Francis' demeanor. Abhorring slanderers above any other kind of sinner, he said that their tongues bear venom with which they poison the others. Thus, if slanderers -- biting fleas -- were speaking, he would avoid listening to them and, as we ourselves have seen, he would turn his ears elsewhere so that they would not be sullied by hearing them.

---

[245] *Rm* 15, 18.

One time, when he heard one brother denigrating another, he turned to his vicar, Brother Peter Catanii, and uttered this terrible sentence: "If no remedy is taken against slanderers, grave danger will come over the Order. Soon the good fragrance of many will be tainted unless those fetid mouths are shut[246]. Come then, look closely and if you find an innocent brother being accused, inflict such harsh punishment on his accuser that it will serve as an example for everyone. If you cannot punish him yourself, then place him in the hands of the boxer from Florence (he referred to Brother John of Florence, a man of imposing stature and great strength, as the boxer). I want you and all the ministers to pay the utmost attention to preventing such a plague from spreading any further."

Sometimes, he would punish anyone who had maligned a brother by taking his tunic away from him and not allowing him to lift his eyes to the Lord until he had returned what he had taken away. Therefore, by renouncing this vice in a singular way, the brothers of those times, had committed themselves to avoiding diligently anything that could undermine some else's honor or sound like slander.

Excellent decision! In fact, isn't a slanderer no more than the bile of men, a turmoil of wickedness, the dishonor of the earth? And what else can a forked tongue be except the scandal of the Order, the venom of the cloister, a rift in unity? Alas! The surface of the earth abounds in these poisonous animals and no good man can avoid being bitten by the envious! Rewards are even promised to informers and the palm of falsehood is often granted for felling innocence, so that when one cannot live off his own reputation, he obtains his food and clothing by destroying the reputation of others.

183. In this regard, St. Francis often said, "This is how a slanderer reasons: I lack perfection of life, I don't have the prestige of knowledge or some special gift and so I cannot excel either

---

[246] *Lev* 1, 9 and 13; *Ex* 5, 21; *Is* 3, 24.

before God or before men. Nevertheless, I know the best thing for me to do: I will stain the chosen ones[247] and win the favor of great men. I know that my prelate is a man and that at times he too uses my very same means, which is to cut down the cedars so that only the thorn bushes can be seen in the woods. Ah wretch! You feed on human flesh and since you cannot live any other way, you gnaw at the bowels of your brothers!

Those men take care to seem good but not to be good, and they denounce the faults of others without correcting their own. They praise only those whose protection they crave and remain silent when they think that their praise cannot touch the powerful.

To gain harmful praise, they sell the pallor of their faces that are bruised by fasting, so that they will appear to be spiritual men[248] and thus be able to judge everything without being judged by anyone. They enjoy the reputation of saints but do none of their works and are called angels but have none of their virtues!

Description of the Minister General and of the other Ministers

CHAPTER CXXXIX
How the minister must act towards his companions

184. When Francis was nearing the goal of being summoned to the Lord, a brother who was solicitous of divine things and loved the Order asked him, "Father, you are about to go away and the family that has followed you will be left in this vale of tears. If you think there is such a person in the Order, designate someone whom you fully trust and who can safely be entrusted with the burden of minister general." Sighing at each word, St. Francis answered, "Son, I do not see anyone who is capable of

---

[247] *Lk* 16, 4; *Sir* 11, 33.
[248] *Mt* 6, 16-18 and *1 Cor* 14, 37 and 2, 15.

being the leader of such a widely varied army and the shepherd of such a numerous flock! But I want to describe one to you and, you might say, depict for you the kind of person who shines with the qualities needed to be the father of this family."

185. He explained, "He must be a man who lives an austere live, with great discretion and who has an excellent reputation, a man free from any special attachments, so that he will not shame the community as a whole by favoring part of it. He must be a man who craves and loves holy prayer, who knows how to divide his time between caring for his own soul and caring for the flock that has been entrusted to him. In fact, he must celebrate the holy sacrifice of the Mass early in the morning and, with a long prayer, place himself and his flock under God's protection. After prayers," he added, "he must present himself in public and be willing to let himself be stormed by everyone, to answer everyone and to see to everyone sweetly. He must be a man who is completely untouched by the stain of partiality, who has the small and simple as well as the scholarly and powerful equally at heart. He must be a man who, if eminent because of his gifts of learning, must be even more of a portrait of pious simplicity in his ways, and he must love virtue. A man who loathes money, the prime cause of corruption in our profession and perfection and who, being the true leader of a poor Order and a model for the others, must never hold the purse strings. He must be content with his habit and a booklet for himself and with a box of pens and a seal[249] for his brothers. He must not be a collector of books, nor must he be overly dedicated to reading, so that the time he would otherwise devote to study will not taken away from his office.

"He is a man who is able to console the afflicted since he himself is the ultimate shelter for the troubled, so that these sick people will not fall into despair for having failed to find a saving

---

[249] The modest attributes and instruments of government.

remedy in him.[250] To subdue the violent to meekness, he must lower himself and give up part of his own right in order to gain souls for Christ. He should not close the innermost part of his mercy[251] to those who desert the Order, little lost sheep, and must bear in mind that the temptations that can drive one to such a bad fall are surely that much stronger.[252]

186. "I would also like everyone to revere him as Christ's representative and provide lovingly for all his needs. However, he must not smile at these honors and must not feel greater satisfaction over these favors than over the offenses. If, out of weakness or fatigue, he should need more substantial food at times, he should not eat it in secret but should do so publicly in order to encourage others to provide for the weakened bodies without shame.

"It will be up to him, above all, to penetrate the innermost conscience, and to close his ears to chatterers. Lastly, he must be such that he will not weaken the manly rule of justice by coveting to keep a place of honor and must understand that such high office is more of a burden to him than an honor. Nevertheless, excessive mildness must not generate laxity, nor must feeble indulgence dissolve discipline: in a word, he must make himself beloved by all, yet at the same time he must make evildoers fear him.[253]

"I would also like him to have virtuous companions who, like him, can set an example of all good[254], unyielding towards pleasure, strong against difficulties, and so fittingly amiable that they will welcome with holy cheerfulness all those who go to them.

"This," he concluded, "is how the minister general of the Order should be."

---

250 *Rule of 1221*, chap. 4, 5, 6; *Rule of 1223*, chap. 7, 10.
251 *Lk* 15, 4-6 and *1 Jn* 3, 17.
252 *Rule of 1221*, chap. 5.
253 *Prv* 10, 29.
254 *Titus* 2, 7.

CHAPTER CXL
Of the Provincial Ministers

187. The blessed father looked for all these qualities in the provincial ministers as well, although the minister general must glow with each quality in a singular way.

He wanted them to be kind to their subjects and to be so full of benevolence that the guilty would not be afraid of committing themselves to their good will. He wanted them to be moderate in commanding, merciful in the face of failure, more willing to bear offense than to return it, the enemy of sin but doctors of sinners. Lastly, they were to act so that their lives would be a mirror of discipline for others. He also wanted them to be honored and loved by their subjects, since they had to bear the burden of worry and effort.

And he said that the ones who governed the souls entrusted to their care in this manner and according to this standard would be worthy of the supreme reward before God.

CHAPTER CXLI
The Saint's answer when he was asked about the Ministers

188. Once when a brother asked him why he had handed the care of all the brothers over to others, as if they no longer pertained to him, he answered, "Son, I love my brothers to the best of my ability, but if they were to follow in my footsteps[255], I would love them even more and would not be estranged from them. There are a few prelates who lead them down other paths, offering to them the example of the ancient monks and giving little consideration to my teachings. But the results of this conduct will be seen in the end."

---

[255] *1 Pt* 2, 21.

After a little while, seriously ill, he sat straight up on his little bed in spiritual fervor and exclaimed, "Who are the ones who have ripped the Order that is mine and my brothers' right out of my hands? If I go to the general chapter, I'll certainly show them what my will is!"

That brother then went on, "And what about those provincial ministers who have been abusing their freedom for so long? Won't you change them?" Sighing, the Father gave this terrible reply: "Let them live as they like, for losing a few is less detrimental than the loss of many!" He did not say this on account of all the ministers, but because of several who seemed to claim the prelacy as if it were an inherited right because they had been in power for so long.

He also urged regular prelates -- of whatever kind -- above all not to alter their behavior unless it was for the better, not to curry favor and not to exercise power, but to fulfill their duty.

Of holy simplicity

CHAPTER CXLII
What true simplicity is

189. Holy simplicity -- the daughter of grace, the blood sister of wisdom, the mother of justice -- was carefully cultivated by the Saint within himself and beloved in others. Nevertheless, he did not approve of simplicity of all kinds but only of the one that, content in its God, spurns everything else.

She[256] is the one that glories in fearing God, and does not know or say or commit evil. She is the one who, through introspection, condemns no one, the one who, in giving the power that

---

[256] Throughout this entire section, Celano has personified simplicity as a woman and I have thus chosen to use personal pronouns in order to render his concepts more closely.

is her due to those who are more worthy, does not desire it for herself. She is the one who, by not considering Grecian glories to be the best ones[257], prefers action over learning or teaching. She is the one who, in interpreting divine law, leaves word games, embellishments and elegant turns of speech, ostentation and subtlety to those who wish to be ruined, and who does not look not at the bark but the pith, not at the shell but the core, not at the many things but at abundance: in other words, she looks at the supreme and lasting Good.

He wanted this simplicity to exist in lettered brothers and in laymen as well, deeming that it was not contrary to wisdom but indeed was its very sister, yet was more accessible to the poor and more practical than science. So that in the *Salutations of the Virtues* he composed, he said, "I greet you, sovereign wisdom, and may the Lord keep you and your sister, pure and holy simplicity!"[258]

CHAPTER CXLIII
About Brother John the Simple

190. While St. Francis was passing by a villa near Assisi, there was a very simple man out plowing a field, a certain John, who ran up to him and said, "I want you to make me a brother, because I have long desired to serve God."[259] The Saint was gladdened by such simplicity and accepted, replying, "Brother, if you want to become our companion, give whatever you might own to the poor[260] and when you have rid yourself of everything, I will welcome you."

The man immediately untied his oxen and offered one to St. Francis, saying, "We will give this ox to the poor, for I have full title to this portion of my father's possessions." The Saint

---

[257] *2 Mc* 4, 15.

[258] This is the opening line of Francis' *Salutation of the Virtues*.

[259] *Acts* 14, 3 and *Mt* 6, 24.

[260] *Rule of 1221*, chap. 1; *Mt* 19, 21.

smiled, approving of his simplicity of spirit, but when the farmer's parents and younger brothers heard this, they hastened over in tears, grieving more over losing the ox than their family member. So the Saint comforted them by saying, "Take heart. Here, I'll give you the ox and take away the brother." Indeed, he led the man away with him, dressed him in a religious habit and made him his special companion because of his great simplicity.

Now, when the Saint would be meditating somewhere, simple John would immediately repeat his every gesture or attitude in imitation. If Francis spat, he would spit; if he coughed, so would he; he would add sighing to sighing and weeping to weeping. If the Saint raised his hands towards heaven, so would he, watching him carefully as an example and making Francis' every action his own. The Saint was aware of this and one day, he asked him why he was doing this. John replied, "I promised that I would do everything you do, so it would be harmful for me to leave something out." Francis was delighted by such pure simplicity, but he sweetly chided him not to do it anymore.

Not long after that, that simple man went on to the Lord in this purity and the Saint, who frequently held his life up as an example for the other brothers to imitate, joyfully called him Saint John instead of Brother John.

You should note that it is characteristic of pious simplicity to live under the rules of one's superiors and to rely always on the examples and teachings of the saints. Who will admit that a wise man of the world[261] can imitate the Saint, who reigns now in heaven, with as much zeal as that simple man who tried to resemble him while he was still on earth?

What then? After he had followed the Saint in life, he preceded him in eternal life.

---

[261] *1 Cor* 2, 4.

CHAPTER CXLIV
How he favored unity in his sons,
and how he told them a parable about it

191. His constant desire and his vigilant concern was to make sure that the bond of unity was always kept intact among his sons, so that those who had been drawn by the same spirit and begotten by the same father[262] would live harmoniously in the womb of a sole mother. He wanted the older ones to be united with the younger and the wise to be bound to the ignorant through brotherly love and that all of them should be drawn close together by the bonds of love, even if they were far away from each other.

One time, he expounded a parable that held an important lesson. "Here, let's hold a chapter of all the religious in the Church, a general chapter! Since the erudite and the unlettered, the scholars and those men who were pleasing to God[263] despite their ignorance, would all be in attendance, one of the scholars and one of the simpletons were asked to give a sermon. The former reflected, for he was wise, and thought to himself, 'This is not the place to flaunt learning, since there are men who have achieved perfect knowledge, nor would it behoove me to draw attention to myself by affecting to treat such matters among shrewd minds. Perhaps it would be more fruitful to speak simply.'

"The appointed day arrived and the assembly of saints[264] gathered together, anxious to hear the sermon. Dressed in a sackcloth and his head covered with ashes[265], the scholar stepped forward and to everyone's surprise, he preached more through his attitude than his words, saying briefly, 'We have made great promises, but have received even greater ones: let us maintain the former and live in wait for the latter. Pleasure is brief, punishment

---

[262] *Eph* 4, 4; *Jb* 34, 14 and *Prv* 23, 22.

[263] *Heb* 11, 6.

[264] *Ps* 111, 1.

[265] *Jon* 3, 5 and *2 Mc* 10, 25.

eternal, suffering limited, glory infinite. Many are called, few are chosen, but all are rewarded according to merit.' Their hearts filled with remorse, those listening burst into tears and venerated that true wise man as a saint.

"The simpleton said to himself, 'There, the scholar has already anticipated everything I had decided to say and do. But I have it![266] I know a few of the verses of the Psalms, so I will act like the learned, given that he has acted like the simple.'

"During the assembly the next day, the simpleton got up to speak, announcing that a psalm would be the subject of his speech, and animated by the spirit of God, he went on with such fervor, insight and sweetness, following that heavenly inspiration, that everyone, stupefied, proclaimed a second truth: '*The Lord speaks to the simple*'[267] ."

192. This was how the man of God commented on this allegory he had set forth. "The enormous assembly is our Order, which is essentially a synod that gathers souls from all over the world under a single rule of life. In it, the wise profit from the virtues of the simple by seeing that, despite the ignorance of the latter, they seek to reach heavenly heights with great ardor and that, without human instruction, they acquire knowledge of spiritual truths through the wisdom of the Holy Spirit.[268] Here, the simple also turn to their own advantage what pertains to the wise when they see that illustrious men, who would have been held in great esteem in the world, bring themselves down to their level. This," he concluded, "illuminates the beauty of this blessed family, whose many gifts are so pleasing to its Father!"

---

[266] *Lk* 16, 4.

[267] *Prv* 2 and 3.

[268] *Gal* 1, 1; *Acts* 11, 28 and *1 Cor* 2, 13.

CHAPTER CXLV
How the Saint wanted the tonsure

193. St. Francis would often say to those who shaved his head, "Be careful not to make my crown too big! In fact, I want my simple brothers to have part of my head too."[269] In addition, he wanted the Order to be open not only to the rich and the scholarly, but also to the poor and the unlettered. "God," he would say, "does not play favorites with people[270] and the Minister General of the Order, or in other words the Holy Spirit, rests equally over the poor and the simple."

Indeed, he would have like to include these words in the Rule, but this was not possible because it had already been approved[271]

CHAPTER CXLVI
How he also wanted the great clerics[272]
entering the Order to renounce their possessions

194. He said once that even a great cleric who entered the Order must renounce his knowledge somehow so that, after stripping himself of that kind of possession, he would be able to offer himself naked to the embrace of the crucified Christ.

"Learning," he would say, "makes many people intractable, maintaining in them a certain inflexibility whereby they will not bend to humble discipline. Therefore, at the beginning I would like the lettered man to address the following prayer to me: 'Here,

---

[269] He did not want to be too different from the lay brothers, who had a smaller tonsure than the clerics. St. Bonaventure (*Major Life* III, 10) wrote that Innocent III also had the lay brothers tonsured.

[270] *Rm* 2, 11.

[271] The bull of approval was dated November 29, 1223: *Bullarium franc.,* I, 15-19.

[272] The word *clericus* is used here in its medieval meaning to intend "scholar or learned man", as opposed to *laicus* or "unlettered".

brother, I have long lived in the word and have not known my God fully. I beg you to grant me a place far from worldly uproar where I can reflect on my past years in sorrow and step away from the distractions of the heart[273] to reshape my spirit for the better.' Now I ask you, if someone starts out in this way, what will he become? Released from his chains, that lion will certainly come out full of vigor and ready for anything, and the spiritual essence that is thus absorbed in the beginning will continue to develop in him. In the end, he can confidently devote himself to the ministry of the word, since he will give off the warmth burning inside him!"

Blessed teachings! What greater need can one who is returning from such a different field have than to eliminate and cleanse, through an exercise in humility, all the mundane attachments that have long penetrated his spirit and taken root there? Once he has entered the school of perfection, he will quickly reach the peak of perfection.

CHAPTER CXLVII
How he wanted them to be educated, and how he appeared to a companion who was planning to devote himself to preaching

195. He would suffer if anyone neglected virtue to seek knowledge, especially if he did not continue in the vocation of his initial calling.[274] He would say, "My brothers who are driven by their thirst for learning will find themselves empty-handed on the day of their reward. I would prefer that they strengthen their virtues so that when days of tribulation and anguish come, they will have the Lord with them. In fact, tribulation is about set in, so that useless books will be thrown out the window and into dark places."

---

[273] *Is* 38, 15; *Ps* 147, 2.
[274] *1 Cor* 7, 20 and 24, included in *Rule of 1221*, chap. 7.

It isn't that he was displeased over studying the Scriptures, but he said this in order to draw everyone away from being overly concerned with studying, wanting them to be good through charity rather than to be know-it-alls through curiosity.

He also had a premonition that the time would soon come in which learning would cause downfall and become the sustenance of the spirit in place of dedication to a spiritual life.

When a lay brother who was anxious to have a psalter[275] asked for Francis' permission to have it, he gave him ashes instead of the psalter. Moreover, after he died, Francis appeared in a vision to one of his companions who wanted to devote himself to preaching, and he forbade him to do so, ordering him to continue on the path of simplicity. After that vision -- and God is a witness[276] -- the brother experienced such great sweetness that for many days it seemed as if the sound of the Father's words, as life-giving as dew, kept ringing in his ears.

Of the Saint's special devotions

CHAPTER CXLVIII
How he would be moved at the mention of the love of God

196. Perhaps it is neither useless nor inopportune to touch briefly on St. Francis' special devotions. While he was indeed greatly favored in this way through the anointing of the Holy Spirit and piously venerated everything, he nevertheless felt a special inclination towards certain devotions.

Of all the words that are usually said in conversation, he could not hear the phrase "the love of God" without being deeply moved by it. As soon as he heard this expression, he would im-

---

[275] Book of Psalms.

[276] *Rm* 1, 9. The fact that God is called as a witness could be taken to mean that Celano is referring to himself here.

mediately be shaken: he would be transformed and inflamed, as if his deepest heartstrings had been plucked by the plectrum[277] of that exterior voice. He said that offering this reward for alms was noble extravagance and that anyone who considered it to be worth less than money was a terrible fool. As for himself, he precisely observed the resolution he had undertaken when he was still entangled in worldly ties, which was that he would never turn away any poor person who asked him for alms out of the love of God. One time, since he had nothing to give a poor man who was begging out of the love of God, he secretly took some scissors and was about to cut up his tunic and indeed would have done so if the brothers had not caught him in the act. Therefore, he had some other alms given to the poor man instead.

He said, "We must greatly love the Love of the one who has greatly loved us!"

CHAPTER CXLIX
Of his devotion to the angels; and of what he did out of love for St. Michael

197. He lovingly venerated the angels, who fight alongside us and walk with us through the shadows of death.[278] He said that they must be venerated everywhere as companions and likewise as our guardians. He taught them that their glance should not be offended and that one shouldn't do before them what he wouldn't dare to do before men. Since, when singing as a choir one sings in the presence of angels[279], he wanted everyone who was able to do so to come to the choir and sing psalms in devotion.

---

[277] A thin instrument made of metal or bone and used to pluck the strings of a mandolin, guitar or other stringed instrument.

[278] *Ps* 22, 4.

[279] *Ps* 138, 1 and 47, 8.

He would often say that St. Michael should be honored even more highly, since it is his duty to lead souls to God.[280] Consequently, from the Assumption until the feast of St. Michael he would fast devoutly for forty days in honor of Saint Michael and he would also say, "Everyone should offer God praise or some other special tribute in honor of such a great Prince."

CHAPTER CL

Of his devotion to our Lady,
to whose special protection he entrusted his Order

193. He surrounded the Mother of Christ with ineffable love for having given us the Lord of majesty as our brother. He sang special praises to her[281], elevated prayers and dedicated so much and such great love to her that it cannot be uttered any human tongue. In addition, something that should make us even happier is the fact that he chose her as protector of his Order and placed under her wing the children he was about to leave, so that she would nurture and defend them until the very end.

Come then, Protectress of the poor brothers, fulfill your office as our Patron until the time set by the Father.[282]

CHAPTER CLI

Of his devotion to the birthday of Our Lord;
and how he wanted all the poor to be succored on that day

199. He celebrated the Birthday of the Christ Child with more ineffable enthusiasm than any other solemnity, referring to

---

[280] This is stated in the offertory of the Mass for the dead and in the liturgical offices of St. Michael the Archangel (September 29).
[281] He composed the *Salutation of the Blessed Virgin* and his other writings are also filled with praise to the Virgin.
[282] *Gal* 4, 2.

that day in which God, having become a little child, suckled a woman's milk as the feast of all feasts. In his eager thoughts, he would caress the image of those little limbs and because of his compassion for the Baby, which made his heart melt, he would stutter tender words, just like a child, and this name was as sweet as a honeycomb in his mouth.[283]

One time during a discussion as to whether or not it was proper to eat meat, since Christmas happened to fall on a Friday, he replied to Brother Morico, "Brother, it is a sin for you to refer to the Child's birthday as a Friday! On a day like this, I want even the walls to eat meat and short of that, then they should be rubbed with it on the outside."

200. On that day, he wanted the poor and the hungry to be sated by the wealthy[284] and the ox and ass to receive food and hay in greater amounts than usual. And he would say, "If I could speak to the emperor, I would beg him to issue a general statute ordering anyone who can do so to scatter wheat and grain throughout the streets, so that on a day of such great solemnity, the birds and our sisters the skylarks, in particular, can have an abundant amount of food."

He could not hold back his tears when he thought about how needy the poor Virgin was on that day. One time while he was seated at dinner, a brother recalled the poverty of the blessed Mother and the hardship of her little son, Jesus Christ. Francis suddenly got up sobbing in sorrow and, his face streaked with tears, he sat down on the bare ground to finish eating his bread.

Therefore, he called poverty a royal virtue that shone so uniquely in the King and Queen. In fact, replying to the brothers who, during a gathering, had asked him which virtue would bring creatures closer to Christ in friendship, he essentially revealed his heart's secret by saying, "Know, my sons, that Poverty is the spe-

---

[283] *Prv* 16, 24.

[284] *1 Kg* 2, 7.

cial way to salvation is, and its fruits are many but they are known only to a few!"

CHAPTER CLII
Of his devotion to the Body of Christ

201. Throughout his every innermost fiber, he was burning with love for the Sacrament of the Body of the Lord and was filled with wonder over such loving kindness and merciful charity. He considered it no slight omission to fail to attend daily Mass, even just once, if he had the chance to do so. He would take communion often and so devoutly that this would make the others devout as well. Paying all reverence to that venerable Sacrament, he would offer all his limbs in sacrifice and in receiving the sacrificial Lamb, he would sacrifice his spirit on that fire that was always burning on the altar[285] of his heart.

This was this reason that he loved France so much, for she was devoted to the Body of the Lord, and he yearned to die there because of the respect that her people had for sacred things.

He would have liked to send his brothers throughout the world with precious ciboria at times, so that wherever they found that the price of our redemption had been put in an unsuitable place, they could put it in a worthy one.

He wanted great veneration to be shown towards priests' hands, since they have the divine power to prepare such lofty mysteries. He would often say, "If I were to meet a saint come down from heaven and some poor priest at the very same time, first I would honor the priest, running to kiss his feet, while I would say, 'Wait, St. Lawrence[286], for this man's hands touch the Word of life and possess superhuman power!'"

---

[285] *1 Pt* 1, 19 and *Lv* 6, 12.
[286] St. Lawrence was a deacon, not a priest.

CHAPTER CLIII

Of his devotion to the relics of the saints

202. In his devotion to divine worship, this man dear to God did not neglect to honor anything that referred to Him.

When he was at Monte Casale, the one in Massa[287], he ordered the brothers to bring back to their convent some relics from a church that had been abandoned by everyone, for it pained him to think that they had already gone for so long without due honor. However, he was then obliged to go elsewhere on urgent business and the brothers neglected the merit of obedience, forgetting the Father's plea. One day when the brothers were preparing to celebrate Mass, they took the cover off the altar as usual and found beautiful bones that gave off a sweet scent. They were astonished by that unusual sight. A short time later, the Saint returned and looked into whether or not his orders about the relics had been followed. The brothers humbly confessed their fault, thus obtaining forgiveness through their penitence, and the Saint said, "Blessed be the Lord my God[288], who has deigned to accomplish Himself what you should have done!"

Reflect carefully over Francis' devotion, admire the care that God give to our dust and praise his holy obedience. Even if man failed to obey the Saint's orders, the Lord obeyed his prayers.

CHAPTER CLIV

Of his devotion to the Cross; and of a mysterious secret

203. Lastly, who can possibly explain, who can even understand, that he did not want to boast of anything but the cross of the Lord?[289] The only one who is given to know this is the one who alone has experienced it. Without a doubt, even if we were to

---

[287] Massa Trabaria, near the Tuscan town of Arezzo.

[288] *Ps* 18, 47.

[289] *Gal* 6, 14.

experience a small part of it, our words, spoiled by daily and base use, could not express such marvelous feelings. Perhaps this is why it had to be manifested in his flesh, because it could not be expressed with words.[290] Thus, let silence speak where words fail, for the thing that has been designated shouts where the signs of expression are lacking.

This is all that can be said to human ears, that it is still not fully clear why that sacred mystery appeared in the Saint.[291] The part of it that he himself revealed draws its explanation and fulfillment from the future. He who has nature, law and grace as his witnesses will be found to be truthful and worthy of faith.[292]

Of the Poor Women

CHAPTER CLV
How he wanted the brothers to treat them

204. It is not fitting to pass in silence over the spiritual edifice, which was much nobler than the material one, that the blessed Father, under the guidance of the Holy Spirit, built at St. Damian's after repairing the little church there, in order to augment the heavenly city.

It is hard to believe that Christ would have spoken to him from the wood of the cross and have done so in a way so prodigious that it fills anyone who hears about it with fear and sorrow, merely to exhort him to restore a perishable and already decrepit building. As the Holy Spirit had foretold[293], an Order of sacred virgins was to be founded there which, like a reserve of living

---

[290] *Eccl* 1, 8 and *Sir* 43, 29.
[291] *1 Tim* 3, 16.
[292] *Jn* 1, 17-18.
[293] *Acts* 1, 16.

stones[294], would be propagated for the restoration of the celestial home.

After the virgins of Christ began to gather there and to flow from various parts of the world to lead a life of utmost perfection in the observance of supreme poverty[295] in accordance with their profession, and clothing themselves in the splendor of all virtues, the Father continued to take care of them and to love them in the Holy Spirit, even though he deprived them of his bodily presence little by little. In fact, since they had given all proof of their great perfection, the Saint could see that they were ready to face any risk and bear any sorrow out of the love of Christ, and that they were resolved never to deviate from the holy institutions. Thus he firmly promised them and the other women who would live under the same Rule that he would always give his help and advice and the help and counsel of his brothers. As long as he lived, he kept that exact promise and when he was close to death, he firmly instructed the brothers to follow his example at all times, for he said that both the brothers as well as those poor women had been led to live outside of the world by one and the same spirit.[296]

205. When the brothers expressed their surprise over the fact that he no longer went to visit the holy maidens of Christ frequently, he responded, "My dear brothers, you shouldn't think that I no longer love them deeply. In fact, if it were a sin to protect them in Christ, wouldn't it be even worse to have them united with Christ? If I had not called them, I could not have been blamed, but neglecting them after having called them would be the height of cruelty. However, I am acting this way to give you an example, so that you will do as I do[297]. I do not want anyone to offer spontaneously to visit them, but I want those who most object to this duty to be given the responsibility of serving

---

[294] *1 Pt* 2, 5.

[295] This is what made Clare's rule unique among the cloistered orders of the times.

[296] *1 Cor* 12, 11.

[297] *Jn* 13, 15.

them. And they must be spiritual men who have been proven through a long and virtuous religious life."

CHAPTER CLVI
How he upbraided several brothers who willingly went to the monasteries

206. One time, a brother who had two daughters who led a saintly life in a monastery, offered to bring a poor little gift that the Saint wanted to send there, but he was reproached very severely with words that I do not want to relate, and the gift was sent through someone else, who accepted the task only after having refused it a number of times.

During the winter, another man went to a monastery, driven by compassion, ignoring the absolute ban imposed by the Saint. As soon as he heard about it, the Saint made him return on foot without a tunic, walking for a number of miles through the rigorous snow.

CHAPTER CLVII
Of the sermon he preached more through his example than his words

207. Compelled by the repeated prayers of his vicar[298], who wanted him to preach to the daughters while staying at St. Damian's, the Holy Father was won over by his and agreed.

The Women gathered together as usual to hear the word of God, but also to see the Father. Lifting his eyes towards heaven, where he always kept his heart, he began to pray to Christ.

Then he asked for some ashes to be brought to him, used them to make a circle around himself and sprinkled some over his head. As the women watched the blessed Father, who had fallen silent in the middle of the circle of ashes, their hearts were over-

---

[298] Brother Elias.

come with great wonder. And at this point, the Saint got up in front of the astonished women and instead of preaching, he recited the *Miserere*. Then, when it was over, he left quickly.

By virtue of this mutual lesson, God's maidservants were so filled with contrition that they poured out a flood of tears and were barely able to keep from punishing themselves harshly at their own hands. That episode taught them that they should consider themselves dust and that no other feeling towards them except this one could draw them close to his heart.

This was his relationship with the holy women. These were his very profitable visits which were nevertheless rare and were performed out of need. This was his will for his friars: he wanted them to serve the women out of love for Christ, whom they themselves serve, but in such a way that, like birds, they would beware of the traps that had been laid out for them.

Praise of the Brothers' Rule

CHAPTER CLVIII
*How Blessed Francis praised the Rule;
and of the brother who carried it with him*

208. He nurtured burning zeal for the common profession of the Rule and bestowed a special blessing upon all those who were also zealous about it.

Indeed, he defined it to his brothers as "the book of life, the hope of salvation, the marrow of the Gospel, the way of perfection, the key to paradise, the agreement of perpetual covenant".[299] He wanted everyone to have it, to know it well and to go over it always in their minds in order to stir them from indolence and keep the memory of the oath they had made alive in their

---

[299] *Sir* 24, 31; *Rev* 3, 5 and 20, 12-15; *1 Thes* 5, 8; *Gn* 17, 3.

hearts. He taught them to keep it in front of them at all times as a reminder of their conduct and, even more, to die with it.

This lesson was remembered very well by a lay brother, whom we believe should be venerated among the martyrs and who gained the palm of glorious victory. In fact, when the Saracens led him to martyrdom, kneeling humbly and holding the Rule up high in his hands, he said to his companion, "For all the sins committed against this holy Rule, I take the blame before God and before you, dearest brother."[300] This brief confession was followed by the sword, which ended his life in martyrdom, and shortly thereafter he was glorified by miracles.

He had entered the Order so young that he could barely withstand the established fasts and, although just a boy, he would wear a hair shirt against his skin! Happy this young man who crowned a blessed beginning with an even more blessed end![301]

CHAPTER CLIX
A vision glorifying the Rule

209. It happened one time that, through a heavenly miracle, the most holy Father had a vision about the Rule.

At the time in which the brothers were being counseled concerning approval of the Rule[302], the Saint, who was quite preoccupied about it, had the following dream. He felt as if he had collected tiny crumbs of bread from the ground and that he had to distribute them among the numerous hungry brothers surrounding him. While he was hesitating over distributing them for fear that, being so small, they would fall through his hands like specks of dust, a voice from above cried out to him, "Francis,

---

[300] The *Rule of 1221*, chap. 20, states that a brother could make his confessions to another brother if there were no priests.

[301] The editors of the Latin text identify him as Brother Electus.

[302] From the general chapter in 1221 and from the pope in 1223.

take all the crumbs and shape them into a single host and give it in that way to anyone who wants to eat some." As soon as he did this, those who did not receive the bread with devotion or who scorned it after they had taken some, immediately appeared to be infected with leprosy.

In the morning, the Saint recounted everything to his companions, grieving that he was unable to grasp the meaning of the vision[303]. A short time later, however, while he was staying awake in prayer, a voice coming down from heaven told him, "Francis, the crumbs last night are the words of the Gospel, the host is the Rule and leprosy is sin."[304]

Because of the faithfulness sworn by the brothers of those times, they did not find the Rule too difficult to observe, being that they were so willing go beyond obligation in all things. Indeed, there is no room for tepidness or laziness where the incentive of love stirs one to ever greater undertakings.

Of St. Francis' illnesses

CHAPTER CLX
How he discussed with a brother about the care for his body

210. Through innumerable sufferings and serious illness, Francis, the herald of God, set off on the path of Christ and did not turn aside until he had happily reached the established end. Although he was tired and his body was completely destroyed, he never stopped his race towards perfection or resigned himself to mitigating the rigor of his austerity. Even when his body was exhausted, he could not offer it even the smallest care without being

---

[303] *Dn* 2, 19, *Tb* 3, 11 and *2 Pt* 1, 17-18.

[304] St. Bonaventure (*Major Life*) adds that the Saint withdrew to a hermitage (Fonte Colombo) with two brothers in order to prepare a more concise version of the Rule. However, as soon as it was completed and handed to Elias, vicar of the Order, it got lost.

reproached by his conscience. Thus, when he was reluctantly forced to try some remedy to soothe his physical suffering, which went beyond his strength, one day he shyly asked a brother whose advice he greatly trusted, "What do you think, dearest son, about the rebukes that I am often given by my conscience over the care I give to my body? It is afraid that I am indulging it too much because it is ill and that I am too prompt to console it with refined things. It's not as if it feels pleasure anymore, for due to my lengthy illness, it has lost all refinement of taste."

211. Feeling that the answer was coming to him from God, the son cautiously responded to his father, "Tell me, Father, if you please, hasn't your body been as diligent as it could in obeying your orders?" And he replied, "I can testify[305], my son, that it has been obedient in everything and has never avoided any suffering to itself. Rather, one could say that in order to accomplish my will, it has rushed at my every command, has not shirked any sort of effort and has not refused any punishment. In this sense, we have always agreed, he and I, to serve Christ the Lord without any hesitation."

The brother said to him, "So then, Father, where is your generosity? Where's your mercy and great discretion? Could this be a fitting reward to a faithful friend, to be willing to receive its benefits without returning the favor to the giver when he is in need? How could you have served your Lord, Jesus Christ, until now without the help of your body? Hasn't he faced all danger for this, as you yourself admit?" The Father replied, "I must acknowledge that this is absolutely true, son!" Then the brother added, "Is it reasonable for you to abandon such a loyal friend who has exposed himself and his own good for you even in the face of death, now that he is in such great need? Far be it from you, Father, who help and sustain the afflicted! Far be it from you to commit such a sin against the Lord!"[306]

---

[305] *Jn* 5, 31; *Col* 3, 20; *Jgs* 9, 54; *Col* 3, 24.
[306] *Gn* 18, 25.

"And may you be blessed, my son," replied the Saint, "for you have offered such wise and healthy solutions to my scruples." Then he gaily turned to his body to say, "Rejoice, brother body, and forgive me, because from now on, here I am ready to satisfy your desires willingly, ready to come to your help in need!".

But what could possibly please that poor worn-out body anymore? What could sustain it, if all of its parts were already melting away? Francis was already dead to the world and Christ was living within him[307]. Earthly delights were a cross for him to bear since he already bore the cross of Christ deeply rooted in his heart, and so the Stigmata shone in his flesh because the roots of the cross were sunken deep into his spirit.

CHAPTER CLXI
What the Lord promised him as a reward for his infirmities

212. It was truly a miracle that, as exhausted as he was by all the suffering throughout every part of his body, he still had to strength to go on. He even referred to these woes not as pain, but as sisters.

There were certainly many reasons for his suffering. Indubitably, in order to increase his glory with triumph, the Most High not only entrusted difficult works to him while he was still at the very beginning of his soldiering, but even once he was a most expert veteran, He gave him cause for triumph. He also served as an example for his followers, for he never slowed down his activities out of old age, nor did he mitigate his rigor on account of illness. Moreover, and not without cause, he achieved perfect purification in this vale of tears so that he could account right down to the last quarter[308] if even the tiniest particle that could be burned were left in him, so that purified in this way, he could ascend more

---

[307] *Gal* 2, 19-20; 6, 14.
[308] *Ps* 84, 7 and *Mt* 5, 26.

quickly to heaven. But, just as he himself declared as far as others are concerned, I believe that the main reason for his anguish was to prepare a great reward for himself in this way.

213. One night, feeling weaker than usual because of the various grave sufferings, in his heart he began to feel compassion towards himself. However, in order to keep that ready spirit from offering the flesh even a minute of physical assent, he steadfastly maintained the shield of patience by invoking Christ. As he was praying and struggling in this way, the Lord gave him this promise of eternal life: "If the world and the entire universe were most precious gold and, eliminating all pain, you were given a treasure of such great glory to compensate for all your woes that the aforesaid gold would be worthless in comparison and undeserving of mention, wouldn't you be happy and wouldn't you want to bear your temporary suffering willingly?" "Certainly, I would delight in it and delight beyond all measure!" exclaimed the Saint. "Then rejoice," the Lord said to him, "for your illness is the pledge of my kingdom and, thanks to your patience, you can surely expect your share in this kingdom."

Now, how much do you suppose the blessed man rejoiced over such a happy promise? With what great patience and, even more so, with how much love do you think he embraced the sufferings of his body? Only he knows fully, for he was unable to express this at the time. He merely recounted something to his companions as well as he could.

On that occasion, he composed several hymns in praise of creation, inviting the creatures to praise their Creator[309].

---

[309] This hymn of praise, better known as the "Canticle of Brother Sun", is traditionally thought to have been composed by St. Francis while he was staying at St. Damian's during the winter of 1224-25.

Of the death of the Holy Father

CHAPTER CLXII
How, on his deathbed, he exhorted his friars and blessed them

214. *When a man dies,* says Wisdom, *his life is revealed*[310] and we have seen this gloriously accomplished in our Saint. Following the path of God's commandments with a prompt spirit, he went through all the stages of virtue to rise to the top and like soft metal that is hammered to perfection by numerous tribulations, he reached the highest limits of perfection[311]. Then indeed did his marvelous works shine with a brighter light and after trampling over the seductiveness of mortal life, his whole life glowed in the light of the truth as if it had been divine and he soared freely to heaven. He considered it shameful to live according to the world, he loved his own to the end[312] and he welcomed death singing.

In fact, as he was approaching his last days and the temporal light was disappearing to be followed by eternal light, through the example of his virtue he demonstrated that he had nothing in common with the world. Overcome by the grave illness that put an end to his suffering, he had himself placed naked on the naked ground, so that in the final hour in which he was given to the enemy to be assailed, he could battle naked against his naked adversary. In fact, he awaited his triumph without a tremor and with his hands crossed over each other, he clasped the crown of justice[313]. Placed on the ground in this way with his sackcloth taken off, he lifted his face towards heaven as he always did, and thus turned towards that glory with his entire spirit, he covered the wound in his right side with left hand so it wouldn't be seen. And he said to the brothers, "I have done my duty. May Christ teach you what is left for you to do."

---

[310] *Sir* 11, 27.
[311] *Ps* 119. 96.
[312] *Jn* 13, 1.
[313] *2 Tim* 4, 8.

215. At this sight, his sons shed a flood of tears, heaving deep long sighs, and they felt as if they would faint from pain and compassion. In the meantime, stifling his sobs as much as he could, his guardian[314], who comprehended the Saint's wishes through divine inspiration, got up. He quickly got a tunic, some underpants and a sackcloth hat, and said to the Father, "You should know that I'm letting you borrow this tunic, the underpants and the hat out of holy obedience, but in order to assure you that you have no right to own them, I forbid you to give them to anyone else."

The Saint was delighted by this and rejoiced heartily when he saw that he had been faithful to Lady Poverty to the very end. In fact, he had done this so that he would not even have his own clothing when he was on the verge of death, but would have a habit lent to him by someone else. He had gotten used to wearing the sackcloth on his head to cover the scars caused by his eye treatment, and also because he greatly needed a cap made of fine soft wool[315].

216. The Saint then turned the palms of his hands towards heaven, magnifying his Christ who was allowing him to ascend to Him free of any burden. And to show himself as the true imitator of Christ, his God in all things, right to the end[316] he loved the brothers and sons, whom he had loved from the beginning.

He summoned all the brothers who were present and with words of comfort to ease the pain they would feel over his death and with fatherly affection, he exhorted them to love God. He spoke at length about patience and the observance of poverty, counseling the Holy Gospel above all other principles. All the brothers surrounded him and, starting with his vicar, he stretched his right hand over them and laid his hand on the head of each

---

[314] Brother Angelo.
[315] This was not the usual hood (*caputium*) but, as indicated in the *Legenda antiqua*, "a large hood... with a cloth made of wool and linen stitched to the hood over his eyes, since he could not stand daylight".
[316] *Jn* 13, 1.

one.[317] "Farewell, all my sons," he said. "Live in the fear of God and remain with Him forever. And since temptation will come and tribulation is already approaching, happy are those who persevere in the work they have begun. As for me, I am hastening to God, to whose grace I entrust all of you." Then he blessed the brothers who were present as well as all the ones spread throughout the world and those who would come after them until the end of time[318].

Let no one encroach upon this blessing that was given to those present for the ones who were absent. The way it has been indicated   elsewhere seemed to draw a distinction, but more for the purpose of   claiming rank.

CHAPTER CLXIII
Of his death and of what he did first

217. As the desolate brothers wept bitterly, the holy Father had some bread brought to him. He blessed it, broke it and gave each one of them a piece to eat[319]. He also had them bring him the book of the Gospel and asked them to read him the Gospel according to John, from the passages that starts: Before the feast of Passover, etc.[320]. He recalled the most holy last supper that the Lord celebrated with his disciples[321]. Indeed, he did all this to commemorate that venerable institution and to demonstrate the love that he bore for the brothers.

After that, the few days that remained until his death were spent by him in hymns of praise and he invited his most beloved companions to praise Christ together with him. Then, singing as

---

[317] *Gn* 48, 14-22.
[318] *1 Cor* 1, 12; *Jn* 1, 15; *Dn* 7, 18.
[319] *Mt* 14, 19; *Jn* 6, 53.
[320] *Jn* 13, 1.
[321] *Mt* 26, 20.

well as he could, he burst out with the Psalm[322] that goes "With a loud voice I cry out to the Lord, with a loud voice I beseech the Lord". With several verses that he had already composed on another occasion, he also summoned all creatures to praise God, urging them to love Him. He even urged death, terrible and painful to everyone, to sing praise and, going happily to meet it, he received it like a welcome guest, saying, "Welcome, my sister death!" To the doctor, he said, "Come, brother doctor, go ahead and tell me that I'm near death, which will be like the door to life for me!" To the brothers he said, "When you see that I'm about to pass away, place me naked on the ground, just as you saw me the day before yesterday, and once I'm dead, leave me lying there for the time it takes to walk a mile unhurriedly."

At last the final hour arrived in which, since all of Christ's mysteries had been accomplished in him, he blessedly ascended to God.

How a brother saw the soul of the holy Father at his death

217a. One of the brothers among his disciples, a man of some renown, saw the soul of the most holy Father as it was ascending straight to heaven[323], like a star yet as big as the moon and as dazzling the sun, hovering over vast waters and being transported on a pure-white cloud. Then a multitude of people gathered together, praising and glorifying God's name. All the citizens of Assisi hastened in droves and the people from the entire district hurried to see the divine marvels that the Lord had manifested in his servant.

Deprived of such a Father, his sons grieved and they poured out the pain and love in their hearts with tears and sighs.

---

[322] *Ps* 142, 2.
[323] *Ps* 29, 3; *Rev* 14, 13.

The newness of the miracle also turned weeping to joy and mourning to song.

They saw the body of the blessed Father adorned with the Stigmata of Christ and that is, in the middle of his hands they saw, not the holes from the nails, but the nails themselves formed out of his flesh, indeed born from his very flesh and they had kept the dark color of iron, whereas his right side was reddened with blood. His skin, which had been dark by nature, now gleamed with extraordinary whiteness, promising the prize of blessed resurrection. Lastly, his limbs became soft and supple and becoming like the limbs of a child again, they were not stiff the way they usually are in the dead.

CHAPTER CLXIV

Of the vision that Brother Augustine had on his deathbed

218. The minister of the brothers in Terra di Lavoro at that time was Brother Augustine[324] and he had come to his final hour. He had lost the power of speech long before, yet he was heard crying out, "Wait for me, Father! Wait for me! Here I am, I'm coming with you!" And in response to the questions of the astonished friars concerning his exclamation, he declared, "Don't you see that our father Francis is going up to heaven?"

And released from its flesh, his sacred soul immediately followed the most holy Father.

---

[324] Brother Augustine, a native of Assisi, was also cited by Dante in *Paradise*, XII, 130.

CHAPTER CLXV
How, after his death, the holy Father appeared to a brother

219. That night at the very same hour, as another brother whose life was praiseworthy was praying intently, the glorious Father appeared to him dressed in a scarlet dalmatic[325] and he was being followed by an immense throng of men. Many of them stepped aside to ask the brother, "Isn't this the Christ, brother?"[326] And he would reply, "Yes, it is he!"[327] And the others asked him again, "Isn't he Saint Francis?" And again, the brother answered that it was. For it seemed to him and to that crowd that Christ and blessed Francis were one and the same.

Anyone who is capable of understanding will not find this judgment rash, because he who is united with Christ becomes one spirit with Him and God himself becomes all in everyone.[328]

In a marvelous procession, the blessed Father arrived at last at a smiling place irrigated by the clearest of water and lush with every sort of plant, rich in splendid flowers and full of trees of all kinds. There was a marvelously large and beautiful palace and the new citizen of heaven went in, and finding many brothers seated there at a table that was sumptuously set with exquisite food, he began to feast with his own in delight.

CHAPTER CLXVI
The vision of the bishop of Assisi
about the death of the holy Father

220. The bishop of Assisi had gone on a pilgrimage to the church of St. Michael[329] at that time. While he was stopping over

---

[325] The liturgical vestments worn by deacons.

[326] *Jn* 7, 26.

[327] *Mt* 26, 48.

[328] *1 Cor* 6, 17 and 12, 6.

[329] The famous sanctuary on Mount Gargano, in southern Italy.

in Benevento on his return, the blessed Father Francis appeared to him on the night of his death and said to him, "Father, now I am leaving the world to go to Christ."[330]

When he arose the next morning, the bishop told his companions about his vision and, calling the notary, he had the date and the time of his vision written down. Feeling very disconsolate, he wept that he had lost such an excellent Father. When he arrived at his diocese, he recounted what had taken place and gave the Lord endless thanks for his gifts.

Of the canonization and translation of St. Francis

220a. In the name of our Lord Jesus Christ. Amen. On the third of October in the year of his Incarnation 1226, on the day he had foretold, twenty years after he had given himself most perfectly to Christ and had followed the life and the footsteps of the Apostles, the apostolic man, Francis, was released from the shackles of mortal life, happily passed on to Christ and was buried near the city of Assisi.[331] He began to shine forth with miracles that were so numerous and so great and so varied that in a short time, he led a large part of the world to admire this new age.

Since he was already becoming famous in various places through the new light of miracles and people who had enjoyed release from their afflictions through him were flocking there from all over, the lord pope Gregory, who was in Perugia with all the cardinals and with the other prelates of the Church, began to discuss his canonization. Thus finding that they agreed, all of them gave the same opinion. They read and approved the miracles that God had worked through his servant and they extolled the

---

[330] *Jn* 16, 28.
[331] Francis was buried in the Church of St. George, which was originally outside the city walls.

exterior and interior life of the blessed Father with the highest of praise.

First of all, the princes of the earth were called to this great solemnity and on the established day, the entire group of prelates, together with an endless crowd of people, entered the city of Assisi with the blessed pope so that his canonization could be celebrated there for the greater honor of the Saint. After everyone had gone then to the place that had been prepared for this solemn occasion, first of all Pope Gregory preached to the entire people and announced God's splendors with sweet affection. Then he also praised the holy father Francis in a most noble speech and, while he was declaring the purity of his life, he was bathed with tears. Finishing his discourse and raising his arms towards heaven, Pope Gregory exclaimed in a resounding voice...[332].

The Prayer of the Saint's Companions

221. Here, blessed Father, in our simplicity we have attempted to sing of your magnificent works as well as we could and to reveal, for your glory, at least some of your innumerable virtues. We are well aware that our poor words have greatly dimmed the splendor of your marvels, for words are powerless to explain the greatness of such perfection. Quite happy that the human pen should be beneath the heights of such a wonderful life, we ask you and our readers to consider our affection as our commitment. And who indeed, o saint among saints, could possibly feel within himself and impart to others the ardor of your spirit, and conceive of those ineffable transports of love that rose incessantly from your heart up to God?

Delighted by the sweetness of your memory, we have written these pages in an effort to make this known, albeit in a stumbling fashion, to others as well, as long as we are alive. Now

---

[332] The *M* codex ends at this point.

you feed on the finest of wheat for which you so greatly hungered, and you drink from the stream of full joy[333] for which you so greatly thirsted, but we are certain that the abundance of the house of God has not inebriated you so much that you would forget your children, since the One in whose vision you are blessed is fully mindful of us. So draw us to yourself, venerated Father, so that we whom you see as tepid through indolence, languid through laziness and virtually dead through neglect can follow your perfume[334]. The little flock is already following you with unsteady footing and our weak and dazzled eyes cannot bear the brilliant rays of your perfection.

Mirror and model of perfection, let us live a new life as in the beginning and do not allow us to be any different from you in life, since we have been true to you in profession.

222. Here, we now prostrate ourselves in humility to beseech the clemency of the eternal Majesty on behalf of our Minister, Christ's servant and successor to your sacred humility and imitator of true poverty, who has attentively cared for your little lambs with sweet affection out of his love for your Christ. We pray to you, o Saint, to help him and love him so that, ever following in your footsteps, he may gain the glory with which you have now been blessed.

223. With all the affection in our hearts, we also pray to you, most merciful Father, for that son of yours who now, like before, has written your praises[335]. He has devoutly composed this little work to the best of his ability, even though it is not worthy of your greatness and together with us, he offers and dedicates it to you. Deign to defend him from all evil, let holy merit grow in him and, through your prayers, allow him to come to enjoy the company of saints for eternity.

---

[333] *Ps* 81, 17 and 36, 9.

[334] *Sg* 1, 3.

[335] Celano is obviously alluding to himself here, and to his double biography of Francis.

224. Father, remember all your children who, tormented by grave danger, can only follow in your footsteps from afar, as you, most holy One, can well see. Give them the strength to go on, purify them so that they will be perfected, make them fertile so that they will bear fruit, inspire them with the spirit of grace and prayer[336] so that they may possess the humility that you had, observe the poverty to which you were always faithful, deserve the charity with which you have always loved Christ crucified.

Who, together with the Father and the Holy Spirit, lives and reigns forever and ever. Amen.

Here ends the Second Life

---

[336] *Zec* 12, 10, *1 Cor* 1, 23.

Treatise of the Miracles

of Blessed Francis

The text of the letter of introduction to the Minister General, Brother John of Parma, has been lost and only the opening words remain: "The religious solicitude...".

Here begin the miracles of Blessed Francis

CHAPTER I
Of the marvelous way in which his Order arose

As we begin to set down in writing the miracles of our most holy father Francis, with regard to the place of honor that we have reserved for the miracles that were manifested in him, we thought it would be proper first of all to emphasize that solemn prodigy that warned, shook and, I would say, terrified the world. This was the rise of the Order, the fertility of the sterile and the generation of many and various people.

He looked pensively at the old world, sullied by the crust of vice, at the deadened sacred orders far from the footsteps of the apostles and, in the depths of the night of sin, at the silence that had been imposed on sacred discipline: and suddenly that new man bounded into the world[1] and at the abrupt appearance of this new army, the people were dumbfounded by the signs of apostolic renewal. The long-buried perfection of the early Church, whose grandeur the world had read about but whose examples it could no longer see was immediately brought to light. Why shouldn't the last be first[2], for the hearts of fathers have been transformed miraculously into their sons' and those of the sons to their fathers'? Could anyone possibly fail to become aware of such a widespread and famous mission of the two Orders[3] without taking it as an omen of some magnificent future event? Since the time of the Apostles, never had the world had such an exceptional or such a marvelous warning.

Moreover, the fertility of the sterile must also be admired. I am referring to this poor religion, devoid of all the humor of worldly things, as sterile and arid land. It is truly sterile, since it

---

[1] *Wis* 18, 1415.

[2] *Mt* 20, 26, followed by *Mal* 3, 6.

[3] Is this a reference to the first and second Seraphic Orders, or does it refer more generally to the Franciscan and Dominican orders?

does not reap and does not store its harvest in the barn[4], nor does it carry a full traveling bag along the way of the Lord. And yet, contrary to every expectation, this Saint harbored the hope of inheriting the world, heedless of his exhausted body and of Sarah's dead womb[5], certain that through this fertility divine power would very soon beget the Hebrew people. For it is not sustained by full storerooms, overflowing warehouses or vast estates, but by poverty itself, through which it has made itself worthy of heaven and is marvelously nurtured in the world. O weakness that comes from God, more powerful than any human strength[6], that brings glory to our cross and offers wealth to our poverty!

In the end, this vine was seen to spread out very quickly, stretching its offshoots from sea to sea.[7] People assembled from all over, flocking in throngs, and virtually all of a sudden, the living stones were gathered for the eminent building of this marvelous temple.[8] Not only did we see that it multiplied in a short time through its numerous children, but it was also glorified, since we know that many of those who were born achieved the palm of martyrdom[9] and we venerate many of those who have been inscribed in the catalogue of the saints because of their perfect confession of all holiness.[10]

But let us return to the Head of all those people, whom it is now our intention to discuss.

---

[4] *Mt* 6, 26 followed by *Lk* 9, 3.

[5] *Rm* 4, 19.

[6] *1 Cor* 1, 25.

[7] *Ez* 17, 6-7.

[8] *Mk* 13, 1 and *1 Pt* 2, 5.

[9] The martyrs of Morocco (1220), Ceuta (1227), Valence (1231).

[10] St. Anthony, canonized in 1232 and perhaps also Brother Roger of Todi. Others from the First Order are unknown, although St. Elizabeth (Third Order) was canonized in 1235. At this time, Innocent IV had started the proceedings to canonize Brother Simon.

CHAPTER II

*Of the miracle of the Stigmata
and of how the Seraph appeared to him*

2. The new man, Francis, shone through a new and stupendous prodigy when he appeared awarded with a singular privilege that had never granted throughout the previous centuries, and what I mean by this is that he was adorned with the sacred Stigmata and, in this mortal body, he was rendered similar to the body of the Christ Crucified.[11] Anything that the human tongue can say of him will never be fitting enough praise.

There is no reason to ask why, for it is arcane, nor should any previous examples be sought, since this is a singular gift. Both publicly and privately, all the ardor of the man of God was turned to the cross of the Lord, and from the time he first started soldiering for the Crucifix, various mysteries of the cross shone over him.

In fact, when at the beginning of his conversion he had decided to bid farewell to the enticements of this life, Christ spoke to him from the wood of the cross while he was praying and this voice came from the image's very mouth: "Francis, go and repair my house which, as you can see, is falling into ruin!" From that point on, the remembrance of the Lord's Passion was imprinted in his heart in deeply-etched letters and, through a deep assimilation received in him, his soul would begin to grow faint as soon as the Beloved spoke.[12] Didn't he perhaps go so far as to wrap himself up in the cross when he chose the habit of penance, which bears the image of the cross?[13] Although this habit was even better suited to his intentions, since he was zealous in poverty, nevertheless the Saint demonstrated the mystery of the Cross even more clearly through it, to the point that, just as his soul had clothed itself with the crucified Lord on the inside, his body was

---

[11] *Phil* 3, 10 and 21; *Rm* 7, 24.
[12] *Sg* 5, 4.
[13] *First Life*, 22.

likewise clothed with the cross of Christ on the outside, and under the same sign with which God had overcome the power of the spirit, his army soldiered for the glory of God.

3. Wasn't it Brother Sylvester, one of the first friars and a man of proven sanctity in every respect, who saw that coming from his mouth was a golden cross which, with its arms outstretched, miraculously marked the whole world?[14] A trustworthy report has also been written and validated that with his bodily eyes, Brother Monaldo, illustrious in his life, behavior and in his practice of virtue, saw blessed Francis crucified while Blessed Anthony was preaching on the subject of the cross.[15]

And wasn't it perhaps customary, indeed established by pious decree that wherever the first sons should happen to glimpse the shape of the cross, they should pay it the honor of due reverence?[16] More than anything else, he knew the "tau" sign best, which was the only way he would sign his letters and which was drawn all over the walls of his cells. And with his bodily eyes, that man of God, Pacificus, contemplator of celestial visions, saw an enormous multicolored "tau" on the father's forehead, shining as brightly as gold.[17]

How worthy of belief through rational persuasion and of acceptance by all, then, is the fact that the man who was armed with such great love for the cross should have become the object of admiration because of his marvelous homage to the cross!

Thus, there is nothing about him that can be declared more truthfully than what is said about the Stigmata of the cross.

4. The way in which this apparition then took place is as follows.

(*What follows is essentially the same description as the one found in the* First Life, *94-95, with just a few variations, such as the indication that the hermitage of Mount La Verna* "is in the province of Tuscany

---

[14] *Second Life*, 109.

[15] *First Life*, 48.

[16] *First Life*, 45.

[17] *Second Life*, 49 and 106.

where, by this time, in his retreat for devout contemplation, he had fully extended himself towards heavenly glory"; *as well as the different way in which he would move from anxiety towards certainty*: "but while he was looking beyond himself and his intellect failed in its capacity to find and answer, all of a sudden this meaning was manifested to him on his very body".

5. Lastly, dying happily two years later, he exchanged this valley of misery for the blessed homeland and when the marvelous fame of this great event reached men's ears, there was an enormous gathering of people who praised and glorified God's name.[18] All the people of Assisi came down in throngs and the residents of the entire area hastened there, avid to see this new sight that the Lord had put on the earth for the very first time. The novelty of the miracle turned weeping to joy and enchanted the eye with astonishment and ecstasy. They saw the blessed body adorned with the Stigmata of Christ and that is, his hands and feet held, not the holes from the nails, but the very nails themselves that, by divine virtue, were made miraculously from his flesh and indeed they were part of his very flesh, so that if one side was pressed, the other side would immediately respond like a single nerve.[19] It could also be seen that his side was turning red with blood.

We saw this: we who are saying this touched what we are describing with our hands, with our tearful eyes we caressed what we are confessing on our lips, and we profess that each moment of what we once swore by touching sacred objects[20] is true. Along with us, many of our brothers also saw this while the Saint was

---

[18] *Acts* 21, 30; *Lk* 2, 20; *Ps* 85, 9.

[19] Although much of these section repeats what was described in the *First Life*, 113 and in the *Second Life*, 217a, the details about how the nail callosities moved in his hands and feet are new.

[20] It is unclear whether the oath was sworn on the Bible or on some other sacred object. Nevertheless, this obviously refers to a ritual oath either for the initial examination during the canonization proceedings or when Gregory IX issued the bulls (1237) affirming that the Stigmata were true. These bulls were then upheld by both Innocent IV and Alexander IV.

alive and, at his death, over fifty of them, together will countless laymen, venerated this.

Thus, let there be no room for any uncertainty, let no one doubt the great gift given by eternal Goodness. Indeed, God willing, may the many members remain united with the head, who is Christ, through this seraphic love so that in the battle they may be found worthy of such armor and that in a similar rank of glory they may be raised to the kingdom of heaven! What sane person can fail to say that all of this is for the glory of Christ?

But let's move on to the punishment that was inflicted on those who were incredulous, thereby convincing those who are not devout and making the devout even more certain.

6. Near Potenza, a city in the kingdom of Apulia, there was a cleric by the name of Roger, an honorable person and a canon at the main church. Tormented by a lengthy illness, one day he went to pray in a church in which there was a painted image of blessed Francis, depicting the sacred Stigmata. Going up to it, he prostrated himself in prayer before the image, imploring with great devotion. While his eyes kept staring at the Saint's Stigmata, however, his mind wandered in vain thoughts and he did not immediately drive out the insinuating thorn of doubt through diligent reasoning. Indeed, through the trickery of that age-old adversary, he broken-heartedly began to say to himself, "Could it be true that this saint became famous through such a miracle, or was it the pious illusion of his followers?" He pressed on, "It was a feigned invention, or perhaps a deception conceived by his friars. It transcends human intellect and is far from all reasonable judgment." O human insanity! Fool! For indeed, the less that divine prodigy could be comprehended, the more you should have venerated it. If you had the flower of wisdom, you should have known that it is so easy for God to continue to renew the world with new marvels and, to His own glory, always to work in us things that are not worked in others.[21]

---

[21] *2 Cor* 4, 12.

What happened then? He who brooded over frivolous thoughts was harshly afflicted by God so that he would learn through his suffering[22] not to take God's name in vain. Just as he heard a noise like a shot from a crossbow, he was suddenly struck on the palm of his left hand (for he was left-handed). Thus stricken with this wound, at the very moment he was astonished by that sound, he immediately took off his glove, for he was wearing gloves, and although his palm had not been struck, in the middle of his hand he saw a wound so that it looked as if he had been struck by an arrow, and it burnt so much that he thought it would kill him. Wondrous to relate! No trace of it could be seen on his glove and so the pain of the hidden wound corresponded to the hidden wound in his heart.

7. Thus, for two days he moaned and roared, driven by the fiercest pain. He told everyone about the veil of incredulity in his heart and confessed his belief that St. Francis had truly had the Stigmata, swearing on oath that the shadows of doubt had now fled. He prayed and beseeched the Saint of God to help him out of respect for the holy Stigmata and his many prayers were further enriched by a great sacrifice of tears. A true wonder! Incredulity cast aside, his mental recovery was followed by physical recovery. All pain subsided, the burning cooled and there was no trace of his ever having been struck. That man became humble before God, devout to the Saint and was the amicable subject of the Order of the friars ever after. This solemn miracle was confirmed and was also corroborated in particular through the oath of the bishop of that place.

May the marvelous power of God, who in the city of Potenza revealed magnificent events, be blessed in all things.

8. It is customary among noble Roman matrons, both widowed and married and especially among those whose wealth can maintain the privilege of generosity and in whom Christ has instilled his love, to set a small room aside in their houses, or in

---

22 *Heb* 5, 8.

other words, a small refuge dedicated to prayer, where they keep painted icons and the image of whichever saint they venerate in particular. Thus a lady, who was noble in the splendor of her behavior and through her family's glory, had chosen St. Francis as her protector. She had a painted image of him in the room that was set aside and there she prayed to the Father in private.[23] One day while she was devoutly attending to prayer, she began to peer very sharply to see the sacred signs, but was unable to find them and was painfully overcome with great astonishment. But it is no marvel that the painting did not have what the painter had omitted. For several days, the woman bore that affliction deep in her heart and did not say anything to anyone, gazing at the image often and always sorrowing over it. All of a sudden, one day the same signs that were normally put in other images appeared on his hands, so that divine virtue compensated for what human art had overlooked.

9. Trembling in great astonishment, the woman immediately called her daughter, who had followed her mother's holy intentions, and showing her what had taken place, she diligently asked if she had ever seen the image without the Stigmata before then. The girl affirmed and swore that, yes, the Stigmata had been missing before and that now the image truly appeared to have it. But since the human mind often drives itself to fall and revokes truth for doubt, the guilty doubt that maybe the image had been marked this way right from the start crept into the woman's heart again. Nevertheless, in order to keep the first miracle from being scorned, the virtue of God added a second one. In fact, those signs disappeared immediately and the image was deprived of that privilege, so that the subsequent sign was proof of the previous one. I saw this married woman full of virtue, I declare, I saw that under her worldly habit, her soul was consecrated to Christ the Lord.

---

[23] *Mt* 6, 6.

10. From the time it is born, human reason allows itself to be enticed so greatly by sensual teachings and coarse specters, that it is forced by changeable imagination to revoke in doubt everything there is to believe. Therefore, not only is it difficult for us to believe these marvelous acts of the saints, but for the most part, faith itself endures objections to the truth of salvation.

Indeed, there was a brother in the Order of the Friars Minor, a preacher by office and influential in his life, who was firmly convinced of the reality of the holy Stigmata. Since one either maintains his usual order of beliefs or begins to look beyond them, the suspicion of doubt about the Saint's miracle began to be titillated in him. You could see the struggle that took hold of his spirit, with reason defending the side of truth and imagination always suggesting the opposite. Reason, backed by much support, determines that things are as they are said to be and if other arguments in favor of credibility also lack, then it rests on the truth believed by the Church. The shadows of common sense conspire in the opposite direction against the miracle, for the miracle appears to be contrary to all laws of nature and has never been heard of throughout the centuries. One night, exhausted by this battle, he went to his room with his reason weakened and his imagination more stubborn than ever in its insolence. While he was sleeping, St. Francis appeared to him with his feet muddied, humbly harsh and patiently irate. And he said, "What are these clashes and conflicts in you? What is this narrow-mindedness of doubt? Look at my hands and my feet!"[24] And although the friar could see the pierced hands, he could not see the Stigmata on his mud-covered feet. "Take the mud off my feet," he said, "and you'll recognize the mark of the nails!" As he gripped the Saint's feet, the friar felt as if he were washing off the mud and were touching the openings of the nails with his hands. As soon as the friar woke up, he was bathed in tears and through public confes-

---

[24] *Jn* 20, 27 followed by 20, 25.

sion, he purified his former love that had somehow become muddied.

11. So that the Holy Stigmata of the invincible soldier of Christ won't be considered of little value, the novelty of a more obvious miracle that took place in Spain, or rather, in the kingdom of Castille, will make it easier to understand what powerful arms those signs were with God, in addition to constituting a sign of special prerogative and an insignia of supreme love that the whole world has never ceased to admire. In fact, there were two people who had long reviled each other in mutual hatred and there was no appeasing their bitterness, no easing their heated insults, and there was not even a moment's solution for the grief that had arisen between them, except for one of them to die a most cruel death at the hands of the other one. Both of them went about covered in armor and, with many companions, each one laid frequent traps for his adversary, since they could not commit the crime in public.

It happened one evening, when it was already deep into twilight, that a very honest man of praiseworthy fame passed along the road on which one of them was lying in ambush to kill the other. While he was hurrying towards the friars' church to pray after compline[25] as he was accustomed to doing since he was very devoted to St. Francis, the children of darkness rose up against the child of light[26], whom they thought was their adversary whom they had long sought to kill. Mortally wounding him from all sides with their swords, they left him there half-dead. Lastly, however, the enemy had thrust his sword deeply into the man's neck and, unable to withdraw it, left it in the wound.

12. People hastened from all over and, crying to the heavens, the entire neighborhood denounced the death of an innocent. And since there was still a breath of life left in the man, the doctors decided not to take the knife from his throat. Perhaps they

---

[25] The last evening prayers.
[26] *1 Thes* 5, 5.

did this out of respect for confession, so that he could at least confess through some sign. Therefore, since the doctors had worked all night long until morning to clean away the blood and close his wounds but did not obtain any improvement because there were so many deep injuries, they gave up treating him. Filled with great sorrow, the Friars Minor were with the doctors around the bed, and awaiting the death of their friend and the friars' bell then rang out for matins. When the man's wife heard the bell, she ran over to the bed wailing, "My lord, get up quickly and go to matins, because you're being called by the bell!" With a repeated murmur coming from his chest, he who was thought to be dying immediately attempted to speak, mumbling his words as well as he could. And raising his hand to the sword stuck in his neck, he seemed to be motioning for someone to pull it out. A truly miraculous thing! The sword, suddenly flying up, bounced to the main door of the house as if it had been flung by the hand of a very powerful man. The man got up and, healed almost as if he had simply gotten up from a deep sleep, he recounted the marvels of the Lord.

13. Such great amazement gripped everyone's hearts[27] that they felt as if they had lost their wits and were seeing what was happening in a phantasmagoria.[28] At these thoughts, the one who had been healed said, "Do not fear. Do not think that what you are seeing is a figment of imagination. In fact, St. Francis, to whom I have always been devoted, has left just this very minute, and he has perfectly healed all my injuries. He placed his most holy Stigmata over my wounds and, one at a time and with their sweetness, he soothed them all. As you can see, that contact has miraculously healed every fracture. Then, while you were hearing the panting in my chest, since the other wounds had been healed with all sweetness, it seemed to me that the most holy Father,

---

[27] *Lk* 5, 9 and *Acts* 1, 24.

[28] A phantasmagoria was a type of magic-lantern show consisting of various optical illusions in which things quickly changed size and blended into each other.

having made the sword go down my throat, wanted to leave. And it was to him that I was weakly gesturing with my hand -- for I couldn't speak -- to extract the sword, which was about to kill me. And gripping it at once, as you all saw, he hurled it aside with a strong hand. Then, like before, he stroked and medicated my wounded throat with his holy Stigmata and healed it so perfectly that the flesh that was cut looks identical to the flesh that has always been intact."

Who then can fail to be amazed by such events, who could invent that everything that is said about the Stigmata is not divine?

CHAPTER III
Of the power he had over inanimate creatures

14. *(With the exception of six words and the omission of three lines at the beginning, this section is identical to the account in the* Second Life, *106, about the cauterization done on Francis' optic nerve).*

15. *(With the exception of one word and the omission of the last gloss, this section is a word-for-word repetition of the miracle of the water that gushed from solid rock on Mount La Verna,* Second Life, *46).*

16. Gagliano[29] is a populous and noble castle in the diocese of Valva (Sulmona) in which there lived a woman named Mary who, having been converted to the Lord through the difficult ways of this world, had dedicated herself to serving St. Francis. One day, when she went up on a mountain that was doomed by a serious drought in order to weed around green maples, she forgot to bring water with her and because of the great heat, she was about to faint from thirst. Unable to work any longer and lying almost lifelessly on the ground, she mentally began to invoke her patron, St. Francis, and then, exhausted, she fell asleep for a while. And here St. Francis came to her and called her by name.[30] "Get

---

[29] Gagliano-Aterno in the province of Aquila, not far from the town of Celano.
[30] *Is* 40, 26.

up," he said, "and drink the water that is offered to you and to many as a divine gift." The woman yawned at the sound of this voice and, overcome with drowsiness, settled down again. Called once again, she fell back to the ground, overcome with exhaustion. But the third time, greatly comforted by the Saint's order, she got up and, picking up a fern that was near her, she uprooted it from the ground. Upon seeing that all its roots were damp, she began to dig around using her fingers and a little stick. The hole was immediately filled with water and the little drop swelled until it had become a spring. The woman drank her full and then she rinsed her eyes which, dimmed by long illness, could not see anything clearly. Her sight cleared and it was as if her eyes had been suffused with new light and wrinkled old age had been driven out. The woman hurried home and, to the glory of St. Francis, showed everyone this wonderful miracle. Its fame spread and even reached the ears of people in other regions. People afflicted with various illnesses[31] hastened from all over and after making their salutary confession, they were liberated from their illnesses. In fact, the blind regained their eyesight, the lame could walk again, those with dropsy became thinner[32] and various diseases were healed in various ways. A clear spring is still there even today and an oratory was built there in honor of St. Francis.[33]

17. During the time he was staying at the hermitage of Sant'Urbino[34] and was suffering from a very serious illness, St. Francis weakly asked for some wine but was told that there was none there to give him. He then asked for some water to be brought to him and when it was given to him, he blessed it with the sign of the cross. Changing its nature, that element immediately lost it own flavor and took on another one. What had been pure water became excellent wine and what poverty was unable to do was offered by sanctity. Upon tasting some of it, the man of

---

[31] *Mk* 1, 34 and *Jn* 5, 4.
[32] Dropsy causes extensive swelling.
[33] The spring is still there, but only the ruins remain of the oratory.
[34] This episode is mentioned briefly in the *First Life*, 61.

God was healed so quickly that while the marvelous cure was caused by that transformation, the wonderful transformation itself testified to the wonderful cure.

18. A very grave pestilence raged in the province of Rieti and it struck all oxen so badly that hardly any of them were left untouched by it. One night in a vision, a God-fearing fellow was instructed to hurry to the friars' hermitage, get the water used to wash blessed Francis' hands or feet, for he was staying there at that time, and spray it over the oxen. When he got up in the morning, the man, very solicitous of his benefaction, went there and, unbeknownst to the Saint, he obtained this washing water through the other friars and sprinkled it over all his oxen as he had been told. From that moment on, through the grace of God the infection ceased and never raged through that land again.

19. In various regions, the fervent devotion of many inhabitants induced them to bring St. Francis bread and other food for him to bless. Through the gift of God, this food would keep for a long time without going bad and the sick who ate it would be healed. It has also been proven that, by virtue of this blessed food, raging thunderstorms and hailstorms had been driven away.[35] And some people who had experienced this can attest that by means of the cord he tied around his waist and the pieces of fabric unstitched from his habits, diseases were driven out, fever fled and long-desired health returned.[36] And when, on Christmas day, he celebrated the commemoration of the Crèche and of everything that had once come to pass with the Baby Jesus in a mystical presentation out of love for the Child of Bethlehem, one of the many miracles that was worked there by God was that the hay taken from that manger became a saving medicine for a great number of people, especially for women with difficult labor and for all animals struck with infection.[37]

---

[35] See *Second Life*, 35-36, with particular reference to the town of Greccio.
[36] See *First Life*, 64 and 63, as well as 96 and 136 below.
[37] See *First Life*, 84-87.

Having said this about inanimate creatures, let us add something about the obedience given by the animate ones.

CHAPTER IV
Of his power over animate creatures

20. The creatures also tried to return St. Francis' love for them and to reciprocate his benefaction with gratitude.... (*What follows is the episode of the swallows at Bevagna, taken from the* First Life, *58, with other elements drawn from the* Legend *by Julian of Speyer, 37*).

21. (*Recounted here is the episode of the swallows at Alviano, as described in the* First Life, *59*).

22. In the city of Parma, a student was tormented so greatly by a swallow's incessant chirping that he could hardly stay there long enough to meditate. Losing his patience somewhat, he began to say, "This must be one of those swallows that, as it has been written[38], would not allow St. Francis to preach until he told them to be quiet." And turning to the swallow, he said, "In the name of St. Francis, I order you to let me catch you." The bird immediately flew into his hands. The astonished student set it free and did not hear it chirp any more.

23-28. [*The episodes in this section are taken either word for word or with slight modifications from the recounts of the river bird of Lake Piediluco (*Second Life, *167), the fish in this lake (*First Life, *61), the hawk on Mount La Verna (*Second Life, *168), the pheasant in Siena (*Second Life, *170), the cricket at the Porziuncola (*Second Life, *171) and the clay pot and the bees (*Second Life, *169)*].

29. Near Greccio, a live and healthy leveret was offered to St. Francis. When the leveret was set free, even though it could have run off wherever it wanted, it raced over when the Saint called it and hopped into his lap. Picking it up kindheartedly and

---

[38] In *First Life*, 39.

gently warning it not to get caught again, the Saint ordered it to return to the woods.[39]

30. (*This is a brief account of the episode that took place with the rabbit, as described in the* First Life, *60*).

31. One time when the man of God was traveling from Siena to the Spoleto valley, he came to a field in which a rather large flock of sheep was grazing. Since he had greeted them sweetly, as was his custom, they all ran over to him, lifting their heads and returning his greeting with loud bleating. His vicar attentively observed what the lambs were doing and, walking behind him with the other companions at a slower pace, he said to them, "Did you see what the lambs did with our holy Father? He must certainly be a great saint," he concluded, "if beasts venerate him as a father and mindless creatures recognize him as the friend of their Creator."

32. The larks are birds that love broad daylight and are terrified of the darkness of dusk, yet on the evening that St. Francis passed on from this world to Christ, even though the twilight of the coming night had already fallen, they went to the roof of the hut and circled around it for a long time, screeching loudly and showing either joy or sadness -- we don't know which -- in their own way through their singing. They resounded with a gladness that sounded both like weeping and jubilant mourning, either to grieve for the orphaned sons or to salute the Father who was approaching eternal glory.

Filled with astonishment, the guardians of the city who were taking turns watching over the place invited the others to marvel over the miracle.

---

[39] See also *First Life*, 60.

CHAPTER V

How divine clemency was always ready
to fulfill St. Francis' desires

33. Not only did creatures obey this man's signals, but the providence of the Creator also condescended to his desires wherever he went. That paternal clemency anticipated his vows and since he had fully entrusted himself to it, it anticipated him by coming promptly to his aid. Want and its receipt, desire and its fulfillment, came at the same time.

(This same section continues with the miraculous supply of food described in the First Life, *55. The brief mention made of his attempt to go to Syria recalls his trip to Spain, which is recounted below).*

34. When he was returning from Spain without having been able to reach Morocco as he had desired, St. Francis fell gravely ill. Afflicted not only with weakness but with dearth, and rudely kicked out of his lodging by his host, he remained speechless for three days. When he finally regained enough strength little by little and continued slowly on his way, he said to Brother Bernard that if he had a little bird, he would eat it. And there, hurrying across the field was a knight, carrying an exquisite bird, who said to St. Francis, "Servant of God, accept with pleasure what divine clemency is sending you." He joyfully welcomed the gift and realizing that Christ was taking care of him, he blessed Him in all things.[40]

35. *(Of the cloth for the cowls brought by a stranger while he lay ill in the bishop's palace in Rieti: see* Second Life, *41 and 43).*

36. *(The dinner that was provided miraculously for the oculist, taken from the* Second Life, *44).*

---

[40] *Tob* 7, 1 and 13, 1 and *1 Thes* 5, 23.

CHAPTER VI
Of Lady Jacoma dei Settesoli

37. Jacoma dei Settesoli[41], who in the city of Rome was equally famous for her nobility and her sanctity, had earned the privilege of the Saint's special love.

In praising her, there is no need for me to recall her illustrious lineage, the rank of her family, her great wealth, nor the marvelous perfection of her virtues or her long chastity as a widow.

Now then, as the saint lay ill with the sickness that, by putting an end to his suffering, ended the happy race of his life[42] with most blessed results, a few days before he died, he wanted to have Lady Jacoma sent for from Rome, so that if she wished to see the one she had so ardently loved during his exile as he was returning to his homeland, she could hasten to his side. The letter was written, a very swift messenger was sought and once he was found, he prepared to set off. But suddenly, the pawing of horses, the noise of soldiers and the sound of a group gathering could be heard at the door. One of the companions, the very one who was giving the messenger his orders, went to the door and found the very woman he was about to summon and who was thought to be far away. Totally astonished, he dashed to the Saint and, beside himself with joy, exclaimed, "I'm bringing you good news, Father!" And the Saint replied at once, hurrying to anticipate his words, "Blessed be the Lord, who has send us our brother, Lady Jacoma! But open the door," he added, "let her in and bring her to me, because the rule of seclusion established for women does not apply to Brother Jacoma."

38. The noble guests rejoiced and in spiritual solace, many tears were shed. And so that nothing was lacking to complete the miracle, they found that the saintly woman had brought every-

---

[41] Of Norman descent, she was the widow of Graziano dei Frangipani of the Settesoli family. She spent the last years of her life in Assisi and was buried in the Basilica of St. Francis. St. Francis referred to her as "Brother Jacoma".
[42] *2 Tim* 4, 7.

thing that the letter prepared for her had told her to bring for the Father's funeral. In fact, she had brought with her an ash-colored cloth in which to wrap the poor body of the dying man, numerous candles, the shroud for his face, a cushion for his head and a certain type of food[43] that the Saint liked, and everything that his spirit had desired had also been suggested by Lord.

I must certainly proceed to speak about the events surrounding this pilgrimage so that I won't leave that noble pilgrim uncomforted. A multitude of people, and in particular the devout group from the City, were waiting for the birth of the Saint to come quickly at the hour of his death. However, this moment was eased by the arrival of these devout people from Rome and it was hoped that he might live just a little longer. Consequently, the lady also decided to send the group away and remain there alone with her children and a few equerries. The Saint was opposed to this, however, and said, "Don't do it, because I'll die on Saturday and then on Sunday you can leave again with everyone."

And this is what happened. At the predicted time, he who had strenuously battled in the Church militant entered the Church triumphant. I will leave out the crowds of people, the songs of joy, the harmony of the bells, the streams of tears, I will leave out his sons' lament, his friends' sobs, his companions' sighs, and I will come to what will console that pilgrim woman, deprived of the solace of her Father.

39. Thus, bathed in tears, she was secretly taken aside and as he placed her friend's body in her arms, the vicar[44] said to her, "Here, hold the one you loved when he was alive, even now that he is dead." And bathing that body with her hot tears, her tears and sobbing doubled and, sorrowfully embracing and kissing him repeatedly, she loosened his veil to see him. What happened then?

---

[43] According to the *Mirror of Perfection* (chapter 112), this was a specialty that Jacoma would always prepare for Francis. These sweet biscuits, known as "mostaccioli", were made of almonds, sugar and other ingredients.

[44] Brother Elias, vicar until May 29, 1227.

She contemplated that precious vase[45] that had concealed the precious treasure adorned with five pearls.[46] She could see the chiseling that only the hand of the Almighty could have wrought for the world to marvel over, and in spite of the death of her friend, she experienced extraordinary joy over this. She immediately decided that this unheard-of prodigy should not be disguised or hidden any longer, but that with providential resolve, it must be shown for all to see. Everyone raced to see this and truly, they found what God had never done for any other nation[47] and admired this in astonishment.

I will pause with my pen, for I do not want to stumble over what I would be unable to explain.

John Frangipani, who was a young man at the time and later became proconsul of the Romans and count of the sacred Palace, has sworn to everything that he saw then with his own eyes, together with his mother, and touched freely with his own hands[48] and he has confirmed this for all those who doubt it.

At this point, the pilgrim returned to her homeland, consoled by this privilege of grace. And now that we have spoken of the Saint's death, let us move on to other things.

CHAPTER VII
Of those who were raised from the dead through the merits of Blessed Francis

40. I will now begin to speak about those who were raised from the dead through the merits of Christ's confessor, asking for the attention of both listeners and readers alike. A student of brevity, I shall omit many circumstances in my recount and I will only make note of miraculous events, keeping my silence about the manifestations of his admirers.

---

[45] *Prv* 20, 15.
[46] The Stigmata.
[47] *Ps* 147, 20.
[48] *Jb* 13, 1 and *Gen* 27, 12; *1 Jn* 1.

At the castle of Monte Marano near Benevento, a woman of noble lineage who was even more noble in virtue, was bound to St. Francis through extraordinary devotion and she rendered him worthy reverence. Afflicted with illness and close to death, she went the way of all creatures.[49] Since she died at around sunset, her burial was put off until the next day so that the company of those dear to her could gather together. During the night, the clergy arrived to sing the exequies of the wake with a psalter and a multitude of people, both men and women, was praying around her when all of a sudden before everyone's eyes the woman sat up in bed and called to one of the priests there and to her parish priest, saying, "I want to confess, father. Hear my sins! In fact, I am dead and I was supposed to be kept in a dark prison since I had not confessed the sin I will reveal to you. But," she went on, "because St. Francis, to whom I was always very devoted, has interceded for me, I was allowed to return to my body to obtain forgiveness[50] by confessing that sin. And here, as you will see, after I have revealed it to you, I will hurry to the rest that has been promised to me."

Thus, she confessed in trembling to the trembling priest and after receiving absolution, she peacefully lay back down on the bed and happily fell asleep in the Lord.[51]

So who is able to celebrate Christ's mercy with worthy praise? Who is worthy of extolling the value of confession and the Saint's merits with a fitting encomium?

41. In order to demonstrate how everyone must lovingly welcome the admirable divine gift of confession and so that it will rightly be proclaimed that this Saint always enjoyed singular merit with Christ, the things that marvelously appeared while he lived in the world and what his Christ demonstrated about him even more clearly after his death, must be reported.

---

[49] *Jos* 23, 14.

[50] *Gen* 4, 13.

[51] *Acts* 7, 60.

In fact, when the blessed father Francis went to Celano one time to preach, a knight devoutly and insistently begged him to dine with him. At first he refused and resisted at length, but in the end, he allowed himself to be convinced, virtually overcome by the man's insistence. The mealtime arrived and a splendid table was set. The devout host rejoiced and the entire family merrily welcomed the poor guests. Lifting his eyes towards heaven, blessed Francis remained on his feet and secreted called his host over. "Here, brother host," he said. "Convinced by your prayers, I have come to eat at your house.[52] Now, obey my advice at once, for you will not eat here but elsewhere. Confess your sins devoutly and contritely, and let there remain no sin in you that you have not revealed through honest confession. Today the Lord will reward you[53] because you have welcomed his poor ones so devoutly." That man was immediately convinced by those saintly words and calling St. Francis' companion, who was a priest, he revealed all his sins in a truthful confession. He gave instructions concerning his household[54] and, without doubting, he waited for the words of the Saint to be accomplished.

They sat down at the dinner table at last and as everyone started to eat, he too, having made the sign of the cross over his chest, reached his trembling hand out for his bread, but before he could pick it up, he bowed his head and gave up his spirit.[55]

O! How the confession of sin should be loved! Here, one of the dead was raised to make his confession and then, so that a living person would not perish forever, he was forestalled through the benefit of confession.

42. A notary in the city of Rome had a son, just barely seven years old who, as children do, wanted to follow his mother as she was on her way to the church of St. Mark for the sermon. Lagging behind his mother and upset over of her refusal, he fell

---

[52] *Lk* 7, 44.
[53] *Is* 59, 18.
[54] *Is* 38, 1.
[55] *Jn* 19, 30.

from one of the windows of the palace -- through I don't know what diabolical instinct -- and as he hit the ground with a final tremor, he found death's door that is common to everyone. As soon as she heard the noise made by the boy's body as it fell and imagining that she had lost her little treasure, the boy's mother, who hadn't gone very far yet, ran home only to find her lifeless son. She immediately began to rage against herself with punishing hands and, at her cries, the neighbors hastened and the doctors were summoned for the little dead boy. But can they possibly raise the dead? The time for prognoses and special diets had past and the doctors could acknowledge the event, in the realm of divine jurisdiction, but they could not remedy it. Thus devoid of heat, life, sensation, movement and strength, he was pronounced dead by the doctors. Brother Rao of the Order of the Friars Minor, a preacher who was very famous throughout Rome, was on his way there to pray and going up to the boy and filled with faith, he said to the child's father, "Do you believe that St. Francis can raise your son from the dead through the love that he always bore for the Son of God, our Lord Jesus Christ?"[56] The father answered, "I firmly believe this and I confess it. I will be his servant forever and will solemnly visit his sacred place." The friar prostrated himself in prayer with his companion and invited everyone to pray. After he had done this, the child began to yawn a bit and lift his arms to get up. His mother ran over and embraced her son, while his father is beside himself with joy[57] and all the people, filled with admiration, magnified Christ and his Saint in a loud voice. The boy immediately walked before everyone and was perfectly restored to life.

43. When the friars of Nocera asked a man by the name of Peter for a cart, which they needed for a short time, he foolishly replied, "I'd sooner skin two of you together with St. Francis than lend you the wagon." The man immediately regretted having ut-

---

[56] *Acts* 17, 31; 8, 37 and 11, 17.
[57] *Acts* 12, 14.

tered such a blasphemous sentence and, slapping himself across
the mouth, he begged them for mercy. In fact, he feared that
punishment would follow and, indeed, it followed at once. At
night, he dreamt[58] that his house was full of men and women
who were dancing most merrily. His son, named Gafaro,
promptly took ill and after a short time, he gave up his spirit. The
dancing he had dreamed about was transformed into funereal
mourning and jubilee was turned into weeping. He remembered
the curse he had flung against St. Francis, so that the punishment
taught him how serious the fault had been. He rolled about on the
floor and never ceased invoking St. Francis, saying, "I am the one
who sinned![59] You should have flogged me. O Saint, give back to
this penitent man what you took away from him who cursed so
irreverently. I give myself up to you, I put myself at your service
forever. And I will always give you every prime offering." Marvelous thing! At these words, the boy got up and, forbidding them to
weep, he related the circumstance of his death. "As soon as I was
dead," he told them, "blessed Francis came and led me along a
dark and very long road. Then he brought me to an orchard that
was so pleasant and so delightful that the entire world cannot
compare to it. Then he brought me down the same road and said
to me, 'Return to your father and your mother: I don't want to
keep you here any long.' And here, just as he wanted, I've come
back."

44. In the city of Capua, while a boy was carelessly playing
near the banks of the Volturno with many others, he fell from the
shore into the depths of the river. The rushing current[60] quickly
swallowed him up, burying him under the sand. At the cries of the
boys who had been playing with him near the river, many men
and women rushed over to them and, informed of the child's
plight, they tearfully cried, "St. Francis, give the child back to his
father and grandfather, who toil at your service!" In fact, the fa-

---

[58] *Gn* 28, 12.
[59] *2 Kg* 24, 17.
[60] *Ps* 46, 5.

ther and grandfather had worked with all their might to build a church in St. Francis' honor. And while the people beseechingly and devoutly invoked the merits of blessed Francis, a swimmer who happened to be nearby heard the noise and approached them. And when he learned that the boy had fallen into the river a good hour before, he invoked the name of Christ[61] and the merits of blessed Francis, set his clothes aside and dove naked into river. Not knowing where the boy had fallen, he began to look carefully on both sides of the river and along the riverbed. At last, through divine will, he found the spot where the slime had covered the boy's corpse like a sepulcher. Digging to get it out, he mournfully realized that the boy was dead. And yet, while the people who were present saw that the boy was dead, they nevertheless wept and wailed, crying, "St. Francis, give the boy back to his father!" And, driven by natural compassion, several Jews who had also hastened there also repeated, "St. Francis, give the boy back to his father!" As the outcome would then show, Blessed Francis, stirred by the people's devotion and prayers, immediately raised the boy from the dead. The child, who was brought back to life while everyone was delighting and marveling over this at the same time, begged to be brought to the church of St. Francis, through whose favor he swore he had been resuscitated.

45. In the city of Suessa in the area referred to as "The Columns", the devil, who loses the soul and kills the body, destroyed a house. Even though he attempted to kill many children who were playing their children's games at the house, he was only able to carry off one boy, who was killed by the sudden collapse. Roused by the rumble of the house as it was being destroyed, men and women came from all over and, picking the beams up here and there, they gave the dead boy back to his mother. Scratching at her face and tearing at her hair, trembling with bitter sobs and streaming with tears, she cried out hoarsely, "St. Francis, St. Francis, give me back my son!" And along with her, all those pre-

---

[61] *Acts* 22, 16.

sent, both men and women, also wept bitterly, saying, "St. Francis, give this poor mother her son!" An hour later the mother, recovering from such deep sorrow and returning to her senses, made the following vow: "O St. Francis, give this wretch her beloved son and I will encircle your altar with a silver frieze, cover it with a new cloth and place candles all around it for your church." And so, since it was nighttime, they placed the corpse on the bed and waited to bury him the next day. Now then, at around midnight, the young boy began to yawn and, warming up his limbs, before it was full daylight, he came back to life and burst into displays of praise. Upon seeing that he was safe and sound, the entire population and the clergy gave thanks to blessed Francis.

46. In the town of Pomarico, located in the mountainous area of Apulia, a father and mother had an only daughter who was tender in age and tenderly beloved. And since they could not hope to have any other children, she was the center of all their attention. Indeed, when she fell mortally ill, her father and mother felt that they too had died. Thus, anxiously keeping constant watch over the girl day and night, one morning they found her dead. Perhaps there had been some inattentiveness due to lack of sleep and to the fatigue of keeping watch over her. Thus deprived of this sweet child and having lost all hope of having other children, the girl's mother felt that she too was dying. The relatives and neighbors gathered for the very tearful funeral and hastened to bury that lifeless body. The forlorn mother, filled with unspeakable sorrow, lay there absorbed in her utter sadness and was unaware of what was happening. In the meantime, St. Francis, accompanied by a sole companion, visited the disconsolate woman and conversed placidly with her. "Don't cry[62]," he said, "for I will bring the light back to your lamp that has gone out completely." The woman got up at once and after revealing to everyone what St. Francis had said to her, she would not allow them to bring the lifeless body anywhere else. Then the mother

---

[62] *Lk* 7, 13, followed by *2 Kgs* 21, 17 and *Prv* 20, 20.

turned to her daughter and, invoking the name of the Saint, picked her up alive and unharmed. We will leave it for others to describe the astonishment that filled the hearts of those who saw this and the joy of her family, greater than anything they had ever experienced before.

47. In Sicily, Gerlandino, a young man who was a native of Ragusa, went out to the vineyard with his relatives during harvest time. As he was leaning under the grape press to pour the wineskins in a vat, the joist device moved and the enormous stones used to press the lees fatally struck him on the head. The father rushed over to his son and he was so desperate when he saw him covered in this way that instead of helping him, he left him there under the weights exactly as they had fallen. As soon as the winemakers heard the mournful wail of his voice, they quickly ran over and, taking pity on the wretched father, they pulled his son from that disaster. Setting him down to one side, they wrapped the corpse and hastened simply to bury him. However, the father obstinately prostrated himself at Christ's feet, begging that He deign to give him back his only son through the merits of St. Francis, whose feast day was approaching. He doubled his prayers, made a vow to demonstrate his devotion and promised to visit the Saint's remains as soon as possible. In the meantime, that evening the boy's mother arrived and, in a frenzy, she dashed to her dead son and her cries moved the others to tears as well. All of a sudden, the young man got up, scolding those who were weeping, and he rejoiced that he had been brought back to life through the help of St. Francis. In turn, the men who had gathered also raise hymns of praise to heaven, praising Him who, through his Saint, had released the dead man from the clutches of death.

48. Another dead man was brought back to life in Germany and in an apostolic letter[63] written at the time the body of blessed Francis was translated, the lord Pope Gregory informed and de-

---

[63] Papal bull *Mirificans* dated May 16, 1230.

lighted all the friars who had assembled for the translation and the chapter meeting. I have not described the events behind this miracle because I did not know about them and I feel that this papal testimony goes far beyond any other authenticating instrument.

But let's move on now to the others that he tore from the jaws of death.

CHAPTER VIII
Of those he brought back to life from the jaws of death

49. In Rome, a noble citizen by the name of Rudolph had a tower that was quite high and, as was the custom, there was a guardian in the tower. One night, the guardian was sleeping soundly at the top of the tower, stretched out on a pile of wood placed right where the wall jutted out, when the winch got loosened and broke on the outside, tossing him down from that high precipice with all the wood, so that he fell onto the roof of the palace and then from the palace to the ground. At that great noise, the entire family woke up and the knight, suspecting an attack, got up and went outside fully armed. He unsheathed his sword, brandishing it at the prostrate man with the intention of striking him, for in his sleepy state he didn't recognize his guardian. But the knight's wife, fearing that it could be her brother whom her husband hated with deadly animosity, kept him from wounding the man by throwing herself over him face down and mercifully defending him. What strange and bewildering drowsiness! Neither that ruinous double fall, nor the uproar and noise aroused the sleeper, yet at the touch of a caring hand, he finally woke up and, as if he had been deprived of pleasant repose, he said to his master, "What's your reason for disturbing my sleep now? I have never slept so sweetly, for I was lying ever so gently in the arms of St. Francis." When the others informed him of his fall and he discovered that he was now below when he had been sleeping above, he was astonished by the event, which he had not felt in the least.

Before everyone, he promptly promised to do penance and, with his master's permission, he undertook a pilgrimage. Out of reverence and homage towards the Saint, the lady then also sent some altar-hangings to the friars who resided in her castle outside Rome.

The Scriptures extol the merits of hospitality, while examples confirm them. In fact, out of reverence for St. Francis, the aforesaid lord had given lodging to two Friars Minor that very night and they too had run outside with the others when the servant fell.

50. In the town of Pofi, in Campania[64], a priest named Thomas went with a number of men to repair the mill of his church. There was a deep whirlpool under the mill and it had an abundantly flowing canal running through it. Thus, while the priest was walking incautiously along the edge of the canal, he suddenly fell in and the quickly rushing water drove him against the notched wood that sets the mill into motion, so that he was all curled up in the device, unable to move. Since he was on his back, the water was rushing over his face, so that his sight and hearing were miserably dulled. All he had left was his heart, not his tongue, and through it he feebly invoked St. Francis. He was stuck in this way for a long time when his companions, fearing for his life by this time, finally prepared to return. "Heave," said the miller. "Let's turn the wheel in the opposite direction so that his body will be released." So saying, they strained to turn the wheel the other way and saw that the man who had fallen into the water was still alive. While the priest, half-dead, was still being twisted around by the whirlpool, along came a Friar Minor dressed in a white cowl and wearing a rope around his waist and, very gently, he took him by the arm and dragged him from the river. "I am Francis, whom you have called." Thus released, the man was completely astonished and began to dash back and forth crying, "Brother, brother!" and asking the others, "Where is he? Which

---

[64] The area around Naples.

way did he go?" Trembling, those men fell to the ground, glorifying God[65] and his Saint.

51. In Capitanata, some boys from the town of Celano[66] had set out in a group to cut grass. In that countryside, there was an old well whose edge was hidden by the green grass and the water in it was four paces deep. While the boys were playing tag with each other, one of them suddenly fell into the well. However, at the very moment that he was suffering ruin on earth, he invoked suffrage from heaven and as he was slipping, he cried, "St. Francis! Help me!" As soon as the boy disappeared from sight, the others turned this way and that[67] to look for him, shouting and crying. At last they came to the edge of the well and seeing the footprints left on the grass, they began to shudder when they realized that the boy must have fallen in. They ran back to town sobbing, gathered a crowd of men together and returned to the boy, whom everyone considered lost. One of the men slid down a rope into the well, only to find the boy sitting stock-still on the surface of the water, completely unharmed. When they pulled him out of the well, the boy said to everyone, "When I fell suddenly, I invoked the protection of blessed Francis. He came to me at once as I was falling to my ruin and, stretching his hands out to me, he picked me up easily and never let me go until, together with you, he pulled me out of the well."

52. All treatment had been suspended on a girl of Ancona who was drained by a mortal illness, and since death was at hand by this time, the funeral preparations were already under way. As she was about to draw her last breath, blessed Francis came to her and said, "Have faith, daughter[68], for in my grace you have been completely freed. Wait until evening before telling anyone about

---

[65] *Nm* 14, 5 and *Lk* 2, 20.

[66] Some documents indicate that this was not the town of Celano in the Abruzzi area but a town by the same name in southern Italy.

[67] *Gn* 37, 30.

[68] *Mt* 9, 22 followed by 8, 4.

the health I am restoring to you." When evening came[69], she suddenly sat up in bed and those who were present fled in bewilderment, believing that a demon had invaded the body of the dying girl and that the perverse usurper had taken over, carrying her soul away. Her mother dared to draw closer to her and, doubling her entreaties against what she thought was a demon, she tried to lay her back down on the bed, but her daughter said, "Please, mother, don't believe it's a demon, for at around nine o'clock blessed Francis completely cured of my illness and ordered me not to tell anyone about it until now."

The name of St. Francis aroused stupendous happiness in those who had been put to flight by the thought of the demon. At that very same moment, they tried to force the girl to eat a bit of chicken, but since it was Lent, she refused. "Do not fear," said she. "Don't you see St. Francis dressed in white? Here, he is urging me not to eat meat because it's Lent and he is instructing that the funeral gown be given to a woman who is in jail. Look now! Look and you'll see him leaving!"

53. In a house near Nettuno[70], there were three women, one of whom was very devoted to the friars and most devoted to St. Francis. Buffeted by the wind, the house collapsed over two of the women, killing and burying them. Invoked in silence, blessed Francis came immediately and did not allow the woman devoted to him to suffer the least injury. In fact, the wall that the woman had been leaning against remained intact up to height of the woman and over her head, a beam had fallen down into such a precise position that it sustained the entire weight of the deadly collapse. The men who had run over at that crashing noise shed tears over the two women who had been killed, giving thanks to St. Francis for the one who had survived, who was a friend of the friars.

---

[69] *Mt* 20, 8 followed by *Mk* 14, 70.
[70] On the coast near Rome.

54. Near Corneto[71] in the diocese of Viterbo, a rather important and powerful city, a large bell was being cast at the friars' residence and since many of the friars' friends had gathered to give a hand with this undertaking, when the casting had been completed, they joyously held a great feast. At this point, an eight-year-old boy named Bartholomew, whose father and uncle had devoutly assisted in casting the bell, brought a special dish to the guests. Suddenly, a raging wind shook the house[72] and hurled the boy against the main door, which was very large and heavy, with such great impetus that the boy was thought to have been crushed to death under that enormous weight. And in truth, he was completely buried under that weight, so that no part of him could even be seen. The casting was followed by confusion[73], and the diners' festivity by the grieving of mourners. Everyone flew up from the table and, invoking St. Francis with the others, the boy's uncle dashed to the wooden door. Instead, the boy's father, unable to move since he was paralyzed by grief, made vows out loud and offered his son up to St. Francis. The deadly weight was lifted from the boy and behold! The one who was thought to be dead happily appeared as if he had just woken up, without even a scratch. Confusion was thus followed by the return of joy[74] and the banquet that had been interrupted was followed by a great show of exultation. The boy himself declared to me that he had been lifeless the whole time he had been lying under that weight. Accordingly, he became a Friar Minor when he was fourteen years old and later became a man of letters and an eloquent preacher in the Order.

55. A little boy from this same town swallowed a silver buckle that his father had given him and the buckle completely

---

[71] Tarquinia, an ancient Etruscan town on the coast near Rome.

[72] *Jb* 1, 19.

[73] Celano's word play is lost here as well, since the Latin for "casting" is "fusio". Thus, "fusion was followed by confusion".

[74] More word play: in Latin, "refusio" for "return", so we go from "fusio" to "confusio" to "refusio".

blocked the opening in his throat, so that he could not breath at all. His father wept bitterly, feeling that he had killed his own son, and he rolled around on the ground, ranting like a madman. His mother tore her hair out and clawed at her skin, weeping over the wretched event. All their friends grieved at the great sorrow that death could whisk a healthy boy away so suddenly. Promising a votive offering, the father invoked the merits of St. Francis to deliver his son. And the boy immediately spat the buckle from his mouth, blessing the Saint's name with everyone.

56. A fellow by the name of Nicholas, who was from the town of Ceprano[75], fell into the hands of cruel enemies one day. These enemies, heaping injury upon injury with ferocious rage, did not stop beating the wretch until they were sure he was either lifeless or on the brink of death. Drenched in blood, they went off, leaving him more dead than alive. At the very first blows, this Nicholas had cried out in a very loud voice, "Help me, St. Francis! Come to my aid!" And many people far off had heard that voice, but didn't get there in time to help him. When he was brought home covered in his own blood, he shouted that he would not die, nor did he feel any pain, for St. Francis had come to his aid and had impetrated from the Lord that he do penance.[76] Thus, contrary to all human expectation, after the blood was washed away he was healed.

57. Several men from Lentini[77] were cutting a large stone slab from the mountain to place over the altar in a church dedicated to St. Francis that was soon to be consecrated. However, while about forty men were straining to put the stone on the vehicle and kept heaving it up, the stone fell on one of them and covered him like a tomb. Since the men did not know what to do in the confusion, most of them ran off in despair. In a mournful voice, the ten who were left invoked St. Francis so that he would not let a man die so miserably while he had been serving the Saint.

---

[75] Near the modern city of Frosinone, in south-central Italy.

[76] *Mk* 6, 12.

[77] Near Syracuse.

The buried man was lying there half-dead and the vital spirit that was left in him yearned for St. Francis' help. The men got their courage back at last and moved the stone so easily that no one had any doubt that the Saint's hand had been helping them. The man got up unscathed and he who was almost dead was fully revived, he whose eyes had been dimmed recovered his sight, so that through him, everyone would be brought to understand the importance of St. Francis' aid in desperate cases.

58. Near San Severino in the Marches there occurred a similar event that is worth recalling. While an enormous stone, which was being transported from Constantinople for the fountain of St. Francis that was being built in Assisi[78], was being dragged along heavily by many people, one of the them slipped under it and not only was he thought to have been killed, but indeed he was thought to have been crushed completely. Instead, just as he immediately appeared to him and as reality indeed demonstrated, St. Francis came to him and, lifting the stone, he pushed the man aside unharmed. And so it happened that a horrible scene became a miracle for everyone.

59. While Bartholomew, a citizen of Gaeta, was toiling to construct a church dedicated to blessed Francis and was attempting to set a beam in place in the building, this beam, which had not been positioned properly, fell and gave him a serious blow to the neck. As he lay bleeding, with the little spirit that was keeping him alive, he asked a friar for last rites. However, since the friar could not find the viaticum right away and it seemed as if the man would die on the spot, the friar suggested that expression of St. Augustine to him: "Believe, and it will be as if you had eaten." The following night, blessed Francis appeared to the wounded man accompanied by eleven friars and, clasping a little lamb to his chest, he went to the man's bedside and called him by name, saying, "Do not fear, Bartholomew. You will not be assailed by the

---

[78] The documents of the city of Assisi mention this ancient fountain, which was built in the thirteenth century.

enemy, who wanted to harm you because you were serving me, for you will now get up completely cured! This is the little lamb you asked for and that you have received by virtue of this good intention. The friar also gave you good advice." And so, passing his hand over the man's wounds, he ordered him to return to the work he had begun. The man got up early the next morning and when he appeared safe and sound to those who had thought he was half dead, he aroused their admiration and amazement. In truth, because of the man's unhoped-for salvation, they thought they were seeing a ghost instead of a man, and not a body but a spirit.

60. One time in the town of Peschici[79] in the diocese of Siponto, two Friars Minor had started to construct a church in honor of St. Francis, which was no small undertaking. Since they did not have everything they needed to build it, one night when they had roused themselves from their sleep to sing praise, they began to hear the thud of stones being piled up. They urged each other to go take a look and when they went outside, they saw an enormous throng of men running about to gather the stones together. All dressed in white robes, the men were going back and forth in silence. The enormous pile of stones that had been collected demonstrated that this was no trick of the imagination, not to mention that there were enough stones there to complete construction. Moreover, any suspicion that these had been men of flesh and blood was dispelled, because after diligent research had been conducted everywhere, they could find no one who had thought of helping them in this way.

61. The son of a nobleman from Castel San Gemignano[80] was afflicted with a grave weakness that had no cure and was on his deathbed. Rivulets of blood streamed from his eyes, the way it would spurt from the vein on your arm. Given that the other real signs of imminent death had also appeared, he was thought to

---

[79] In the Gargano area in southern Italy.
[80] In Tuscany.

have passed away. Since friends and relatives had gathered in customary mourning, the funeral was arranged and all that was left to do was bury him. In the meantime, the father, surrounded by a weeping throng, remembered a vision he had heard about before. He ran quickly to the church of St. Francis that had been built in that very town and with a cincture around his neck, he very humbly threw himself down before the altar. And thus promising votive offerings and multiplying his prayers with his wailing and sobbing, he gained St. Francis' patronage with Christ. He promptly went back to his son and when he found that he had been restored to health, mourning was transformed to joy.

62. In the village of Piazza in Sicily, the soul of a young man that, according to Church ritual, had been entrusted to the intercession of the holy Father when it was offered up by a maternal uncle, was called back again when it was just a step away from death.

63. In this same town, while a young man named Alexander was playing tug-of-war with his friends on a cliff, the rope broke and he fell from the cliff. He was carried off and gave every appearance of being dead, but when the boy's father, weeping and sobbing, offered him to Francis, the Saint of Christ, he got his son back safe and sound.

64. A woman from this same town was afflicted with consumption and, on the verge of death, her soul was commended. However, the people around her invoked the most holy Father and she was immediately cured.

65. Near Rete, in the diocese of Cosenza, two children from that town had had a fight at school and one of them received such a serious chest injury that his stomach was perforated and undigested food seeped from the wound, so that the child could not hold any nourishment. Indeed, his food was not digested, nor would it remain in some pocket, but it would come out through the wound. Since no doctor was able to offer him any remedy, following a friar's advice, the boy and his parents forgave the boy who had wounded him and they vowed to blessed Francis that if

the wounded boy, whom the doctors had given up on, were snatched from the clutches of death, they would send the boy to his church to fill it with candles. As soon as the vow was made, the boy was healed so perfectly and marvelously that the doctors of Salerno[81] considered it no small miracle that he had been brought back to life.

66. As two men were going to mountain of Trapani on business, one of them fell deathly ill. The doctors who had been summoned to cure him hastened to his side, but they could not offer him any relief. Instead, his healthy companion vowed to St. Francis that if, through his merits, the sick man should regain his health, then every year he would observe Francis' feast day with a solemn mass. Thus making this vow, he went home to find that the sick man, whom he had left speechless and senseless and whom he thought had already departed from this life, had regained perfect health.

67-69. [*This section recounts three miracles that were already described in the* First Life, *specifically, the stories about Matthew of Todi (139), about the anonymous young man who fell and about Walter of Arezzo (140)*].

CHAPTER IX
Of those afflicted with dropsy and paralysis

70-71. (*The dropsical man from Fano and the paralytic woman from Gubbio, from the* First Life, *141-142*).

72. A young girl from Arpino[82], in the diocese of Sora, had such great fits of paralysis[83] that her limbs hung limply and her nerves were contorted, and since she had no rational activity whatsoever, it seemed that she was oppressed by the demon rather than being pervaded with any human spirit. In fact, the ill-

---

[81] A reference to the famous medical school there.

[82] In south central Italy.

[83] Based on the description, it would appear that she was suffering from polio.

ness had attacked her so violently that she seemed to have reverted to living like a baby in a cradle. At last, inspired by God, her mother carried her in a cradle to the church of blessed Francis near Vicalvi, where she shed many tears and redoubled her prayers. As a result, the girl was freed from all the injuries caused by the disease and recovered the health she had had in her earlier years.

73. In this same town, there was a young man who was so severely paralyzed that his mouth was completely shut and his eyes rolled around and his mother brought him to this church. That young man could not move at all, but since his mother had prayed on his behalf, he recovered perfect health even before they had gotten home again.

74. In Poggibonsi[84], a little girl named Umbertina was afflicted with a very serious and incurable case of epilepsy. Her parents, who had lost all hope in human remedies by then, assiduously implored blessed Francis' help. Moreover, they agreed that if their daughter were freed from such a terrible illness, they would vow to fast each year on the eve of the blessed Father's feast day and feed a number of poor people on the actual feast day. As soon as they uttered this vow, the girl, completely liberated, was healed and never suffered from any other effects of the disease thereafter.

75. Peter Manganella, a citizen of Gaeta, lost the use of his arm and hand because of paralysis and his mouth twisted up towards his ear. After he had followed the advice of his doctors, he then lost his sight and hearing as well. In the end, he beseechingly consecrated himself to blessed Francis and was liberated through the merits of this most holy man.

76-80. (*These miracles were described in the* First Life, *and are recounted here in this order: n° 141, the arthritic man from Todi; n° 142, Bontadoso and the woman from Gubbio; n° 141, the young man and woman, both from Narni, who were cured of paralysis*).

---

[84] In Tuscany.

CHAPTER X

Of those who were saved from shipwrecks

81. Some sailors were in great danger while they were still about ten miles from the port of Barletta and since the fury of the storm was becoming more intense, they laid their anchors, doubting that they would survive. Since the spirit of the tempest was getting stronger and the swollen sea was seething, however, the cables broke and the anchors were lost, so that they wandered unsteadily and uncontrollably over the water. At last, the sea became calm again through divine will and they undertook every effort to recover the anchors, whose shrouds were floating on the surface. Therefore, they put all their strength into pulling up the anchors and invoked the help of all the saints but, soaked in sweat, they were unable to recover even one anchor that whole day. There was a sailor by the name of Perfetto[85] who was not perfect in any way, however, and he was a man who disparaged anything that had to do with God. Thinking thoughts to the contrary, he said to his friends with a sneer, "You've invoked the help of all the saints, but as you can see, not one of them has come to our aid. Let's call that Francis, who's a new saint, so that he'll plunge into the sea with his hood and get our lost anchors back. If we find that he has helped us, we can donate an ounce of gold to his church that they are building now in Ortona."[86] The others fearfully consented to the mocker and although they condemned his scoffing, they agreed with his vow. In just a split second, the anchors floated to the surface without the use of any instruments, as if iron's very nature had been transformed into light wood.

82. A pilgrim, who was disabled in body and was not even sound of mind since he had also suffered from dementia, was returning from overseas with his wife by ship. Still not perfectly cured of his disease, he was afflicted with a burning thirst and

---

[85] Perfect.

[86] A small town in the province of Chieti in south-central Italy, which has a lovely cathedral.

began to cry out in a loud voice, "O you faithful, go draw up a glass of water for me, for St. Francis has filled my flask with water." Truly marvelous! They found the container that they had left empty and useless was filled with water. Then another day, a storm arose and the ship was covered by the waves and tossed about in a real tempest. This same sick man suddenly began to shout throughout the ship, "Everyone get up and go out to meet blessed Francis, who is coming! He's here now to save us!" He threw himself fell face-down and weeping loudly, he worshipped him.[87] As soon as he saw the saint, the sick man regained his health and calm then followed.

83. Brother James of Rieti wanted to ford a river by boat. Letting his companions get off on the riverbank first, he was getting ready to be the last one off when unfortunately, the little raft capsized, and while the driver could swim, the friar instead sank to the bottom. The brothers who had disembarked invoked blessed Francis with their affectionate words and with tearful prayers, they urged him to help his son. Likewise, since he could not cry out with his mouth, the friar, who was submerged in the immense depths of the whirlpool, cried out deep in his heart as well as he could. Thus, with the Father helping him in person, he walked through deep water as if it were dry land and gripping the sunken raft, he took it to the shore. Marvelous to relate! His clothes were not wet and not even a drop of water clung to his cowl.

84. As two men were sailing on the lake of Rieti together with two women and child, the little boat happened to tip over and was immediately filled with water, so that they thought they were about to die. While all of them began to shout, certain by now that they would die, one of the women cried out with great faith, "St. Francis, while you were alive you granted me the benefit of your friendship. Now that we are about to perish, help us from heaven." The Saint who had been invoked appeared immediately

---

[87] *Mt* 26, 39 and *Jn* 9, 38.

and pulled the boat filled with water safely to the port. They had brought a sword with them on the boat and, floating miraculously, it followed the boat across the waves.

85. Tossed about by a perilous squall, several sailors from Ancona could easily see that they were in danger of drowning. Despairing that they could survive at this point, they imploringly invoked St. Francis when a great light appeared on the sea and with this light, calm was divinely granted. As a votive offering, they gave their savior a valuable pallium and rendered great thanks to him.

86. A brother by the name of Bonaventure was sailing on a lake with two men when a hole appeared in the boat and the in-rushing water submerged them. Invoking Francis from the bottom of the lake, that boat full of water promptly took them to the port. Likewise, a brother from Ascoli who had sunken to the bottom of a river was also saved through St. Francis' merit.

87. A fellow from Pisa, from the parish of Saints Cosmas and Damian, confirmed in a declaration that while he was on a ship at sea with many other people, a great storm was driving the ship up against a promontory, so that it would have been shattered. As soon as they saw this, the sailors wove a bridge using lateens and planks and they pulled themselves onto it with the others, using it as a shelter. However, the aforesaid Pisan, who was not holding tightly onto the bridge, was struck by a violent wave and tossed into the sea. Since he did not know how to swim, nor could the others help him, he sank wretchedly to the bottom. Unable to speak, as he was devoutly entrusting himself to St. Francis in his heart, he felt as if a hand had immediately picked him up from the seabed, bringing him back to that bridge, and he and the others were saved from being shipwrecked. The ship was then shattered against the mountain and completely destroyed.

CHAPTER XI
Of those who were bound and imprisoned

88. In the Byzantine empire, it happened that a Greek servant of a certain master was wrongly accused of theft. The governor of the city ordered that he be put into strict confinement and chained harshly and then, in the enforceable sentence, that one of his feet be cut off. The lord's wife anxiously pleaded that the innocent man be released promptly, but the magistrate's obstinate severity would not give in to her pleas. The woman thus turned to imploring St. Francis and she entrusted the innocent man to his mercy with her vows. The helper of the wretched immediately helped him and as soon as he grasped the hands of the imprisoned man, his bonds were loosened, his imprisonment ended and the innocent man was led outside. "Here I am," said Francis, "the one to whom your master's wife has devoutly entrusted you." While that man, stricken with fear, had to descend from that high cliff overlooking any abyss, without knowing how, he suddenly found himself down on the ground. Then, returning to the lady of the house, he told her about the miracle that had taken place. She immediately had a wax image made as a votive offering and had it hung over a painting of the Saint for everyone to see. As the mean husband, upset by this, was striking his wife, he himself was struck with a serious illness for which he could not be cured until, confessing his fault, he magnified Francis, the Saint of God, with devout praise.

89. In Massa San Pietro, a poor man owed a certain amount of money to a knight, and since he was unable to repay it due to his utter poverty, the debtor was imprisoned upon the knight's request. He begged the knight to take pity on him and asked for a extension out of love for St. Francis since, as he prayed, he believed that the knight revered the famous Saint. The proud man scorned the prayers addressed to him and vainly defamed the love of the Saint as being useless. Instead, he arrogantly said, "I will have you locked up in such a place and will lock you up again in such a prison that neither Francis nor anyone else will be able to help you." He found a dank prison and threw the man into it in chains. A short time later, St. Francis came and, opening the prison and breaking his shackles, he led the man home safely. Afterwards, the man brought those chains to the church

of blessed Francis in Assisi so that with the objects through which he had experienced the Father's clemency, he could demonstrate that marvelous power. Thus, by frustrating the proud knight, the power of Francis delivered the prisoner from the evil to which he had been subjected.

90. Five officials of a great prince, imprisoned on the basis of suspicion, were not only tied up with tight bonds, but they were also kept in prison under very close watch. Since they had heard that St. Francis shone everywhere through his miracles, they devoutly entrusted themselves to his care. Thus, one night St. Francis appeared to one of them and promised him the benefit of freedom. The one who had had the vision was heartened by this and he revealed the promised grace to his companions in prison. Although they were in darkness, they wept and rejoiced, making vows and praying even more. One of them soon began to chip at the wall of that well-fortified tower with a bone and that tenacious wall gave way so easily that it seemed as if it had been made of ash. Having made a hole in the wall, he attempted to slip through it and, breaking their bonds, one after the other they escaped to freedom. There was still an immense precipice left before they could complete their escape, but audacious Francis, their guide, gave them the audacity to descend it. Thus going off unharmed, they left placidly, singing great praises to this Saint's greatness.

91. Albert of Arezzo, kept in strict confinement for debts that had been wrongly attributed to him, humbly commended his innocence to St. Francis. He dearly loved the Order and of all the saints, he held special veneration for the Saint. His creditor had blasphemously said that neither God nor St. Francis would be able to release the man from him. On the eve of the feast of St. Francis, since the prisoner had not eaten anything but had given his food away to a poor man, St. Francis appeared to him the next night as he was keeping his vigil. As soon as he entered, the shackles fell from the man's feet and the chains from his hands.[88] The doors opened spontaneously and the planks fell from the roof and, thus freed, the man departed to return home. Afterwards, he fulfilled his vow by fasting on the eve of St. Francis' feast day and

---

[88] *Acts* 12, 7.

each year he added an ounce to the church candle of the yearly offering.

92. A young man from the district of Città di Castello who had been accused of being an arsonist and was tightly shackled under close guard, entrusted his cause to St. Francis. One night as he was lying bound in chains between the guards, he heard a voice saying to him, "Get up quickly and go wherever you want, for your chains have been undone!"[89] He carried out this order without delay and, led out of the prison, he began to walk to Assisi to offer his liberator the sacrifice of praise.

93. When the lord Pope Gregory IX was reigning at the See of blessed Peter, proceedings had to be initiated against heretics in various places. Among them, there was a certain man named Peter from the city of Alife and, accused of heresy, he was captured in Rome. Pope Gregory handed him over for custody to the bishop of Tivoli who, taking him under the penalty of losing his episcopate, had shackles put on the man's feet. However, since his simplicity betrayed his innocence, he was kept under more lenient custody. It has been recounted that several noblemen from the city wanted the bishop to incur the penalty that the pope had threatened and, out of their inveterate hatred toward the bishop, they secretly advised Peter to flee. Consenting, he escaped one night and immediately fled far away. When this was discovered, the bishop became deeply worried about it and although he fearfully awaited his punishment, he was equally as grieved that his adversaries' desire had been accomplished. Therefore, he had diligent searches conducted and, sending spies all around, the wretch was found and the bishop had the ingrate handed over to be more closely guarded in the future. He had a dark prison prepared, surrounding it with sturdy walls, and he had the inside braced with enormous planks that had been joined together with iron bolts. He had heavy shackles weighing many pounds put on him and gave him limited food and carefully measured drink.[90]

Since any remaining hope of freedom had been denied to him by this time, given that He would not allow that innocent man to

---

[89] *Ibid*, 12, 10.
[90] *Ez* 4, 16.

perish, God, in His mercy, came to his aid. With considerable tears and prayers, the man began to invoke blessed Francis to take pity on him, for he had heard that the eve of his solemn feast day was at hand. That man had great faith in St. Francis because, as he himself related, he had heard the heretics loudly railing against him. As the night of his feast day was approaching, at around twilight, blessed Francis took pity on him, went down into the prison and, calling him by name, ordered him to get up immediately. Terrified, the man asked himself who on earth it could be and he sensed that St. Francis was there. Nevertheless, he got up and called a guard over, saying, "I am very afraid[91], because there is someone here who is ordering me to get up and he says he is St. Francis!" The guard replied, "Be still down there, you wretch, and go to sleep! You're actually ranting because you didn't eat well enough today." Towards noontime, however, when the Saint of God again ordered him to get up, he saw that the shackles on his feet had been broken and had dropped quickly to the ground. Moreover, when he turned to look around the prison, he saw that the planks were being opened, for the nails were falling out by themselves, and the way out had been cleared for him. Although he was no longer bound, he was so astonished that he was unable to run away and, standing at the door and shouting, he frightened all the guards. As soon as they announced to the bishop that he had been released from his chains, the bishop, who thought the man had escaped again when he heard the miracle being recounted to him, became so frightened that, being unwell, he promptly fell off his chair. However, once he was able to understand the events that had taken place, he devoutly went to the prison and recognizing that divine power was manifest,[92] he worshipped the Lord there. Lastly, the chains were brought to the pope and the cardinals and when they saw what had happened[93], they greatly admired and blessed God.

94. Guidalotto of San Gemignano was falsely accused of having killed a man by poisoning him and of planning then to kill that man's

---

91 *Gn* 45, 3.
92 *Mk* 5, 30 and *Gn* 24, 26.
93 *Lk* 23, 47.

son and entire family with the very same poison. The podestà[94] of that place had him imprisoned and, weighing him down with very heavy chains, threw him into a horrific tower. The podestà was devising which punishments they should use to wear him down so that, through torture, they could wring a confession from him for the crime for which he had been accused. Therefore, they heaped numerous iron weights on him, which finally made him faint. They ordered that he be lowered to the ground repeatedly and then raised again so that by adding suffering upon suffering, he would be brought more quickly to confess his crime. However, through his spirit of innocence, he kept a peaceful face and did not demonstrate any despair over his torment. Then they lit quite a large fire under him, but not even one hair was touched despite the fact that he was hanging head down. Lastly, he was covered with boiling oil, but because he was innocent and had entrusted himself to blessed Francis from the very beginning, he laughingly passed all these tests. In fact, the night before he was to be led to his punishment, he was visited by St. Francis in person and surrounded by a dazzling light until morning, he basked in that splendor full of joy and faith. Blessed be God, who will not allow the innocent to perish and, in the flood of great waters, is ready to come to the aid of those who place their hope in Him.[95]

CHAPTER XII

Of the women who were delivered from the difficulties of childbirth and of those who do not celebrate his feast day

95. A countess from Slavonia, who was as famed for her nobility as she was for her love of goodness, burned with devotion for St. Francis and with attentive piety towards the brothers. When the time came for her to give birth, in the throes of tremendous suffering, her labor was so difficult that the rise of her offspring in the future seemed to be the setting of their mother in the present. It seemed that she was unable to bring the child forth into this life without leaving it

---

[94] The local authorities.
[95] *Ps* 66, 20; *Jb* 4, 7; *Ps* 32, 6.

herself and so through this effort, not to give birth but to perish.[96] Francis' fame, virtue and glory came to her mind and her faith was enlivened and devotion kindled. She turned to this efficacious aid, to her faithful friend, to the relief of the devout, the refuge of the afflicted. "St. Francis," she said, "I beseech your mercy with all my heart, and I vow in my mind what I cannot express in words." Mercy was miraculously quick! As soon as she stopped speaking, she stopped suffering, so that she came to the end of her labor pains and the beginning of her delivery. In fact, her labor ended immediately and she happily gave birth to the little baby. She did not forget her vow and did not fall back on her resolution. She had a most beautiful church built and then bestowed it to the brothers in honor of this saint.

96. In the area around Rome, a certain Beatrice, who was about to give birth, had been carrying a dead fetus in her womb for four days and was suffering great anguish and afflicted by mortal pain. The dead fetus was driving its mother to her death and since she had not miscarried it yet, it was putting the mother's life in danger. Her doctors' attempts to help her failed and any human remedy was in vain. Thus a large part of the original curses had fallen on the wretch[97] so that, having become the tomb of the offspring she had conceived, her own tomb was surely not far behind.

At last, going through intermediaries, she entrusted herself to the Friars Minor with every devotion and very faithfully begged them for some relic of St. Francis. It happened by divine will that a piece of cord that the Saint had once used as a belt was found. As soon as the cord was placed on the suffering woman, she was immediately released from her pain, the dead fetus -- cause of death -- was expelled and she regained pristine health.

97. The wife of a noble citizen of Calvi, by name of Juliana, had been mourning the death of her children for years and wept constantly over the unfortunate events that had occurred. All the children she had borne had been received into the earth and these new scions had quickly been cut down by the hatchet. Therefore, since she

---

96 Celano's word play is lost in the translation: "parere" (to give birth) is juxtaposed with "perire" (to perish).
97 *Gn* 3, 16.

now bore in her womb a child that had been conceived four months before, she abandoned herself more to sadness than to joy, fearing that the illusion of happiness over this birth would be nullified by subsequent sadness over its death. Now, one night while she was sleeping, a woman appeared to her in a dream, and in her arms she was bearing a lovely child, whom she happily offering to her, she said, "Lady, take this little one that St. Francis is sending you!" However, almost as if she were unwilling to accept what she would immediately lose again, she refused, saying, "Why should I want this child that I am sure will die soon like the others?" At this, the other woman responded, "Take this child that St. Francis is sending you, for he will live." After this conversation had been repeated three times, the lady took the child being offered to her into her arms and then she woke up immediately and told her husband about the vision. They both were both delighted by this great joy and offered many vows so that they would gain the grace of having children. When her time was up, the woman gave birth to a little boy who was bursting with vitality and he made up for the grief over his siblings who had died.

98. Near Viterbo, a woman was about to give birth, even though she herself was close to death. She was tormented by intestinal pain and with every other type of suffering that women have. Physicians were consulted and midwives were summoned, but since there was no improvement, only the worst could be expected. The afflicted woman invoked blessed Francis and vowed to celebrate his feast day for the rest of her life. Immediately healed, she joyfully brought her pregnancy to term. Although she had obtained what she wanted, however, she forgot her promise. In fact, she went to do the washing on the feast of St. Francis, not because she was unmindful, but because she turned her back on her recent vow. She was soon overcome with unusual pain and, warned by this suffering, she went home. As soon as the pain ceased, however, since she was one of those people who change their minds ten times an hour, as soon as she saw her neighbors bustling about, emulating them rashly, she dared to do even worse than before. Suddenly, she was unable to pull back her right arm, which was stretched out to work and had to keep it stiff and immobilized. She tried to use her other arm to lift it, but then the other one also turned stiff through a similar curse. By this time, the unlucky woman had to

be fed by her son and was unable to use her hands for anything else. Her husband was dumbfounded and upon questioning her as to why this had occurred, he realized that the reason for her affliction was her failure to observe her vow to St. Francis. When the man and woman fearfully renewed their vow, the Saint had mercy on them nevertheless, for he is ever merciful, and he gave the penitent woman the use of her limbs that she had lost through negligence. Thus, when her sin was revealed as the reason for her punishment, the woman became an example for all those who fail to observe their vows, instilling fear in those who presumptuously violate the saints' feast days.

99. In the city of Tivoli, a judge's wife who had borne six children angrily decided not to have intercourse with her husband any more, since she did not want to continue to sowing a harvest that was so unpleasant to her. The woman detested the fact that she kept bearing little girls and, disappointed in her desire for a little boy, she even blamed divine will. However, one should never rebel against the judgment that falls upon men through the laws of almighty God. Therefore, in her indignation she stayed away from her husband for a year. After a while, she came to regret this and her confessor admonished her to be reconciled with her husband[98], persuading her to ask blessed Francis for a son who, if conceived through the Saint's intercession, was to be named Francis. Not long thereafter, the woman conceived and, while she had asked for just one child, she bore twins. One of them was named Francis and the other one was called Blaise.

100. In the city of Le Mans[99] a very noble woman had a servant who was not of noble birth and whom she forced to do menial work on the feast of St. Francis. But the servant woman, who was nobler than the other woman in spirit, refused to do it out of respect for that day. Human fear prevailed over the fear of God, however, and although she was unwilling, the girl submitted to her orders. She put her hand to the distaff and her fingers plied the spindle[100], but her hands immediately stiffened in pain and her fingers began to burn intensely. The fault is revealed by its punishment, for she was unable to keep still because

---

[98] *1 Cor* 7, 11.

[99] In northern France.

[100] *Prv* 31, 19-20.

her pain was so sharp. The servant ran to the sons of St. Francis, revealed her sin, showed them her punishment and asked to be pardoned. The brothers went to the church in procession and invoked the clemency of the Saint for her salvation. As the brothers were imploring their Father, she was immediately cured, but the burn left a scar on her hands.

101. Something similar took place in upper Campania.[101] A woman was reproached by her neighbors because she did not refrain from working on such an important feast day and stubbornly continued to work until vespers without stopping. However, when her hands suddenly went weak and she was unable to do any kind of work, she was overcome with pain and astonishment. She immediately got up and, declaring that she should venerate the feast day that she had scorned, she went to a priest to make a solemn vow to observe the Saint's feast day in perpetual reverence. After making her vow, she was brought to a church built in honor of St. Francis and weeping copiously, she was completely restored to health.

102. In Valladolid[102], a woman who had been warned by a neighbor that she should honor the feast day of St. Francis without working replied quite arrogantly, "If there were a saint for each craft, the saints would outnumber the days." As soon as this foolish sentence was uttered, she was immediately driven mad through divine punishment and completely lost her wits and her memory for many days until, thanks to the prayers that some people said to blessed Francis, her madness subsided.

103. In the town of Piglio in Roman Campania, a woman was hurriedly doing some work on the feast of St. Francis, but when she was scolded for this by a noblewoman because everyone was observing the feast in divine adoration, the woman replied, "I'm almost finished doing my work. If I'm sinning, the Lord will take care of it." She immediately discovered that she had been punished severely through her daughter, who was sitting next to her. The girl's mouth became twisted up to her ears and her eyes, which looked as if

---

[101] It is unclear whether this took place in the Campania region in southern Italy or in the Champagne region in France.

[102] In Spain.

they were about to bulge out of her head, rolled around miserably. Women came from all over the place and they cursed the mother's wickedness for her innocent daughter. The girl's mother immediately prostrated herself on the ground in sorrow, promising that every year she would observe that day as a feast day and feed the poor on that day out of reverence for the Saint. Without further delay, her daughter's affliction ceased and the woman repented of the sin she had committed.

104. Matthew of Tolentino had a daughter by the name of Frances. Very upset over the fact that the brothers were moving elsewhere, he began to call his daughter Mathea, depriving her of the name Frances. However, as soon as she was deprived of her name, she was also deprived of her health. Indeed, since he was acting out of contempt towards the Father and out of hatred towards his sons, his daughter became gravely ill and was in danger of dying. Now, while he was afflicted with such bitter sorrow over his daughter's imminent death and was blamed by his wife for his hatred towards the servants of God and his contempt towards the Saint's name, with ready devotion he turned first of all to that name and then gave his little girl the original name of which he had deprived her. At last, when girl's sobbing father brought her to the brothers' residence, the girl fully regained her health together with her name.

105. Unaware that she was pregnant, a woman from Pisa sweat all day long while working on the foundations that were being laid in that city for the church being built to St. Francis. St. Francis appeared to her one night, preceded by two brothers who were carrying candles, and he said to her, "Here, my daughter, you have conceived and will bear a son.[103] You will delight in him if you name him after me." It came time to deliver and she bore a son. "He is to be named Henry," said her mother-in-law, "after a certain relative of ours." "Absolutely not," replicated the boy's mother, "instead he is to be named Francis." The woman's mother-in-law mocked the noble name as if it were vulgar. A few days went by and the baby, who hadn't been baptized yet, weakened to the point of death. The household grieved and their

---

[103] *Lk* 1, 31 and 57.

happiness turned to mourning.[104] That night, as the mother anxiously kept watch, St. Francis came to her with two brothers, just like the first time and, upset, he said to the woman, "Didn't I tell you that you will not delight in your son unless you name him after me?" The woman then began to shout, swearing that the boy wouldn't be given any other name. The boy was healed at last and was baptized by the name of Francis. Indeed, he was given the grace of never crying and grew into childhood without any trouble.

106. In Tuscany, near Arezzo, there was a woman whose life had been in danger for seven days because of labor pains. Already deathly pale and given up for lost by everyone, she made a vow to St. Francis, invoking his help as she was dying. After saying her vow, she quickly dropped off to sleep and St. Francis appeared to her. Calling her by her name, Adelasia, he asked her if she recognized his face. When she replied, "Truly, father, I recognize you," the Saint added, "Do you know how to say 'Hail, Queen of mercy'?" When she replied, "I do, Father," the Saint said, "Then start, and before you finish the prayer you will happily gave birth." Having said this, the Saint cried out in a loud voice[105] and as he was crying out, he left. That voice woke the woman up and in awe, she began to recite, "Hail, Queen" . As she began to invoke "your merciful eyes", before she could even finish she gave birth to a beautiful baby boy in joy and health.

107. A woman from Sicily, heedless about abstaining from menial work even though she knew that the solemnity of St. Francis was imminent, prepared a kneading trough in front of her. As soon as she had put the flour in and had piled it up with her bare arms, the flour immediately looked like it was covered with blood. When she saw this, the woman called her neighbors in astonishment. And the more they came there to see this scene, the more the veins of blood grew in the pile. The woman repented about doing what she had done and vowed that she would never again do menial work on his feast day. Thus having made her promise, the bloodstains disappeared from the pile of flour.

---

[104] *Jas* 4, 9.
[105] *Mt* 27, 46.

108. While the Saint was still alive... (*with just a few minor variations, this recount is the same as the one in n° 63 of the* First Life, *about the woman who was saved by holding the reins that St. Francis had held in his hands*).

CHAPTER XIII
Of the herniated who were healed

109. Brother James of Iseo, a very celebrated and well-known person in our Order, testifying himself[106] to the glory of our Father, gave thanks to the Saint of God for the benefaction of his cure. When he was a young boy in his father's house, he was stricken with a very serious hernia and because of the problem caused by the painful lesion, the hidden parts of his body that nature had concealed, would move about. His father and his family, who knew what it was, grieved for him and while doctors' remedies were attempted repeatedly, there was no improvement. At last, divinely inspired, the boy began to meditate on the salvation of his soul and studiously to seek God, who heals those who are contrite of heart and continue in their contrition.[107] Therefore, he devoutly entered the Order of St. Francis, but did not disclose the illness with which he was afflicted. However, when he had been in the Order for a while and the friars learned of the young man's illness, they were frightened and although they regretted it, they wanted to send him home to his parents. However, the boy's great constancy overcame this pressing insistence. Therefore, the friars took care of him until, sustained by grace and giving off the fragrance of goodness through the probity of his ways, he was given the duty of caring for souls and he observed regular discipline in a praiseworthy way. It then happened that when the body of St. Francis was transferred to its current place, this brother was present when the translation was celebrated, together with many others. Going up to the tomb in which the remains of the most holy Father lay, he began to pray at length about his chronic illness. All of a sudden, his organs

---

[106] *Jn* 1, 15.
[107] *Ps* 147, 3.

went back into place and, feeling that he was cured, he took off his belt and from that time on, he was completely relieved of all the pain of the past.

110. There was a man from Pisa and since all his intestines came out onto his genitalia, he came up with a diabolical plan against himself on account of the very sharp pain and horrible sense of shame. In fact, plunged into the abyss of desperation, he decided that he no longer wanted to live and would kill himself by hanging. In the meantime, however, driven by his conscience, which was not dead yet, the name of St. Francis started to become etched in his mind and he began to invoke his name, albeit weakly. All his evil intentions promptly changed and he prayed that the enormous sore be healed instantly.

111. The son of a fellow from the town of Cisterna on the seacoast, overcome by the rupture of his genitals, could not use any sort of contrivance to hold his intestines in. In fact, the lumbar band that usually heals this type of hernia caused new multiple ruptures. His distressed parents were anguished over this and the horrendous sight of this illness was enough to make friends and neighbors weep. After attempting every sort of remedy in vain, the boy's mother and father consecrated him to St. Francis. Thus, on the feast of St. Francis, bringing him to the church built in his honor near Velletri, they set him before the Saint's image and, making their vows together with the rest of the crowd, they offered up all their tears for him. While the Gospel was being sung and the sentence that goes "what you have hidden from the learned and the clever you have revealed to the merest children"[108] was being recalled, the boy's lumbar belt suddenly burst and all the useless remedies dissolved. The wound went down immediately and his yearned-for health was restored. There was a great uproar and the people who were there praised the Lord and venerated his Saint.

112. Near Ceccano, a castle in Campania, while the sacristan, Nicholas, was entering the church early in the morning, he tripped suddenly, falling so heavily that all his intestines fell out onto his groin. The clerics and other neighbors hurried over to him, lifted him up and put him to bed. He lay there immobilized for eight days and

---

[108] *Mt* 11, 25.

was unable to get up even when nature called. The doctors were summoned and undertook all the remedies of their art, but his pain grew and instead of being cured, his illness got worse. His intestines, which had come out monstrously, had become localized out of place, causing the man such pain that the wretch was unable to eat for more than eight days. Desperate at this point and approaching death, he turned to St. Francis for help. He had a religious and God-fearing daughter and he exhorted her to implore St. Francis' suffrage on his behalf. The blessed daughter went outside for a while and, her face bathed in tears, she started to pray to the Father for her father. The enormous value of prayer! While she was still praying, her father promptly called her and announced the joy of his unhoped-for cure. Everything had gone back to its proper place and he felt better than he had before his fall. He thus made a vow that blessed Francis would always be his patron saint and that he would celebrated his feast day every year.

113. In Spello (*this recount is essentially identical to the one in the* First Life, *144*).

114. A young man named John, who was from the diocese of Sora, had such a serious intestinal hernia that the remedies prescribed by his doctors gave him no improvement. It happened one day that his wife went to a church dedicated to blessed Francis. While she was praying for her husband's health, one of the friars said to her with simplicity of spirit, "Go tell your husband that he should consecrate himself to blessed Francis and then make the sign of the cross over his hernia!" She recounted this to her husband when she returned. Consecrating himself to blessed Francis, he made the sign of the cross over that area and his intestines immediately went back into place. The man was amazed over how quickly this unhoped-for cure had taken place and he began to do many tests to find out if what had aided him so suddenly could have been a real cure. While he was suffering from a high fever, blessed Francis appeared to him in a dream and, calling him by name, said, "Do not fear, John, because you will be healed of your illness." This miracle was widely believed because blessed Francis also appeared to a religious named Robert and when he was asked who he was, he replied, "I am Francis and I have come to heal a friend of mine."

115. In Sicily, a fellow by the name of Peter, who was suffering from an inguinal hernia, was miraculously cured when he promised to visit the Saint's sanctuary.

CHAPTER XIV
Of the blind, deaf and dumb

116. At the convent of the friars of Naples, there was a brother by the name of Robert, blind for many many years, who developed a fleshy growth in his eyes that kept him from moving or using his eyelids. Since many foreign brothers had gathered there to go off to different parts of the world, blessed Francis, the mirror and model of saintly obedience, healed this brother in their presence in the following way in order to urge them on the journeys through the uniqueness of this miracle. One night, Brother Robert was lying deathly ill and his soul had already been commended to God, when the blessed Father went to him with three brothers who were perfect in their saintliness, and that is St. Anthony, Brother Augustine and Brother James of Assisi[109], all of whom, just as they had followed him to perfection while they were alive, also accompanied him soon after his death. Taking a small knife, St. Francis removed the excess skin, restored his previous sense of sight and saved him from the jaws of death, saying, "Robert, my son, the grace I have given you is a sign for the brothers who are going to far-off peoples so that they will know that I am going ahead of them and will guide their steps. They should go forth cheerfully," he said, "and carry out the obedience assigned to them with a ready spirit. May the sons of obedience delight, especially those who have forgotten their terrestrial homeland, for they have a hardworking and solicitous predecessor as their leader!"

---

[109] St. Anthony died in Padua in 1231 and was canonized in 1232. Brother Augustine was minister of the province of Terra di Lavoro and he died at the same time as St. Francis (*Second Life*, 218). Lastly, the third brother, who died in Foggia, was one of Francis' closest companions and he was the one who saw Francis' soul ascending to heaven on a white cloud (*Second Life*, 217 and *First Life*, 110).

117. In Zancati, a town near Anagni[110], a knight named Gerard had lost his sight completely. It happened that two Friars Minor who were coming from foreign lands, went to his house to ask for lodging. Received honorably by the entire family and treated with all kindness, they did not notice their host's blindness at all. After a short time, they went on to the friars' residence six miles away and stayed there for eight days. One night, then, blessed Francis appeared to one of the brothers in a dream and said, "Get up and hurry with your companion to the house of the host who honored me through you and who demonstrated such great piety to you out of respect for me. Repay his cheerful welcome and honor him who has honored you! In fact, he is blind and cannot see and this came to him through his sins that he has not confessed yet. The darkness of eternal death[111] awaits him and unending torment is ready for him. Indeed, he is bound for this because of the faults he has not abandoned yet." When the Father had disappeared, his son got up and hurried with his companion to carry out this order. The two of them went back together to their host and the one who had had the vision told the man everything, going in order. The man was more than a bit astonished and confirmed that what he had just heard was indeed the truth. He was contrite to the point of tears, willingly made his confession and promised to mend his ways. Thus renewed deep inside, his eyesight was promptly restored on the outside as well. The fame of this miracle spread, leading those who heard about to do honor to their guests.

118. In Greece, near Thebes, after a blind woman had fasted only on bread and water for the eve of the feast of St. Francis, her husband brought her to the friars' church on the morning of Francis' feast day. While the Mass was being celebrated, when the Body of Christ was lifted up, she opened her eyes, seeing clearly and worshipping it most devoutly. During the Elevation, she loudly exclaimed, "Thanks be to God and to his Saint, because I can see the Body of Christ!" All those present turned at her cries of gladness[112]

---

[110] Anagni, the "City of Popes", is outside Rome. Some scholars have indicated Zancati as the birthplace of Innocent III.

[111] *Jb* 3, 5.

[112] *Ps* 47, 2.

and when the celebration was over, the woman returned home[113] guided by her own eyesight. Christ was Francis' light during his lifetime and just as He delegated each one of His marvelous manifestations to him then, now He wants glory to be given to his body.

119. In Roman Campania, a fourteen-year-old boy from the town of Pofi lost his left eye completely due to a sudden trauma. This intense pain gouged his eye from his socket so that, hanging for eight days dangling from the end of a thin finger-long peduncle, it was deadened completely. Even though there was nothing left to do but sever it and the doctors had completely given up hope by this time, his father nevertheless turned his mind[114] entirely to the help of blessed Francis. That tireless helper of the wretched did not fail to answer the supplicant's prayers. He put that dead eye back in its place and illuminated it with the beams of desired light, giving it pristine efficacy.

120. In this same region, near Castro, a large beam fell down and seriously struck a priest on the head, blinding him in the left eye. Falling down to the ground, he began to moan, calling loudly to St. Francis, "Help me, most holy Father, so that I can go to your celebration as I promised your brothers," for in fact, it was the eve of Saint's feast day. Getting back up, he was promptly healed perfectly and burst into songs of praise and joy, turning all those present, who were commiserating with his plight, to feelings of amazement and jubilee. He went to the celebration and told everyone about the Saint's clemency and power, which he had experienced first-hand. Therefore, let everyone learn to honor devoutly the one whom all of them know will readily help those who honor him.

121. While blessed Francis was still alive, a woman from Narni who had been struck blind made the sign of the cross over her eyes and by virtue of this same man of God, she immediately and miraculously regained the eyesight she had lost.[115]

---

[113] *Lk* 1, 56.

[114] *Mk* 12, 30.

[115] This episode was also described in the *First Life*, 67.

122. While a man from Mount Gargano, whose name was Peter Romano, was working in his vineyard, he was splitting wood with an iron bar and injured his eye, cutting it in half so that his pupil, split in two, was hanging out. While he despaired that it was not humanly possible for anyone to come to his aid in such grave peril, he vowed that if he were helped, he would eat nothing on St. Francis' feast day. The Saint of God immediately restored the man's eye to its proper place, putting back together again what had been split in two and restoring the gift of sight.

123. Through the merits of blessed Francis, a nobleman's son who was blind from birth was given the eyesight he so desired and he became known as Illuminatus in honor of this event. When he came of age, he entered the Order of St. Francis and completed this holy beginning with an even holier end.

124. The noble castle of Bevagna is located in the Spoleto Valley. A saintly woman lived there with an even saintlier daughter and with a niece who was very devoted to Christ. St. Francis honored their hospitality several times by staying with them. In fact, this woman had a son in the Order, a man who had achieved perfection. However, one of them, the niece that is, had been deprived of exterior sight, although the inner eyes that observe God shone with a marvelous ability to see. One time when she prayed to St. Francis, who had taken pity on her illness, and asked that he also be mindful of their efforts, he sprinkled his saliva over the blind woman's eyes three times in the name of the Trinity and restored to her the sight she had desired.

125. Near Città della Pieve... (*What follows is a summarized version of the miracle of the deaf and dumb beggar who was taken in by Mark and healed through the vow of his benefactor,* First Life, *147-148*).

126. A woman from the Apulia area had lost the power of speech a long time before and was unable to breathe freely. One night while she was sleeping, the Virgin Mary appeared to her and said, "If you want to be healed, go to the church of St. Francis in Venosa and there you will regain the health you so desire!" The woman got up and, unable to speak or breathe, she gestured to her family that they should go to Venosa soon. They consented and went there with her. When the woman entered the church of St. Francis and asked for help with all

her heart, she coughed up a fleshy mass and was miraculously cured before everyone's eyes.

127. In the diocese of Arezzo, a woman who had been dumb for seven years pleaded her case to divine ears with zealous desire, asking that God deign to loosen her tongue. Now while she was sleeping, two brothers dressed in red robes came to her and sweetly counseled her to consecrate herself to St. Francis. She willingly obeyed their advice and making her vow in her heart -- for she could not speak -- she woke up immediately and thus regained wakefulness and speech all at the same time.

128. Men were amazed that a judge by the name of Alexander had been rendered speechless for over six years for having spoken badly about the miracles of blessed Francis. Since he had been punished in the part of his body with which he had sinned[116] and had been drawn to profound repentance, he regretted that he had railed against the Saint's miracles. Accordingly, the Saint did not remain angry but he assisted the man who, now penitent, was humbly invoking him, by giving him back the power of speech. From then on, that blasphemous tongue was consecrated to praising the blessed Father and was rendered even more devout because of its punishment.

129. Since we are the subject of blasphemes, this brings to mind a story that may be useful to relate. A knight named Gineldo from Borgo San Sepolcro very impudently denigrated the works and prodigious signs of blessed Francis. He greatly insulted the pilgrims who traveled to venerate his memory and in public he twittered mad things against the friars. One day while he was playing dice, filled with stupidity and disbelief, he said to those around him, "If Francis is a saint, then let eighteen come up on the dice!" The six on the dice was immediately tripled and, tossing them as many as nine times, he got six times three each time. However, the madman would not cease and, sinning upon sin and heaping blaspheme upon blaspheme, he said, "If it's true that this Francis is a saint, then let my body be felled today by the sword. Instead, if he is not a saint, then let me remain unharmed." In its divine judgment, God's ire did not hesitate the consider his

---

[116] *Wis* 11, 17.

words a blaspheme.[117] When the game was over and he then also offended a nephew of his, this nephew picked up his sword and bloodied it with his uncle's bowels. The wicked man died that very day and became the servant of hell and a child of darkness. Blasphemers beware, and do not believe that words disappear into thin air, nor that there is no avenger for offenses against the saints.

130. *(This section is taken word for word from the* First Life, *136, about the miracle of Sibyll, the blind woman).*

131. In the town of Vicalvi in the diocese of Sora, a little girl who had been blind from birth was brought to the oratory of blessed Francis by her mother and when the name of Christ was invoked, through the merits of the blessed one, she received the eyesight she had never had.

132. In the city of Arezzo, in a church built near the city in blessed Francis' honor, a woman who had been blind for seven years regained her eyesight.

133. In this same city, a poor woman's son was illuminated by blessed Francis, to whom she had consecrated him.

134. *(This is identical to the brief recount of the blind man from* Spello, First Life, *136).*

135. In Poggibonsi, in the diocese of Florence, inspired by a revelation a blind woman set off to visit the oratory of blessed Francis. Once she was brought there, as she was lying before the altar, the object of pity, she suddenly regained her eyesight and returned home without any guidance.

The following miracles have been taken almost literally from the First Life*:*

136. *The blind woman from Camerino (*First Life, *136).*

137. *The blind woman from Gubbio (*ibid., *136).*

138. *The blind man from Assisi who had been Francis' friend while he was alive (*ibid., *136).*

139. *Albertino of Narni, who was blind (*ibid., *149).*

140. *Young Villa, who was mute and paralyzed (*ibid., *149).*

141. *The mute man from the diocese of Perugia (*ibid., *149).*

142. *The woman with a stone in her throat (*ibid., *136).*

---

[117] *Ps* 78, 21 and 109, 7.

143. Bartholomew, from the castle of Arpino in the bishopric of Sorano, had lost his hearing seven years before, but regained it upon invoking the name of blessed Francis.

144. In Sicily, a woman from the district of Piazza Armerina who did not have the power of speech prayed to blessed Francis in the language of her heart and was given the grace of speaking that she had desired.

145. In the little town of Nicosia[118], a priest got up for matins as usual and upon being asked a question by the one who had to read the usual blessing, he gave I don't know what uncouth reply and began to gnash his teeth. He was brought home demented in this way and he completely lost the power of speech for a month. Through the advice of a man of God, he consecrated himself to St. Francis and, freed of his insanity, he regained the power of speech.

CHAPTER XV

Of lepers and of those with hemorrhages

146. Near San Severino, a young man named Atto was covered with leprosy. Since all his members were stiff and swollen, this made him look at everything with a horrible stare. Since the wretch was constantly stretched out on his sickbed, his parents were filled with enormous sadness. One day, the boy's father tried to persuade him to consecrate himself to blessed Francis and joyously getting the boy to consent, he obtained a candlewick that he used to measure his son's height. The boy vowed that every year he would bring blessed Francis a candle of that size. As soon as the votive offering was made, he immediately arose, cleansed of leprosy.

147. Another one by the name of Buonomo from Fano who was afflicted with paralysis and leprosy was brought by his parents to the church of blessed Francis and was completed healed of both diseases.

148. A noble woman by the name of Rogata, who was from the diocese of Sora, had suffered from hemorrhages for twenty-three years. When she heard a boy who was singing in the Italian

---

[118] In Sicily.

language[119] about the miracles that God had worked during that time through blessed Francis, spurred by her great pain, she burst into tears and thus kindled by faith, she began to say to herself, "O blessed father Francis, through whom so many miracles are shining forth, deign to deliver me from this disease! So far you have not worked a miracle this great." In fact, because she had lost so much blood, this woman often looked as if she were dying and if her blood stopped circulating, her whole body would swell up. What else can I say? After just a few days had gone by, she felt herself she was cured through the merits of most blessed Francis. Also her son named Mario, whose arm was numb, was healed through a simple vow to the Saint of God.

149. A woman from Sicily who was debilitated by hemorrhaging, was cured by blessed Francis, Christ's standard-bearer.

CHAPTER XVI
Of the insane and the possessed

150. Peter of Foligno[120], who went once to visit the temple of blessed Michael, felt as if he had swallowed demons after he had sipped some spring water. Possessed then for three years, his body was torn apart and he said terrible things and did horrible deeds. Finally, as soon as he put his hand on the tomb of the blessed Father and humbly invoked his virtue, he was marvelously liberated of the demons that had cruelly tormented him.

151. A woman from the town of Narni, who was possessed by the devil, was visited by him in a dream and ordered to make the sign of the cross. Since she was feeble-minded and did not know how to bless herself, the blessed Father made the sign of the cross over her and drove all diabolical suffering from her.

152. In Marittima, a woman struck with insanity had been deprived of sight and hearing for five years. She would tear at her clothes with her teeth, had no fear of water or fire and would fall into horrible attacks of epilepsy. One night, since divine mercy was

---

[119] As opposed to Latin.
[120] This episode is described at greater length in the *First Life*, 137.

prepared to take pity on her, she fell fast into healthy sleep. In fact, she saw blessed Francis seated on a beautiful throne and, prostrate before him, she implored him to heal her. Since he still would not answer her prayers, the woman made a vow, promising that as long as she had the wherewithal, she would not deny alms to anyone who asked out of love for him. The Saint immediately acknowledged this pact, which was similar to the one that he had once made with God[121] and making the sign of the cross over her, he restored her completely to health.

153. A little girl who lived near Norcia[122] had long been afflicted by illness when at last it was understood that she was vexed by the devil. In fact, often screeching she would bite herself and would not avoid high places or feel afraid of any danger. Indeed, since she had lost the power of speech and the use of her limbs, she did not seem to be a rational being. Her parents, anguished over their offspring's derangement, tied her bed to a mule and brought her to Assisi. On the day of the Lord's Circumcision, as she was lying on the floor before the altar of St. Francis, as High Mass was being celebrated she suddenly vomited I don't know what evil thing.[123] She then promptly got up and kissed the altar of St. Francis and, completely liberated of all ill, she burst out and exclaimed, "Praise be to God and to his Saint!"

154. The son of a noble man was prey to the torment of falling sickness, which was at least as horrible as it was painful. He foamed at the mouth, looked threateningly and, abusing his body, he would spit I don't know what diabolical thing. His parents invoked the Saint of God, imploring a cure, and they offered their miserable son to his compassionate love. Thus, that merciful one appeared to the boy's mother one night in her sleep and said to her, "Here, I've come now to save your son." The woman awoke in trembling at that voice and found that her son had been perfectly healed.

---

121 As indicated in the *First Life*, 17, in the *Second Life*, 123 and in the *Legend of the Three Companions*, III, 8, before his conversion Francis had decided that he would never deny alms to anyone who asked out of the love of God.

122 This town, which is the birthplace of St. Benedict, is not far from Assisi.

123 In the Pisa *Tavola* dating to the thirteenth century, the painter represented this miracle as a completely new occurrence, depicting a little black winged devil coming out of the girl's mouth.

155. I don't believe I should pass over the marvelous power he had over demons while he was still alive.[124] One time in the castle of Sangemini, the man of God, announcing the kingdom of heaven, went to stay with a God-fearing man whose wife was vexed by the devil, as everyone knew. When blessed Francis was implored on her behalf, he firmly refused to have anything to do with this since he was afraid of being applauded by men. In the end, supplicated by numerous prayers, he had three brothers who were with him sit in three corners of the room, while he himself went to the fourth one to pray. When his prayers were over, he confidently went over to the woman, who was writhing miserably, and ordered the devil to leave in the name of Jesus Christ.[125] At his command, the demon furiously withdrew so quickly that the man of God thought he had been tricked and therefore, he left the place red-faced. When he was then passing through that same town another time, the woman, who was outside in the square, began to call after him, kissing his footsteps so that he would deign to speak to her. Reassured by many people about her liberation, only then, after many people had begged him to do so, would he agree to speak to her.

156. When he was in Città di Castello another time[126], a woman possessed by the devil was brought to the house in which he was staying. She stayed outside and, as she gnashed her teeth, she vexed everyone with her howls. Many people beseeched the Saint of God to liberate her, complaining that they had been disturbed by her madness long enough. Blessed Francis sent the friar who was with him over to her, for he wanted to see if the devil were really involved or if the woman was deceiving him. However, knowing that he wasn't St. Francis, she mocked him and gave him little consideration. The holy Father was inside praying and as soon as he was done, he went outside to the woman. Since she could not stand his presence, she began to

---

124 F. Casolini, who translated this work into Italian, indicates that she included this episode in its entirety, despite the fact that it was also described in the *First Life*, 69, because although briefer, it not only differs somewhat from the original recount due to the influence of the *Legend* written by Julian of Speyer, n° 50, but it also makes the Saint's hesitation easier to comprehend.

125 *Heb* 6, 16 and *Acts* 3, 6.

126 The same episode as the one recounted in the *First Life*, 50, but again with numerous changes that were influenced by Julian's *Legend*.

shudder and writhe about on the floor. The Saint of God ordered the demon to come out in obedience and it departed immediately, leaving the woman unharmed.

CHAPTER XVII
Of those with crippled and broken limbs

157. A son was born to a certain fellow in the territory of Parma and the boy's foot was turned backwards, so that his heel faced front and his toes were turned towards the back. This fellow was a poor man, but he was devoted to St. Francis. Every day, he lamented to St. Francis about his son born with such a disgrace, continually stressing his poverty. Since he would go around daydreaming that he would brutally turn the little baby's foot around into the right position, after conniving with the midwife this was exactly what he planned to do while the baby's limbs had been softened in the bath. Before such a rash deed could be attempted, however, through the merits of St. Francis, the baby was discovered to be healthy when his swaddling clothes were taken off, as if he had never had any deformity at all.

158. In Scoppito near Amiterno, a husband and wife who had an only son deplored him as a disgrace to their posterity. Indeed, he did not seem human but looked like a monster since, by a fluke of nature, his forelimbs were twisted to the back. With his arms attached at the neck, his knees joined to his chest and his feet to his buttocks, he truly looked like a ball of wool rather than a bust. Consequently, they kept him away from the eyes of their relatives and neighbors so that no one could see him, for they were not only wounded by grief, but even more so by shame. In addition, the husband was so overcome with grief that he reproached his wife, saying that she had not begotten children like other women, but a monster that could not even begin to compare with the very ugliest ones, and he tormented her with the accusation that this punishment of God was due to one of her sins. The wife, torn apart with anguish and out of her mind with shame, called out to Christ with her constant sobbing, invoking the help of St. Francis so that he would deign to come to the aid of such an unfortunate woman who had been reduced to such disgrace. One night

while, in her sadness, she was engrossed in sad dreams, St. Francis appeared to her, consoling her with pious expressions. "Get up," he said, "and bring the boy to a place nearby that is dedicated to my name and bathe him in the water from that well. In truth, as soon as you pour water over the boy, he will be healed completely." The woman neglected to fulfill the Saint's instructions for her baby and would not agree to do so even when he appeared to her a second time and repeated these very same words. The Saint, however, mercifully taking pity on her simplicity, added new proof of his mercy in a marvelous way.[127] In fact, the third time he appeared to her with the glorious Virgin and the noble procession of apostolic saints and, taking her with the child, in the space of a moment he transported her before the door of this place. And since dawn was already starting to appear and that entire bodily vision had disappeared the woman knocked on the door, dumbfounded and amazed beyond belief. While she awaited in complete faith for the boy to be healed, as had now been promised with this third prophecy, she aroused no small wonder among the friars over the uniqueness of what had happened. In a short time, several noble women from the same province arrived out of devotion and upon hearing what had happened, they were quite astonished. Without any delay, they drew some from the well and the noblest of them bathed the baby with her own hands. All his limbs immediately went back into place and he was healed, and the greatness of the miracle inspired everyone's admiration.

159. Near the castle of Cori in the diocese of Ostia, a man had lost the use of his leg to such a degree that he could not walk or move it at all. Thus, in such great anguish and despairing of any human aid, one night, as if he could see St. Francis in person, he began to moan before him, "Help me St. Francis. Reward the service and devotion I demonstrated to you. In fact, I carried you on my mule and kissed your feet and your sacred hands. I was always devoted to you, I always remained close to you and here I am dying from the very sharp torment of this pain." Struck by this lament and immediately recalling the man's favor, out of gratitude for his devotion, together with a friar he appeared to the man, who was now awake. He said he had been

---

[127] *Hs* 1, 6.

summoned by him to bring him a saving cure. He touched the sore
area with a small stick shaped like a "tau" and the abscess opened up
immediately and he was healed and the sign of the "tau" is still there
even today. It was with this sign that St. Francis signed his letters
whenever he had to send anything in writing on account of need or
charity.

*The subsequent sections were taken almost word for word from
the* First Life *and describe the following miracles:*

160. *The girl who was cured at his temporary tomb* (First Life,
127).

161. *The boy in the district of Narni* (ibid., 128).

162. *Nicholas of Foligno*(ibid., 129).

163. *The boy with the crippled leg* (ibid., 130).

164. *The crippled man from Fano* (ibid., 131).

165. *The little girl from Gubbio* (ibid., 132).

166. *The little boy from Montenero* (ibid., 133).

167. *The man from Gubbio who brought his son in a basket*
(ibid., 134).

168. In the diocese of Volterra, a man named Riccomagno, who
was   barely able to drag himself along the ground and had been
abandoned by his mother because of his monstrous swelling, humbly
consecrated himself to St. Francis and was immediately liberated.

169. In this same diocese, two women named Verde and
Sanguigna[128] who were so severely crippled that they could not move
at all and had to be carried by others, and whose hands were scraped
because they had to lean on them in order to move, regained their
health simply by making a vow.

170. A certain James of Poggibonsi, who was so wretchedly
bent over and crippled that his mouth touched his knees, was brought
by his widowed mother to the oratory of blessed Francis and after
tearfully begging to the Lord to deliver him, she brought him home
safe and sound.

---

[128] These names are quite odd: Verde means "green" and Sanguigna means
"bloody". Perhaps the women were given these cruel nicknames on account of
their illness.

171. In Vicalvi, a woman's withered hand became just like the other one through the merits of the holy Father.

172. In the city of Capua, a woman vowed that she would visit St. Francis' tomb in person. Because of her housework, however, she forgot about the vow she had made and all of a sudden, she was paralyzed on the left side. Because her nerves had contracted, she couldn't turn her head or her arm in any direction. Thus wracked with pain, she wore her neighbors out with her continuous howling. Now, two brothers who were passing by house were begged by a priest to go in to see the wretched woman. Confessing that she had failed to fulfill her vow, she received their blessing and in that very same hour, she got up healed and, made wiser by her punishment, without any further delay she fulfilled the vow she had made.

173. While Bartholomew of Narni[129] was sleeping under a tree, he completely lost the use of his shin and foot because a demon had insinuated himself in him. Being very poor, he didn't know which way to turn, but Francis, lover of the poor and standard-bearer of Christ, appeared to him in a dream and ordered him to go to a certain place. He dragged himself there, but when he turned down the wrong road, he heard a voice telling him, "Peace be to you! I am the one to whom you have consecrated yourself." As he led him to the place, it seemed to the man that Francis had placed one hand on his foot and the other one on his shin, reviving his paralyzed limb in this way. At that time, the man was well on in years and had been crippled in that way for six years.

174. St. Francis worked many similar miracles while he was still alive. Thus, as he was passing through the diocese of Rieti one time, he came to a village where a woman in tears went out to meet him with her eight-year-old son in her arms, and she placed him at Francis' feet. The little boy had already been swollen enormously for four years by then and could not even look down to see his feet. Picking him up lovingly, St. Francis ran those truly sacred hands of his up and down the boy's belly. At his touch, the swelling went down

---

[129] This episode was also described in the *First Life*, 135, but this recount is much briefer.

and, immediately cured, the boy gave great thanks to God and to his Saint, together with his mother, now happy,

175. In the city of Toscanella... (*identical to the episode in the* First Life, *65, with a few words drawn from Julian's* Legend, *47*).

176. Having arrived in Narni... (*Peter, the paralytic, as in the* First Life, *66, with a few words drawn from Julian's* Legend, *48*).

177. Near Gubbio... (*the woman with the crippled hands, as in the* First Life, *67, with a few words drawn from Julian's* Legend, *48*).

178. He arrived once in the city of Orte to lodge there, when a little boy named James, who had long been completely curled up, went to the Saint together with his parents and began begging to be healed. Because of his lengthy illness, his head was bent down to his knees and some of his bones were broken. Therefore, at the very instant that he received St. Francis' blessing, he began to uncurl and, perfectly outstretched, he was completely healed.

179. Another inhabitant of the same city who had a gland the size of a large roll of bread between his shoulder blades was blessed by St. Francis and was immediately cured so completely that not even a trace of it remained.

180. In the hospital of Città di Castello, there was a young man whom everyone knew who, crippled for seven years, had to drag himself along the ground like an animal. His mother had prayed to St. Francis many times on his behalf, asking that he give her crawling son the ability to walk. The Saint, hearing the praying mother's vow and answering her sobs, relieved her son's monstrous contraction all at once and gave him back his natural freedom.

181. Praxedes[130] was very famous among the religious women of Rome and throughout the entire Roman world. From a very tender age, out of love for the Eternal Groom, she had closed herself off in a narrow prison for almost forty years by this time and had earned the special grace of St. Francis' friendship. In fact -- and this is something that he did not do with any other woman -- he received her in obedience, granting her the religious habit, or in other words, the robe and cord, because of her devout piety.

---

[130] It is important to note that Praxedes was not one of St. Clare's followers, nor did she live in a convent, but it seems that she was a Tertiary.

Now, one day when she climbed up onto the scaffold in her cell to get something she needed, she had a dizzy spell and fell down heavily. Not only did she break her leg and her foot, but she also dislocated her shoulder completely.

At this point, the virgin of Christ, who had not seen anyone's face for many years and had firmly resolved never to see one, was lying on the floor like a lump. Not wanting to receive help from anyone, she didn't know which way to turn. Despite the fact that, through a cardinal's order and on the advice of several religious, she was urged to break her vow of seclusion to benefit from the help of a female religious in order to avoid the danger of death, which she would have risked if she let herself go. Refusing to do this, however, she resisted in every way possible so that she would not break her vow in the least. Consequently, she threw herself at the feet of divine mercy and when evening came, she turned to the most blessed father Francis with pious laments, saying, "My most holy Father, you who kindly help the needs everywhere of many people whom you did not even know while you were alive, why don't you come to my help too since, although I was unworthy, I was deserving of your sweet grace during your lifetime? Now, as you can well see, o blessed Father, I must go back on my resolution or die." While she continued to address similar words to him with her heart and her lips, she was suddenly overcome with sleepiness and went into a sort of ecstasy.[131] And then the most benevolent Father, dressed in the while robes of glory[132], descended into that dark prison and began to speak in a sweet tone, saying, "Get up, blessed daughter, get up and fear not. Receive the gift of perfect health and keep your vow unbroken." Then, taking her by the hand, he got up and disappeared.

She then started to turn to and fro in her cell and could not understand what the Servant of God had done to her, for she thought she was still dreaming. At last, she went to the window and made her usual summoning gesture. A monk quickly ran over to her and, astonished beyond all belief, he said to her, "What happened to you, o mother, that you were able to get up?" Thinking that she was still

---

[131] *Acts* 11, 5.
[132] *Is* 52, 1.

dreaming and not recognizing him, she asked to have the fire lit. As soon as the light was brought to her, she returned to her senses and, no longer feeling any pain, she recounted the entire occurrence in order.

CHAPTER XVIII
Of several different miracles

182. In the diocese of Sabina, there was an eighty-year-old woman who had two daughters, and she gave the son of one of her daughters, who had died, to the other daughter to be breast-feed. In the end, however, since this daughter and her husband also conceived, her milk ran out and there was no one who could take care of the little orphan, no one who could give the thirsty baby a drop of milk. The grieving old woman worried about her grandson and since she was unfortunately quite poor, she didn't know which way to turn. The little baby grew weak and faint and out of compassion, his grandmother was dying along with him. The old woman wandered about the streets[133] and houses and no one was spared her laments. One night, in order to soothe his crying, she put her withered breast into the baby's mouth and tearfully asked for St. Francis' counsel and help. This lover of the age of innocence was immediately ready and, with his usual mercy, he took pity on the wretched. "Woman, I am Francis," he said, "the one you have so tearfully invoked. Put the baby to your breast, for the Lord will give you plenty of milk." The old woman followed the Saint's counsel and soon the breasts of the eighty-year-old woman were flowing with milk. Everyone heard about this, for their eyes bore witness to it, and they were filled with amazement, whereas the bent old woman herself was reinvigorated with the warmth of youth. Many people hastened to see this and among them was a count from that region, who was forced to acknowledge that, based on his own experience, he couldn't believe the news that had been reported to him. In fact, when the count came in person and, standing before her, wanted to examine this singular occurrence, the wrinkled old woman squirted a stream of milk onto him, driving him away from her with

---

[133] *Sg* 3, 2.

this sprinkling. Therefore, everyone blessed the Lord, who alone does great wonders[134], and with eager homage, they venerated his servant, St. Francis. The boy grew rapidly because of this marvelous nourishment and quickly grew taller than normal for his age.

183. A man by the name of Martin had led his oxen to pasture far from town. One of the ox fell and broke its hoof so badly that Martin could think of no solution. While he was worrying about how to skin it, since he didn't have any tools with him, he went home, leaving the ox in blessed Francis' care so that the wolves wouldn't devour it before he returned. Early the next morning, he went back to the woods with the skinner, but he found the ox grazing and could not distinguish the broken hoof from the others at all. He thanked the good shepherd[135] who had taken such good care and granted that cure.

184. Another man from Amiterno, whose mule had been stolen from him three years before, turned to St. Francis with his protests, prostrating himself before him with his woeful prayers. One night when he dozed off, he heard a voice telling him, "Get up[136], go to Scoppito and you'll get your mule back." Roused by that voice, he was dumbfounded and then fell asleep again. Called a second time and having a similar vision again, he turned around and asked who was there. "I am Francis, the one to whom you have prayed." Fearing that this was still a dream, he hesitated to carry out his order, but when he was called again for the third time, he devoutly obeyed Francis' counsel. He headed to Scoppito and, finding the mule sound and getting it back for free, he led it home. He told everyone everywhere what had happened and became St. Francis' servant for the rest of his life.

185. A man from the people of Antrodoco had bought a very lovely basin, which he gave to his wife so she would take good care of it. One day, his wife's maid took the basin and put the laundry in it to wash it with lye. However, the warmth of the sun, together with the heat of the lye, cracked the basin so that it was not good for anything.

---

134 *Ps* 103, 20 and 135, 4.
135 *Jn* 10, 11 and *Lk* 10, 35, but used here in reference to St. Francis instead of Christ.
136 *Acts* 11, 7.

Trembling, the maid brought the basin back to the lady and, more through her tears than with words, she explained what had happened. The woman was just as frightened as the maid and, terrified of her husband's anger, she surely expected to be beaten. In the meantime, she carefully concealed it and invoked the merits of St. Francis, imploring his grace. Through the Saint's intervention, the parts were joined together and the basin that had been cracked was made whole again. The woman's neighbors, who before had felt compassion for the fearful woman, were delighted by this and the man's wife was the first one to inform her husband about the marvelous occurrence.

186. In the Marches, while a fellow from Monte dell'Olmo was setting the plowshare into the plow one day, the entire share broke into pieces. The man became downhearted and began to weep copiously, as much for the broken plowshare as for the day's work he had lost. "O blessed Francis," he said, "come to my aid, for I have faith in your mercy. I will give your friars a measure of wheat every year and will put myself at their service, if I can only experience your kindness now, just as countless other people have." As soon as his prayer was over, the plowshare was made whole again and the iron was joined together so that there was no trace of where it had broken.

187. Since a cleric from Vicalvi named Matthew had drunk some deadly poison, he fell so seriously and visibly ill that he could not speak in the least and was simply waiting for death to come. A priest advised him to make his confession, but he wasn't able to get one word out. In his heart, however, he humbly prayed to Christ to deliver him through the merits of blessed Francis. As soon as he weakly invoked the name of blessed Francis, he promptly vomited the poison in the presence of witnesses.

188. During the time that Don Trasmondo Annibaldi, consul of the Romans, was acting as podestà of the city of Siena, in Tuscany[137], he had with him a certain Nicholas, who was very dear to him and who handled all his household affairs. Since the man had suddenly contracted a deadly jaw disease, the doctors announced that his death

---

[137] This was in 1234, after the body of St. Francis had already been translated from St. George's to the new church that was being built. Trasmondo was related to Innocent III.

was at hand. After he had fallen into a deep sleep, the Virgin Mother of Christ appeared to him and instructed him to consecrate himself to St. Francis and to visit his temple without delay. When he got up the next morning, he recounted this vision to his master who, astonished by it, immediately wanted to put it to the test. Consequently, he took him to Assisi and before the tomb of St. Francis, his friend was immediately restored to health. The return of his health was marvelous, but even more marvelous was the kindness of the Virgin, who deigned to take pity on the sick man and to exalt the merits of our Saint.

189. This Saint can come to the aid of all those who invoke him and does not look down on human needs, whatever they may be. In Spain, near San Facondo[138], a man had a cherry tree in his garden that produced rich fruit each year, giving the farmer a profit.[139] One time, however, the tree dried up and withered from its roots. Since the master wanted to cut it so it wouldn't take up any more of that space, when a neighbor advised him to entrust it to St. Francis, the man agreed. Then, against every expectation, in due time the tree marvelously turned green, blossomed, sprouted branches and produced fruit as it used to do. Thus, in recognition of this miracle, he sends this fruit to the friars every year.[140]

190. Since the vineyards in Villasilos had been damaged by an epidemic of certain worms, the inhabitants of the town asked a brother from the Order of Preachers for his advice on how to remedy this situation. The friar instructed them to pick whichever two saints they wanted and then to choose one of these two by lot as their patron saint to get rid of the epidemic, and so they chose St. Francis and St. Dominic. When they drew lots, St. Francis was picked and when those men turned to him to intercede, the pestilence soon disappeared. Therefore, they honored him with special reverence and venerated his order with great affection. Indeed, because of this miracle, each year they too send the friars a special donation of wine.

---

[138] Modern-day Sehagún in the ancient kingdom of Castille.

[139] *Lk* 12, 16 and 2, 52; *Wis* 15, 12.

[140] This donation, as well as the one described in the next paragraph, was apparently still being made at the time Celano was writing the *Treatise*.

191. Near Palencia, a priest had a barn in which to store his wheat, but each year, to the priest's loss, it would be overrun with weevils, or wheat parasites. Distressed by this great loss, the priest devised a plan and entrusted the barn to blessed Francis' care. Having done this, a short time later he found all the dead parasites gathered together and put outside the barn and he no longer had to bear this plague. Subsequently, the priest, who was devoted since his prayer had been answered and was not ungrateful for this benefaction, offered an annual tribute of grain to the poor out of love for St. Francis.

192. During the time in which the abominable scourge of worms had devastated the kingdom of Apulia, the lord of a castle known as Pietramala imploringly entrusted his land to blessed Francis and through the Saint's merits, it was left untouched by that cursed plague, even though the land all around it was devoured by it.

193. A noblewoman from the castle of Galete was afflicted with a fistula between her breasts, and suffering from its stench as much as the pain, she had not found any remedy to heal it. One day, she went to pray in the church of the friars where, finding a little booklet about the life and miracles of St. Francis[141], she carefully studied its contents. As soon as she had comprehended the truth, her face bathed in tears, she took the book and held it open over the diseased part of her body. "O St. Francis," she said, "just as the things recounted about you in these pages are true, so now let me be delivered of this sore through your holy merits!" She wept and kept repeating these devotions and when the bandages were taken off shortly thereafter, she was healed so completely that no trace of a scar could later be found.

194. A similar thing happened near Romania, when a father called upon St. Francis with pious invocations for his son, who was covered with sores caused by a serious ulcer. "O Saint of God," he said, "if the marvels that are being spread throughout the world about you are true, let me experience the mercy of your goodness in my son, to God's praise." The bandaging suddenly burst open and before everyone's eyes, the drainage burst from the wound and the boy's skin healed over so that there was no sign of the illness he had had.

---

[141] This must either have been Celano's *First Life*, his *Legenda ad usum chori*   of the *Life* written by Julian of Speyer.

195. While blessed Francis was still alive, a brother was tormented by a horrible illness that often left him so enervated that all his limbs seemed to go around in a circle. At times, in fact, when he was completely stiff and tense and his feet were curled up to his head, he would rise up to the height of a person and then, falling back down immediately, he would roll about foaming at the mouth. Since the holy Father took great pity on his illness, he said a prayer and healed him by making the sign of the cross over him, so that afterwards he suffered no further problems from this illness.

196. After the death of blessed Francis, another friar had such a serious fistula in his lower abdomen that there was absolutely no hope of his being cured. Although he had asked his superior for permission to visit the place of blessed Francis, he was turned down to save him from incurring even greater risk due to the fatigue of the trip and the friar became very downcast. However, blessed Francis appeared to him one night, saying, "Do not trouble yourself any longer, son, but throw away the piece of leather you are using to cover yourself, take the poultice off the sore, observe your rule and you will immediately be delivered." When he got up the next morning, he did what the Saint had instructed him to do and immediately regained his health.

197. A man who had received a serious head injury from an iron arrow could find no relief through medical assistance, for the arrow had entered through his eye socket and was stuck in his skull. Consecrating himself to St. Francis with devout prayers, while he was resting and sleeping a bit, he heard blessed Francis tell him in a dream to have the arrow removed from the back of his skull. Doing what he had been told in the dream, the next day he was ridden of it without any great difficulty.

CHAPTER XIX
Closing remarks to the miracles of Blessed Francis

198. Thus, since through Christ's infinite mercy, the things that have been written and revealed about His Saint and our Father have been confirmed as true based on the succession of miracles and since,

rightly so, it seems absurd to submit to human judgment[142] what has
been approved by divine miracle, I, the suppliant and humble son of
this Father, beseech everyone to accept them benevolently and to listen
to them with devotion. And even though they have not been
expounded as well as they deserve to be, they are nevertheless worthy
of being held in the most profound veneration, in and of themselves.
Thus, do not scorn the narrator's lack of skill, but consider his faith,
his love, his effort. We cannot coin novelties every day, nor can we
turn a square into a circle, nor yet can we take what we hold as the sole
truth and adapt it for such a wide range of eras and needs. In no way
have we thrown ourselves into writing this out of guilty vanity, nor
have we become involved in such extraordinary teachings out of
selfish instinct, but this effort was wrung from us by the brothers'
insistent prayers and the authority of our superiors then ordered us to
complete it. As to our reward, we are awaiting it from Christ the Lord.
What we ask of you, brothers and fathers, is tolerance and love. So be
it, then. Amen!

The end of the book, praise and glory to Christ

---

[142] *Acts* 15, 11; *Jn* 20, 30; *Mk* 16, 20; *1 Cor* 4, 3.

INDEX

FIRST LIFE

Prologue

PART ONE

PART TWO

PART 3

SECOND LIFE

PART TWO

Treatise of the Miracles of Blessed Francis

TIPOGRAFIA METASTASIO
ASSISI
Stampato in Marzo 2007